THE I TATTI
RENAISSANCE LIBRARY

James Hankins, General Editor

FICINO

COMMENTARIES ON PLATO

VOLUME 2, PART I

ITRL 51

MARSILIO FICINO

COMMENTARIES ON PLATO

VOLUME 2 • *PARMENIDES*, PART I

EDITED AND TRANSLATED BY

MAUDE VANHAELEN

THE I TATTI RENAISSANCE LIBRARY
HARVARD UNIVERSITY PRESS
CAMBRIDGE, MASSACHUSETTS
LONDON, ENGLAND
2012

Printed in the United States of America

Series design by Dean Bornstein

ISBN 978-0-674-06471-3

Library of Congress Cataloging-in-Publication Data

Ficino, Marsilio, 1433–1499.
[Selections. English & Latin. 2008]
Commentaries on Plato / Marsilio Ficino ;
edited and translated by Michael J. B. Allen.
p. cm.—(The I Tatti Renaissance Library ; 34)
Includes bibliographical references and index.
ISBN 978-0-674-03119-7 (cloth : alk. paper)
1. Plato I. Allen, Michael J. B. II. Title
B395.F4713 2008
184—dc22 2008037878

Contents

Introduction

Plato's Parmenides *in the History of Philosophy*

No other dialogue of Plato has provoked more controversy than the *Parmenides*. Modern commentators still wonder whether Plato presented us with a facile exercise in logic or expressed some deeper moral or theological message. In the first part of the dialogue, the old and venerable philosopher Parmenides is having a discussion with Socrates, who is presented as a promising young man. Parmenides challenges Plato's central doctrine, the theory of Ideas, which states that the objects that we see around us are the imperfect copies of higher and eternal models called Ideas. He draws Socrates on to consider a number of issues that arise from the existence of Ideas. For instance, Parmenides objects, if we were to postulate the existence of absolute, perfect models for everything on earth, should we also postulate them for evil or ugly things, such as dirt, hair, or mud? The young and talented Socrates is incapable of defending the doctrine when faced with Parmenides' searching questions. Plato explains to us that Socrates cannot answer Parmenides' questions because he is insufficiently trained in a specific method of inquiry, which Plato calls dialectic. In the second part of the dialogue, Parmenides offers to give a demonstration of how this dialectical method works. He chooses the youngest in the audience to act as a respondent, a young man called Aristoteles (not to be confused with Aristotle the philosopher). In the course of the ensuing discussion, Parmenides and Aristoteles enter into a long and rather puzzling exchange of questions and answers regarding the relation between a mysterious subject, called "the one," and something called "the others." They draw on a series of hypotheses, in which they examine all the pos-

sible ways in which "the one" and "the others" can relate to one another. However, they often use obscure reasoning and draw conclusions that are blatantly contradictory. For instance, in one hypothesis Parmenides concludes that if the one is, the one *is* multiple, at rest or in motion; in another, he concludes that if the one is, the one *is not* multiple, at rest or in motion.

The *Parmenides* thus confronts all interpreters since antiquity with great difficulties. Why does Plato demolish his own theory of Ideas in the first part of the dialogue? What do "the one" and "the others" represent, and what do the expressions "is" and "is not" mean? What is the purpose of this exercise, which is so different from the dialectic practiced in other Platonic dialogues? Is it simply logical, examining all the possible relations existing between unity (the one) and multiplicity (the others), or does it mask some deeper, mystical truths about a "one" that might well be another name for "God"?

All these questions were already being asked in antiquity by the first interpreters of Plato and are well documented by an important text, the fifth-century commentary on *Parmenides* by the Neoplatonic philosopher Proclus (412–85 CE). Proclus provides us with the most complete record of the history of the exegesis of the *Parmenides*.[1] He reviews in great detail his predecessors' exegeses of the dialogue and shows that his master Syrianus developed the best and most conclusive interpretation. From his and other accounts we know that the Neoplatonists established a tight connection between philosophy, theology, faith, and revelation; like the Christians, they had their own "holy scriptures," called the Chaldaean Oracles, some mysterious texts dating from the second century CE. They believed that these texts constituted the supreme revelation that the gods had made about themselves and the world, and they founded the practice of certain religious rituals, called theurgy, on these sacred texts.[2] They thought that Plato's dialogues were in fundamental agreement with the Chaldaean Oracles

and were thus religious texts.[3] As such, they saw Platonism as a theology, a series of "revelations" made by the gods, rather than as a rational discourse describing the place and role of men in the world. In this context, they argued that the *Parmenides* was the supreme expression of Platonic theology and the most sacred of Plato's dialogues. According to them, Plato had deliberately hidden, beneath the *Parmenides'* apparent contradictions, divine mysteries about the highest principle, the One, and the hierarchy of gods.[4] This was not a unanimously accepted interpretation: we know that earlier interpreters of the *Parmenides*, like Albinus (or Alcinous, second century CE), favored a logical reading of the second part of the dialogue. It is, however, the Neoplatonic interpretation, which advocated a theological reading of the dialogue, that historically superseded all the others and still determines, at least in some part, our modern understanding of the dialogue.[5]

As demonstrated by E. R. Dodds, the philosopher Plotinus (ca. 204–70 CE), who is generally considered the founder of Neoplatonism, was the first to adopt a theological interpretation of the dialogue. In his treatise "On the Three Hypostases" (*Enneads* V.1.8), Plotinus establishes a correspondence between the *Parmenides'* first three hypotheses and the first three principles of the universe. According to him, the meaning of the term "One" varies according to the different hypotheses of the *Parmenides*: the first hypothesis describes the first principle, called the One; the second describes the second principle, called the intellect; and the third concerns the third principle, which he calls the soul. Plotinus' successors, Amelius (second half of third century), Porphyry (234–305), Iamblichus (245–ca. 325), Plutarch of Athens (ca. 350–430), and Syrianus (d. 437), developed this interpretation further, making some adjustments to Plotinus' framework. The last two main Neoplatonic commentators, Proclus and Damascius (ca. 458–538), provided the most complete interpretation of the dialogue, from which they drew a comprehensive metaphysical system. Thus Pro-

clus reads in the *Parmenides* the hierarchy of all the gods of the Greek pantheon. He discerns in Plato's description an elaborate structure of nine propositions, which correspond to the nine degrees of reality (or hypostases), from the highest principle, the One, down through the intellect and soul to form and matter. Proclus also reinterprets positively Parmenides' puzzling critique of the theory of Ideas. According to him, Parmenides does not by any means refute Plato's theory of Ideas, but rather plays the role of devil's advocate to test the robustness of the young Socrates' arguments. Proclus describes this initiation as "maieutic" (from the Greek *maieutikos*, pertaining to midwifery): he compares Parmenides to a midwife who encourages Socrates to give birth to progressively more complex thoughts about the One and the Ideas. Similarly, Proclus argues that the final discussion about the One, far from being a logical exercise, actually concerns the principles of all things. Again, Proclus argues, Parmenides uses contradictory arguments to test his interlocutor's ability to think in a rigorous, logical way.

Parmenides' method, Proclus explains, which consists in investigating the consequences that follow and do not follow from the existence and nonexistence of the "one" and the "others," corresponds to the highest form of dialectic; it is comparable to the dialectic of the *Sophist* and the *Phaedrus* and is superior to Aristotelian syllogism, because it is the only reasoning that brings the initiate to the contemplation of Truth.[6] With this interpretive tour de force, Proclus transforms the *Parmenides'* paradoxes and contradictions into an initiation into the highest principles of the universe. It is on the basis of this interpretation that he elaborates an entire philosophical system describing the divine world, which is expounded in another of his works, the *Platonic Theology*.

The Neoplatonic commentators taught philosophy in Greece, Rome, Alexandria, and Syria; some of them, like Syrianus, Proclus, and Damascius, succeeded one another as head of Plato's

Academy in Athens. They saw themselves as the direct successors of Plato. However, while Socrates and Plato practiced philosophy by establishing everyday dialogues between the master and his pupil, the Neoplatonists taught philosophy by interpreting Plato's dialogues in a more or less systematic way. Their interpretation was thus to a large extent conditioned by their teaching: they did not write dialogues, but commentaries; they did not develop their thought through conversations in the streets of Athens, but through scholastic reasoning and exegesis.

In the school curriculum the *Parmenides* was the last step in the pupils' initiation into Plato's divine doctrine; it was seen as encompassing all the truths that had been adumbrated in Plato's previous dialogues. This meant that Plato's other dialogues were systematically reinterpreted in the light of their reading of the *Parmenides*, as clearly exemplified by Proclus' *Platonic Theology*. Two dialogues were considered as having a special affinity with the *Parmenides*: the *Sophist*, seen as a *proteleia*, that is, a preparation, to the *Parmenides*, and the *Timaeus*, whose description of the world was seen as the complement to the *Parmenides'* theology.[7] Aristotle too was integrated into the Neoplatonic curriculum. Despite the fact that Aristotle's philosophy was founded upon a demolition of Plato's theory of Ideas, the Neoplatonists made various attempts to establish a harmony between Aristotle and Plato. This enabled them to adopt some of Aristotle's most attractive doctrines (one of which was his doctrine of the categories) and adapt these to a Platonic framework, where Platonism was presented as the crowning philosophy of Aristotle's description of the physical world.[8] In this context, the Neoplatonists usually combined strong criticisms of Aristotle with more moderate statements, underlining that Aristotle's work was the necessary yet not sufficient propaedeutic to Plato's philosophy.[9]

Such was, in essence, the interpretive framework that was transmitted outside the Platonic schools to the Middle Ages and the

Renaissance.[10] While Byzantine scholars read the *Parmenides* in both Plato's Greek text and Proclus' commentary,[11] the *Parmenides* came to the West as it was understood by the Neoplatonists; it was always associated, directly or indirectly, with Proclus' interpretation.[12] It first entered the medieval world indirectly through the writings of Dionysius the Areopagite. Dionysius was a sixth-century Christian writer, possibly a Monophysite, and a follower of Proclus, but he claimed to be the first-century Athenian pagan Saint Paul converted to Christianity while preaching at the Areopagus (as mentioned in Acts 17:34) and thus to have anticipated Proclus' attractive description of the universe.[13] In two important works, *On the Divine Names* and the *Celestial Hierarchy*, Dionysius adapted Proclus' interpretation of the *Parmenides* to a Christian framework. Dionysius' works were transmitted in the Middle Ages first through the ninth-century translations of John Scotus Eriugena, then through the high medieval versions of John Sarracenus, Robert Grosseteste, Hugh of St. Victor, and others.[14] Proclus' indirect influence via Dionysius' writings can be measured by the success of negative theology, which played an important role in the development of Christian mysticism. According to this doctrine, God can be characterized only by negations, because He is infinitely superior to all things. So we can only describe God by that which He is not, because our reason and our language are insufficient to fully grasp Him in His perfection. Dionysius also adopted Proclus' hierarchy of gods but substituted for the Greek gods a hierarchy of angels, thus adapting the Greek polytheistic pantheon to a monotheistic vision of the world.

Proclus' philosophy also made its way into scholasticism via the *Liber de causis*, an Arabic paraphrase of Proclus' *Elements of Theology* falsely attributed to Aristotle and translated into Latin by Gerard of Cremona in the second half of the twelfth century. Both Albert the Great (ca. 1200–80) and Thomas Aquinas (1225–74) wrote im-

portant commentaries on the *Liber de causis* and on Dionysius' *Divine Names*.

The direct transmission of Proclus' *Parmenides* commentary into the Latin-speaking world began in the second half of the thirteenth century, when the Dominican William of Moerbeke rendered the work into Latin, possibly at the instigation of Thomas Aquinas, whom he had met in Viterbo and Orvieto. Despite its excessively literal character, making it barely understandable to someone with no knowledge of Greek, this version is fundamental because it preserves a large section of the text that is now lost in the Greek original.[15] Moerbeke's translation of Proclus' *Parmenides* commentary had a profound impact on the medieval philosopher Nicholas of Cusa (1401–64), who subsequently ordered a translation of the dialogue to be made by the Greek émigré George of Trebizond (1394–ca. 1472/3). A decade later, the Greek Bessarion (ca. 1403–72) used the Neoplatonic interpretation of the *Parmenides* to convince his Italian audience that Plato was superior to Aristotle and closer to Christianity.[16]

It was only at the end of the fifteenth century, however, that Proclus' interpretation of the *Parmenides* became accessible in a more readable version than that of Moerbeke. In 1496 the Florentine humanist Marsilio Ficino (1433–99) published a commentary on the *Parmenides*, reviving a tradition that had been extinct since the end of antiquity. Ficino is most famous for his translation of the complete works of Plato (1484) and of Plotinus (1492), but his commentaries on Plato are fundamental to understanding the dissemination of Platonism in the centuries preceding the birth of modern scholarship. Given the importance of the *Parmenides* in antiquity and the Middle Ages, Ficino's interpretation—the first to provide a complete interpretation of the text since antiquity—represents an important chapter in the history of philosophy, which still determines, at least in some part, our modern under-

standing of this problematic text. Thanks to Ficino, Plato's *Parmenides* continued to be read through Neoplatonic lenses for nearly five centuries, until modern scholars started to distinguish the meaning of the Platonic original from that of its Neoplatonic commentators.[17]

Ficino started interpreting the *Parmenides* at the age of thirty, when he produced a translation of ten Platonic dialogues at the request of Cosimo de' Medici in 1464.[18] In the introduction preceding his Latin version of the dialogue, Ficino makes it clear that he already knew Proclus' interpretation: he states that the dialogue concerns the One, principle of all things (*de uno rerum omnium principio*); like Proclus he argues that the first part is an initiation into the theory of Ideas, while the second part is arranged in nine hypotheses demonstrating both the transcendence of the absolute One and the procession of all things from it.[19] Ficino's knowledge of Proclus' *Parmenides* interpretation is attested by his marginal annotations in Riccardianus 70, a manuscript in the Riccardiana Library in Florence containing another work by Proclus, the *Platonic Theology*, which is based on a theological interpretation of the *Parmenides*.[20] The annotations, coupled with what Ficino says in the introduction to the dialogue, show that the Florentine philosopher had developed as early as 1464 a profound understanding of Proclus' method and doctrine. This is clear, for instance, from the link he establishes between Plato and the ancient theologians Orpheus, Aglaophemus, Pythagoras, and Philolaos; the status he ascribes to the *Parmenides*, the theological dialogue par excellence, containing all the truths outlined in Plato's other dialogues; and his interpretation of the hierarchy of divine orders proceeding from the supra-essential One.

Three decades later Ficino undertook a much longer, more detailed commentary on the *Parmenides*. According to Kristeller's reconstruction, Ficino started this commentary after November 7,

1492, and finished it before August 1494, as shown by the letters he sent to his friends Filippo Valori and Germain de Ganay.[21] It is possible, however, that some portions of the text, including the passages that draw on Proclus' *Platonic Theology* and the "seven discourses" Ficino writes against Pico, were written earlier and incorporated in the commentary later on.[22] The *Parmenides* commentary was eventually published in 1496 in the *Commentaria in Platonem*, along with the commentaries on the *Sophist*, *Timaeus*, *Phaedrus*, and *Philebus* and the section on the fatal number in Book VIII of the *Republic*.[23] In the period between the redaction of the 1464 *Parmenides argumentum* and that of the full-scale commentary, Ficino intensively studied, translated, and commented on major works of other Neoplatonic philosophers, including Plotinus, Iamblichus, Porphyry, Proclus, Michael Psellos, and Dionysius the Areopagite, and this had a profound impact on his understanding of the *Parmenides*.[24]

Ficino's personal copy of Proclus' *Parmenides* commentary has not yet been identified. At least two complete copies of the Greek text circulated in Florence: Laurentianus Conv. Soppr. 103, a Byzantine manuscript which was purchased by the Florentine Antonio Corbinelli and bequeathed after 1425 to La Badia, and Laurentianus Pluteus 85.8, copied by John Rhosos in 1489 at the request of Lorenzo de' Medici.[25] Ficino also had access to William of Moerbeke's translation and used it at least for the final part of Proclus' commentary, which is now lost in the Greek original.[26] To date, no textual or codicological evidence suggests, however, that Ficino read the rest of Proclus' commentary exclusively in Moerbeke's translation. Examination of Ficino's copies of other Greek texts shows that the humanist generally worked from the Greek original, identifying passages of special interest, before writing up his own commentary on, or paraphrase of, the text.[27] Given that the Greek text of Proclus' commentary was available in Quattro-

cento Florence, it seems reasonable to suppose that Ficino read Proclus' commentary both in the original and in Moerbeke's translation, and that his working copies are now lost.[28]

Ficino's *Parmenides* interpretation continued to play an important role well into the sixteenth century. Giles of Viterbo (1469–1532) requested his protégé Nicolaus Scutellius (1490–1542) to establish a translation (in fact a paraphrase) of Proclus' *Parmenides* commentary, which allowed him to continue the work of Ficino and underline the affinity between Neoplatonism, Christianity, and the Kabbalah; Francesco Patrizi (1529–97) invoked Ficino's theological interpretation of the *Parmenides* to confirm the absolute superiority of Plato over Aristotle.[29]

Character and Themes of Ficino's Commentary

A cursory glance at Ficino's commentary is sufficient to see that the humanist follows very closely the text of Proclus, paraphrasing entire passages of the *Platonic Theology* and the *Parmenides* commentary. A closer reading demonstrates, however, that Ficino is not merely the mediator of Proclus' interpretation.[30] In fact, his reliance on Proclus enables us to discern more clearly the passages where he does not follow the Neoplatonic philosopher. To start with, Proclus' commentary is preserved only until the end of the first hypothesis; the rest of his commentary has not come down to us. Ficino cannot, therefore, simply paraphrase Proclus in the final part of his commentary. Second, Ficino is by no means a professor of philosophy like Proclus.[31] As we have seen, Proclus considered the *Parmenides* as an essentially religious text leading the initiate to the contemplation of divine Truth. However, he also intended to establish the definitive system describing reality, to refute the interpretation of his predecessors, and to provide students with the appropriate tools and methods to study philosophy. In contrast, Ficino sees little utility in establishing a philosophical system like

Proclus' and teaching pupils the different steps in the explication of a text. When he delves into the processes of demonstration, division, and resolution (i.e., the different steps of dialectic), he never does so in a systematic way. Rather, Ficino is interested in the mystical nature of the *Parmenides,* in the path that will enable the soul to ascend toward God. Here Ficino is influenced by Dionysius the Areopagite, who emphasizes, through a mystical reading of the *Parmenides,* the soul's supra-intellectual union with God.[32]

This is very clear from the two passages reproduced below. In the first passage, Ficino insists that he does not intend to derive a hierarchy of gods from the different hypotheses of the *Parmenides* but to elevate our soul toward God by awakening the part of the divine that is within us:

> Finally, the purpose of the first hypothesis will be to separate the absolute One from all the properties and conditions of the intellectual unities [henads], that is, the gods, and to make clear by this separation that all things proceed from it. *But let our purpose be* [emphasis added], in order to attain these mysteries, to reach, through the discursive logic of our reason, the simple intelligences of beings, and through them to stir up the one that is within us (or rather transcends us, since it is divine) in order to perceive this absolute One. For after having in due form denied of the first principle, through discursive reason and intelligence, all the conditions that are proper to beings, we might find ourselves in danger of being deceived by our imagination, and think that, after having denied so many divine realities and powers, we have reached nothingness, or something that is void and vain, indeterminate, formless and confused—unless we balance our negations by stimulating the divine force of our unity through an erotic affect, a force that will immediately transport us to the

> very unity that transcends us, and enable us to enjoy divine Unity through our own unity, when we have let go of the motion of reason and the multiplicity of intelligence, striving solely through unity toward the One, and toward the Good through love.[33]

In the passage paraphrased by Ficino, Proclus describes how the soul can ascend by divine inspiration to "the ineffable and incomprehensible intuition of the One": The soul awakens the unity that lies dormant in its innermost part, whereby it can be reunited with the supreme One.[34] This Neoplatonic doctrine, which had a profound influence on Christian mysticism, supposes that we cannot reach the One (God) by intelligence or reason, but rather by transcending intellectual knowledge and identifying ourselves with the One through love.[35] In the passage quoted above, Ficino is at pains to distinguish the general (that is, Proclean) purpose of the *Parmenides* from his own ("But let our purpose be . . ."). Indeed, in the passage paraphrased by Ficino, Proclus presents the awakening of the soul's inner unity as a means for his pupils to arrive at the true understanding of the text; the different stages of the soul's ascent, from logical reasoning to divine inspiration, inform the way in which Proclus intends to interpret the text. By contrast, Ficino considers the spiritual awakening of the soul as the only and ultimate goal of his interpretation of the *Parmenides'* secret mysteries. In other words, he is not a professor of philosophy or a theologian but a visionary—a man in search of the path that will lead him to God.

This marked difference between Proclus and Ficino is further confirmed by a second text, where Ficino reinterprets one of Proclus' most important doctrines, that of the henads, in a way that notably differs from Proclus. Neoplatonic commentators had always wondered how multiplicity could derive from the totally transcendent and simple One without the One being affected or

corrupted by the process. Proclus had tried to answer this question by postulating the existence, between the absolute One and the multiplicity of the Ideas, of an intermediate and separate level of unities called henads.[36] These henads produce multiplicity on behalf of the One, thus preventing the One from being contaminated; they are also responsible for sowing in each thing the unity that derives from the One.[37] When Ficino paraphrases Proclus, however, he presents the henads not as separate unities between the One and the Ideas but as unities *within* the soul:

> Thus it is through intellectual light that it [the sun] creates visible light—not through its own multiplicity, but rather through the unity of its intellect. This unity lies *at the summit of the intellectual part of its soul* [emphasis added], as the character of that simple Unity which is the principle of the universe and to which the intellect is also supremely united through its own unity. It is through this same unity that it is and is called God. Thus the divine unity of the sun is the principle of the world's uniform light, just as absolute Unity and Goodness are responsible for intelligible light.[38]

In the passage paraphrased by Ficino, Proclus describes the henad of light as a separate principle of unity, which lies between the One and the intellect. By contrast, Ficino considers that the henad of light is the character of divine unity present in each thing, whereby each principle is called God. In other words, Ficino reinterprets the doctrine of henads in the light of the (equally Proclean, but also Plotinian) doctrine of the "one in the soul": the henads are unities within the soul of each thing and render union with God possible. By stressing the presence of the principles of unities within reality, Ficino emphasizes the mystical rather than the metaphysical dimension of Proclus' henology: it is by entering into intimate contact with the "one within us" that the

soul can overcome its own imperfection and enter into unity with the universe.[39]

One might argue that Ficino's reluctance to establish a strict separation between the One and the intellectual world is motivated by a Christian view of the universe. Christians considered that God (the One) was the creator of the world and thus necessarily contained all the Ideas; for them there was no strict separation between the One and the Ideas. As Ficino himself states, "Any Idea is God itself."[40] However, Ficino also introduced, within God, a distinction between the Good and the intellect, stating that "it pertains to the Good to impart unity, goodness, and essence to all things, while it pertains to the intellect also to adorn all things with forms through the intermediary of Ideas."[41] This being the case, it might be more useful to suggest that Ficino was, like Dionysius the Areopagite, simply more concerned with mysticism (i.e., achieving union with God) than metaphysics (i.e., establishing a rational system to describe reality). More specifically, while Proclus' concern was to bridge the gap left by Plotinus between unity and multiplicity, Ficino's concern was to describe the way in which the divine presence could be manifested at every stage of reality and enable us to ascend toward God, because of both our innate desire for the Good and God's illumination.

The Pico-Ficino Controversy

Ficino's insistence that the soul's inner unity was the sole way to reach God's supreme unity can also be interpreted as a direct reply to his young colleague and rival Giovanni Pico della Mirandola (1463–94), who had challenged Ficino's position on Neoplatonic theology.[42] Ever since he started translating Hermetic and Pythagorean writings in the 1460s, Ficino had developed the notion that there exists an "ancient theology" (the famous *prisca theologia*) transmitted, from Persia, Egypt, and Greece, by a succession of

divinely inspired theologians, from Zoroaster, Hermes Trismegistus, Orpheus, and Pythagoras to Plato and his successors, and whose inheritors were the Byzantine George Gemistus Pletho (ca. 1355–1452/54), Bessarion, and Ficino himself.[43] This tradition was based upon a Platonic rather than an Aristotelian vision of the world. Within this framework, the thought of Aristotle occupied a subordinate position: it was not seen as an "ancient theology" that could help us reach God but, following the Neoplatonic tradition, as a propaedeutic to the study of the ancient theologians. In this context, Ficino presents Aristotle as a silent and respectful follower of Plato:

> Aristotle will rightly call the Good "the cause of the causes," as does his master [Plato], and also give it the name of "end," since the final cause precedes all the others. So when he makes being equal to the one and the good, he might mean the one and the good that can be perceived by the intellect and comprehended by being. But the more eminent One, which his master Plato reveals as completely ineffable and unknowable, he does not approve of with words, but rather honors in silence.[44]

According to this view, Aristotle's philosophy is inferior to Plato's theology; yet it is also a form of training that is necessary to the apprehension of Platonism. While Plato had uniquely revealed the truth about the nature of the highest principle, the One-above-being, Aristotle had only treated of the second principle, the one-equal-with-being, respecting in silence the superior wisdom of his master. This view was to be immortalized visually two decades later by Raphael in his celebrated fresco *The School of Athens*, which represents Plato pointing toward the heavens and Aristotle extending his hand toward the earth.[45]

Ficino is at pains, however, to underline the agreement between Plato and Aristotle, even if Aristotle is presented as a mere imita-

tor of Plato. For instance, reflecting on the status of Parmenides' dialectic, Ficino follows Proclus in stating that the exercise in the second part of the dialogue, although different from the method described in the *Sophist* and the *Phaedrus*, constitutes the highest form of dialectic; it consists in *both* arguing on both sides *and* contemplating the Ideas and Truth.[46] Thus for Ficino, as for the Neoplatonists, the *Parmenides'* dialectic is not only a method of reasoning (like Aristotelian logic) but also metaphysics itself, or theology, since its object is the structure of the divine realm and its relation with the human world. Where Ficino does not follow Proclus, however, is when he stresses that Aristotle, like Plato, has blended dialectical method with theological matters:

> Aristotle himself blended the highest form of dialectic (I prefer the Latin word *dialectica* to the Greekish *dialektikè*) with divine matters, in imitation, I believe, of Plato, who used the term "dialectic" to designate theology in the *Republic*. In other words, the subject of the *Parmenides* is theological above all, yet its form is particularly logical.[47]

Similarly, Ficino considers that Aristotle's philosophy is a preparatory exercise to the highest Platonic dialectic, just as the contradictions Parmenides uses to train his pupil constitute a preparation to the contemplation of truth:

> It is to train the noble young man in this method, therefore, that Parmenides leads him through a series of obstacles and forces him to either admit what is false, or use these abstractions, wherein, as stated by the one whom you know, "There is no lie."[48]

The hierarchy that Ficino established between Aristotelian logic and Plato's higher dialectic is precisely what bothered the young Giovanni Pico della Mirandola. Although Pico adopted Ficino's notion of ancient theology, he strongly opposed the subordinate

status Ficino attributed to Aristotle. According to Pico, it does not make sense to exclude Aristotle and scholastic philosophers from the tradition of divinely inspired theologians; they are equally valid philosophers, to be placed at the same level as Plato and the others. In 1485 Pico had already opposed the general trend of the humanistic movement of rejecting medieval scholasticism in toto. Humanists like Lorenzo Valla, for instance, claimed that medieval scholastic philosophy and terminology were not adequate for describing reality, and that one needed to go back to the original Aristotle and use Cicero's Latin. In contrast, Pico argued in his famous letter to Ermolao Barbaro that scholastic terminology was as good and valid as Cicero's Latin and had served to express a philosophical movement as worthy of consideration as ancient philosophies.[49] One year later Pico explicitly challenged Ficino's Neoplatonic interpretation of Plato's *Symposium* in his *Commento sopra una Canzone d'Amore* (1486), a commentary on Girolamo Benivieni's love poem; he insisted on the need to distinguish between Plato's text and the Neoplatonists' interpretations of Plato. Pico's criticisms of Ficino were so virulent that they were deliberately suppressed in the printed version by Pico's contemporaries, only to be rediscovered in modern times in three manuscripts, first by Eugenio Garin, then by Franco Bacchelli.[50] In a treatise entitled *On the One and Being,* written in 1491, shortly before Ficino undertook his *Parmenides* commentary, Pico rejected Ficino's claim that Neoplatonism was the only philosophy that could lead to the contemplation of divine Truth. On the basis of a careful reading of Plato, Aristotle, Simplicius, Dionysius the Areopagite, and scholasticism, Pico argued that the philosophies of Aristotle, Plato, the Neoplatonists, and the Scholastics were equally valid ways to describe divine reality.[51]

As noted above, Ficino considered that when equating one and being Aristotle had only treated of the second principle, while Plato had gone further and revealed in the *Parmenides* the existence

of a higher principle, the One. In contrast, Pico considered that Plato was certainly not the only one to see the truth regarding divine matters. To refute Ficino, Pico's strategy consisted in demonstrating that Plato and Aristotle had called the highest principle *both* one *and* being (*ens et unum*) *and* One *superior* to being (*super ens*).[52] In this way, Pico was striking a deadly blow at Ficino's interpretation of the *Parmenides* as the supreme expression of Plato's theology. Indeed, Pico argued, Proclus' interpretation of Plato's *Parmenides* was the result of a distortion of Plato's original; if one were to read Plato's dialogues as they really were, one would immediately see that Plato and Aristotle were in total agreement with one another. One should dismiss the *Parmenides*, Pico argued, which is only a logical exercise without any serious content, and turn to Plato's *Sophist*, where Plato, like Aristotle, holds that the supreme principle is not only One, as claimed by the Neoplatonists, but also one *and* being.[53]

Ficino was very well aware of Pico's attacks on his interpretation of Plato. In his *Parmenides* commentary he makes one explicit allusion to his rival:

> I wish that admirable young man [i.e., Giovanni Pico della Mirandola] had considered with attention the arguments and discussions above, before attacking his master with such audacity and claiming without fear, in opposition to the doctrine of all Platonists, that the divine *Parmenides* is simply logical and that Plato, like Aristotle, has identified the One and the Good with being![54]

Ficino's reference to "the arguments and discussions above" unmistakably points to a series of seven "Discourses" embedded in the *Parmenides* commentary. I have shown elsewhere that these "Discourses" consist in a point-by-point rebuttal of Pico's arguments.[55] In these seven discourses, Ficino concludes that unity is essential in the process of the soul's elevation toward God. Ficino bor-

rows arguments from the Neoplatonic tradition, using both Proclus and Plotinus, to underline once again the fact that the supra-intellectual union with God necessarily implies that the first principle transcends being and the intellect.[56] How, Ficino asks, can one fully attain God without losing one's sight, reason, and intelligence? The response is that it is only through unity, and not through intellect, that union with God, which constitutes the ultimate goal of mysticism, is possible. In other words, the superiority of unity over being is the *necessary condition* for the soul's ascent toward God. This constitutes the coup de grâce for Pico's audacious claim that the One was not *necessarily* superior to being.

Ficino's "Middle Path," between Plotinus and Proclus

The use of both Plotinus' and Proclus' doctrines to describe the process of mystical union also points toward Ficino's acute understanding of the Neoplatonic tradition as a whole. While modern scholarship tends to emphasize the distinctions between Plotinus' and Proclus' descriptions of the soul's elevation toward God, Ficino prefers to underline the affinity between the two doctrines, an affinity which has recently been noted by John Bussanich.[57] Indeed, beyond the fundamental differences between Plotinus' and Proclus' doctrines and Proclus' sharp criticisms of Plotinus, which Ficino was at least partially aware of, both philosophers describe a state of ecstatic, pure thought that transcends the intellect. Ficino exploits this in his commentary to refute Pico's thesis.[58]

In fact, trying to establish a harmony between Plotinus and Proclus is one of the most important characteristics of Ficino's *Parmenides* exegesis. Numerous passages show that Ficino is often reading Proclus' interpretation of the *Parmenides* through the lens of Plotinus' *Enneads*, a text that Ficino had translated and commented upon in the years preceding his completion of the *Parmenides* commentary. Right at the start of the commentary Ficino

states that although he largely follows the Neoplatonic (that is, theological) interpretation of the *Parmenides,* he does not fully endorse what he considers to be Proclus' "overinterpretation" of the dialogue, which consists in interpreting each attribute of the One as a god of the Greek pantheon. Instead Ficino has chosen a "middle path," according to which the *Parmenides* blends allusions to theological matters and dialectical exercise:

> Proclus himself, like his master Syrianus, thinks that mysteries are hidden in each word, and that the number of conclusions in the dialogue corresponds almost exactly to the number of divinities. For my part I have followed a middle path, and I consider that there is at least as much theology in this dialogue as is permitted by the art that is commonly called dialectical. In my opinion, therefore, allusions to divine matters are not everywhere continuously present, but divulged on occasions.[59]

Throughout the commentary Ficino repeatedly dismisses Syrianus' and Proclus' interpretation of each attribute of the *Parmenides* as a separate god of the Greek pantheon. He characterizes this interpretation as "more poetic than philosophical" (*poeticum potius quam philosophicum*), "more laborious than useful" (*laboriose potius quam utiliter*), and the result of some "inquisitiveness" (*curiositas*).[60] Much has been said of Ficino's reluctance to adopt Proclus' interpretation, which is often seen as a Christian reaction against a pagan polytheistic framework — especially the fact that, following Dionysius' angelic interpretation of Proclus, Ficino identifies the Neoplatonic gods with intellects, or angels, spheres, planets, and stars. And yet, despite the apologetic undertones of some of the passages (*curiositas* has a clear Christian connotation here),[61] the reason Ficino rejects Proclus' interpretation has little to do with the need to conform to Christian dogmas. Other passages suggest that Ficino rejects Proclus' interpretation because he follows Plotinus.

Proclus' interpretation was based upon a strict distinction between the "intelligible" and "intellectual" orders of reality. In contrast, Plotinus did not distinguish between the intellectual and intelligible levels. Ficino follows Plotinus in stating that the intelligible and the intellectual orders cannot be distinguished in terms of substance but only mentally:

> We agree that the first propositions concern more the superior gods and the following propositions, the following gods, but they also in some way concern both orders of gods. For we do not distinguish the intelligible order from the intellectual in substance, but according to reason.[62]

Proclus had rejected the Plotinian doctrine of the direct derivation of the intellect from the One on the grounds that it introduces multiplicity within the One. His own solution was to multiply the various degrees between the One and multiplicity, by placing between the One and intellect the universal principles of limit and unlimited and the henads, and by establishing a distinction between the intellects and the intelligibles.[63] Ficino was well aware of the tensions between Plotinus and Proclus and chose to adopt Plotinus' description of the intelligible world, rejecting Proclus' distinction between the intelligible and the intellectual realms:

> We have often shown in our commentary on Plotinus (whom I follow more readily than Proclus on this matter, as well as on many others) that the intellect, the intelligible, the first being, essence, and the first life constitute in reality one single substance, but that they differ in the intelligible realm in that the five genera of things and the Ideas are formally distinct from one another.[64]

In other words, Ficino's rejection of Proclus' interpretation does not correspond to a need to preserve an "orthodox," monotheistic description of the world (one could anyway argue that Proclus'

supreme principle, the One, is no less "one" than the Christian God), but to a decision to adopt Plotinus' doctrine, according to which the intellect and the intelligible are one unique reality, only formally distinct from one another. As in the case of the henads doctrine, Ficino clearly shows himself to be an unsystematic philosopher, less interested in providing a rigorous description of the universe based on a somewhat rigid and systematic interpretation of the *Parmenides'* final part than in finding some way to achieve mystical union with God.

Throughout his commentary, however, Ficino repeatedly acknowledges his indebtedness to Proclus, referring to him as *saepe noster.*[65] Two-thirds of the way into the commentary, Ficino alludes to the fact that he has closely followed Proclus' commentary until it breaks off toward the end of the first hypothesis. He recognizes that without the final part of Proclus' commentary (which is lost), he can only rely upon God's guidance:

> Through these paths, or rather these impassable regions, we have hitherto had the guidance, or at least the indications, of Proclus and Syrianus. From this point on, however, since nobody guides us, we must proceed with the guidance of God and then trust solely the power of divine inspiration.[66]

While Ficino could not rely on Proclus' commentary for the final part of the *Parmenides,* he could have a fair idea of Proclus' interpretation by reading another of Proclus' texts, the *Platonic Theology.* This explains why he continues, throughout the rest of the commentary, to rely on Proclus' interpretation of the subsequent hypotheses, as the examination of his sources indicates.[67] Again, however, Ficino privileges Plotinus' interpretation of the cosmos over Proclus' hierarchies, considering for instance that the triad being-life-intelligence corresponds to three distinct moments or aspects of being rather than three successive stages in the unfolding of the cosmos.[68]

Links between the Parmenides *and the* Sophist

Plato's *Sophist* is, after the *Parmenides,* by far the most often quoted dialogue in Ficino's commentary. Modern commentators tend to consider the *Sophist* as the text that questions in very definite terms the validity of Parmenides' thesis regarding the One. By contrast, the Neoplatonists, always eager to establish an agreement between Plato's dialogues, considered that the *Sophist,* far from refuting Parmenides' doctrine, anticipated and confirmed the thesis of the supremacy of the One over being expounded in the *Parmenides.*[69] Like Proclus, Ficino considers that the *Sophist* is a preparation for the higher mysteries of the *Parmenides:* the *Sophist* treats of the second principle, being, rather than the supreme One above being of the *Parmenides.*[70] Similarly, Ficino considers that the *Sophist*'s protagonist, simply referred to as the "Eleatic Stranger," is in fact Melissus, a disciple of Parmenides, whose thought was necessarily subordinate to his master's wisdom. As such, he considers that the relationship between the master and his disciple is reflected in their treatment of divine principles:

> Just as Plato always gives Parmenides, who discusses here the One, precedence over Melissus, who discusses being in the *Sophist,* in the same way he is very likely to give the One priority over being, since we would expect Plato to follow in the *Parmenides* the decorum he generally establishes in his dialogues between topics and interlocutors.[71]

As shown by Allen, the interpretation of the *Sophist* was central to the debate between Pico and Ficino.[72] As we have seen, Pico had argued that in terms of theological content Plato's *Parmenides* should be dismissed in favor of the *Sophist,* which (according to him) states the same doctrine as Aristotle. In this context, Ficino uses the Neoplatonic exegesis of the *Sophist* to reject Pico's thesis. Far from demonstrating the equivalence between being and the

One as stated by Pico, he argues, the *Sophist* explicitly shows that being is necessarily one, because it derives from the supreme principle, the One:

> In the *Sophist* it is shown that, since all things partake of the One, the One must truly exist, given that the truer all other things are, the more they partake of the One, and that, since all the beings that partake of the One are not truly One (for they each possess their own multitude), yet truly exist, the true One, that is, the One that does not partake of multitude, must truly exist in nature, and the more precedence it has over all the rest, the more truly One it is. For in every case what is true according to a certain nature always has precedence over that which is false. In the end, the *Sophist* concludes that there will be no beings if the true One does not exist, and that the true One is completely indivisible. Yet the doctrine which, according to the *Sophist*, has been developed by Parmenides' disciple, Melissus, corresponds exactly to the first hypothesis, which first shows that the One has [no] multitude and no parts [137C–D], and all the conclusions deriving from this first conclusion are interwoven in a series which unfolds in a necessary sequence. As a result, it is clear that both the *Parmenides* and the *Sophist* do not treat of a certain one that would only be a name imagined for the sake of logic, and of a being that would simply be the product of imagination, but of the One and being that have, as it were, existence or subsistence.[73]

Similarly, Ficino uses both the *Timaeus* and the *Sophist* to explain the nature of the Ideas and their presence in our world:

> Indeed Plato develops three doctrines, partly in the *Timaeus* and partly in the *Sophist*, on the basis of which the Platonists rightly establish three contemplative truths: the power of the

> world's architect, matter's readiness to be formed and its eternal simplicity, and, finally, the somewhat insubstantial and illusory character of natural things when compared to divine realities. Thus if you say that the participation in Ideas by matter is like impressions made by a seal upon wax, or like reflections on the surface of water or of a mirror, or like paintings, we will have established a comparison that is appropriate (as far as this is right) and in agreement with Plotinus and the [other] Platonists.[74]

In this text, which echoes a number of passages from Ficino's other commentaries, Ficino attempts to address the vexed question of the participation of earthly realities in the Ideas, by describing natural objects as images of the Ideas.[75] Both Plotinus and Proclus had drawn upon the *Sophist* and the *Timaeus* to explain the way in which we can participate in the Ideas. They considered that earthly objects related to the Ideas as images, and described these images as mirror reflections, seal impressions, and images made by painting and sculpture. However, they considered that these comparisons could only be used as teaching tools and did not correspond to reality.[76] By contrast, Ficino fully endorses the comparisons as the most appropriate images to describe the presence of the Ideas in this world. In this way he emphasizes the immanence of the World's Architect, who inscribes onto matter the form of the Ideas.[77]

Ficino's Indebtedness to Medieval Scholasticism

As we have seen above, Ficino considered that scholastic philosophy was inferior to Plato's higher mysteries. However, Ficino remains heavily influenced by scholasticism.[78] Indeed, he often draws upon scholastic terminology to describe Proclus' doctrines. For instance, Ficino uses the medieval dichotomy *actus directus/actus reflexus* to express the notion, developed by Proclus and adopted by

Thomas Aquinas, that knowledge varies according to the nature of the object of knowledge rather than that of the knowing agent. Paraphrasing Proclus, Ficino explains that God can only know human matters in relation to the Ideas, both on a secondary level and in a manner corresponding to God's worth. Proclus' *deuterôs* (secondarily) Ficino renders by *consequenter, per consequentiam,* or *per reflexionem,* using Thomas Aquinas' terminology:[79]

> Human cognitive power relates to human, natural, and suchlike matters through an act that is primary and direct (*actu quidem primo directoque*). For this reason such matters can be known through the mode proper to scientific knowledge, that is, through a conclusion that is appropriately drawn from causes to effect. By contrast, divine matters cannot be comprehended by a primary and direct gaze, nor in the manner of scientific knowledge; it is rather by a kind of reflexive act (*actu quodam reflexo*), through earthly things, which are the images and the effects [of the Ideas], that one can have an intuition of divine matters and of the Ideas, which are the causes and paradigms of these earthly things—or one can at least apprehend the Ideas, not through the usual ratiocination, which is the cause of scientific knowledge, but in an extraordinary way, through the simple intelligence that has been perfectly purified, appropriately exercised, and divinely illuminated.[80]

Other passages seem to indicate a more deliberate use of scholastic philosophy, a controversial one even, especially when it comes to refuting Pico's arguments. In both the following passages one gets the sense that Ficino exploits his knowledge of scholasticism to refute Pico on his own ground. In the first passage, Ficino uses Thomas' notion that essence "does not admit of degrees of more or less" (*essentia non suscipit magis aut minus*), to show, against Pico, that essence can vary only according to degrees of goodness, and

that being and good are therefore not the same. Ficino's use of Thomas' doctrine is particularly interesting, since Thomas had used this distinction to defend the opposite thesis: the convertibility of good and being (*ens et bonum convertuntur*).[81]

In another passage, Ficino uses scholastic terminology to refute Pico's contention that making positive statements about the nature of God, as defended by some scholastic philosophers—for example, through analogy—is as valid as negative theology. Ficino's strategy consists of describing in scholastic terms the doctrines of some "older Platonists" that Proclus had criticized in his commentary:

> Some of the older Platonists used absolute assertions to characterize God: they assumed that since God is the absolute cause of all things (especially the most extended and first ones), He rightly possesses within Himself the powers and the roots of these things, by virtue of which some utterly absolute attributes can be asserted of God—not by any means concrete appellations (for instance, God is being, living or intelligizing), nor abstract appellations, which are very close to concrete appellations (for instance, God is essence, life or intellect), but rather the very abstractions of these abstract appellations (*abstractiones abstractorum*)—for instance (if one can say or hear these neologisms without laughing), "essentiality," "vitality," "intellectuality" and so on for all the other eminently perfect appellations in their several genera. They say that these attributes are within God in the most unified way, a way that is utterly hidden from us and known only to God.[82]

Ficino describes the appellations "essentiality" (*essentialitas*), "vitality" (*vitalitas*), and "intellectuality" (*intellectualitas*) as "abstractions of abstract things" (*abstractiones abstractorum*), an expression without equivalent in Proclus. As such, Ficino may well have intended

to echo Lorenzo Valla's criticism of the scholastic use of words ending with *-itas,* on the grounds that these terms were attested neither in Aristotle nor in classical Latin authors.[83] But above all, Ficino is directly attacking Pico. Pico considered that negative theology, central to Neoplatonism and Christian mysticism, was not the only way to describe God. He argued that one could also make positive statements about God in ways defended by some scholastic philosophers. Thus Pico stated that God can be said to be *plenissima entitas, individua unitas, solidissima veritas, beatissima bonitas,* in accordance with medieval philosophers, and that at the same time He is "above" these attributes, as maintained by the Neoplatonists.[84] To refute Pico, Ficino thus uses Proclus' testimony and expresses the doctrine of these "very ancient commentators" in scholastic terms.

Following Proclus, Ficino considers that the negation of these attributes is the sole way to express God's absolute transcendence, while comparisons or analogies can be used to express the way in which realities are disposed toward God, a notion that was also central to Christian mysticism:

> As to the later Platonists, after the negations, which they privilege more than anything else, like Plato, they admit the use of assertions — not the absolute ones, but only the relative ones [i.e., comparisons]. They do not admit the absolute ones, I say, lest these define something within God, or attribute to God what is akin to us, something that is with great foresight forbidden by Plato in his *Letter to Dionysius,* where he says that this error is the source of all errors regarding God. They consider, however, that relative assertions [i.e., comparisons or analogies] do not signify what God is and what His nature is, nor express His name or concept (which according to Parmenides is impossible for us), but they reveal the way in which realities are related to God. For

> instance, when we call God beginning, middle and end, we understand that nature is created, preserved and achieved by God; when we call Him Good, we understand that, as an end, He perfects all things and is desired by all things. Well then, even if we sometimes appear to assert that He is One, then either we relate things in our experience to God, inasmuch as they are united by Him, or we deny that He is many and composed in any way.[85]

Ficino's recourse to scholastic terminology is particularly notable in his interpretation of the second hypothesis of the *Parmenides*. According to the Neoplatonic tradition, the second hypothesis concerns the second degree of reality after the One, i.e., the intelligible world, called intellect or being. In this context, Ficino is confronted with a double difficulty: the need to describe the emergence of the intelligible and multiple world from the One, and the need to preserve the One's absolute transcendence. This constituted, as we have seen, a fundamental Neoplatonic and, to some extent, Christian aporia—how can one explain and describe the derivation of an imperfect multiplicity and being from the absolutely transcendent and perfect One?

Both Plotinus and Proclus had come up with distinct doctrines to solve this issue. Plotinus had described the derivation of the intellect through the One's overflowing productive power (*dunamis*), while Proclus, as we have seen above, considered that an extra level of unities, the henads, could explain the emanation of multiplicity from the One without contaminating the One's supreme unity.[86] However, even if Plotinus and Proclus stated that the One was strictly separated from the intelligible world, neither really managed entirely to remove multiplicity from it:[87] they were often unclear as to how this could really occur and be described, and they often resorted to the images of goodness and beauty, light and splendor to represent the procession of being from the

One. Ficino too represents the procession of being from the One as the emergence of beauty from God's pure unity and goodness, like the splendor emerging from the pure light, which he associates with the Augustinian distinction between inner light (*lux*) and outer light (*splendor*).[88] To explain the fact that multiplicity can derive from unity, however, Ficino introduces the notion that the intelligible world is structured and limited by what he calls a double "total form" (*forma totalis*):

> Since the first being, which is the closest to the absolute One, is one to the highest degree, any multitude, whatever its quality and quantity are, is reduced within the first being to the unique form of the whole. In things that are composed of different causes and only depend on another cause, the total form (*forma totalis*) is usually subsequent to the multiplicity of their parts. By contrast, within the first being, which is generated by a unique principle, but also somehow exists in itself, the total form is necessarily double. The first precedes the multitude of its parts; the second follows, or rather accompanies, them. The first is called supra-essential Unity and Goodness and is the summit of the intelligible world; the second is called beauty, that is, the arrangement, order and series of Ideas.[89]

The expression *forma totalis* has no exact parallel in Neoplatonism, although the science of whole and parts was central in Plato's *Parmenides* and abundantly exploited by Plotinus and Proclus.[90] The notion of *forma totalis* actually echoes the expressions *forma totius* and *principium formale* in medieval mereology (i.e., the science of parts and wholes), often used to express the nonidentity of the whole (here, the One) and its elements (in this case, intellect and being).[91] Ficino uses this notion to reconcile the tension between God's absolute transcendence (as One and Good) and

His immanence (as beauty). In this context, Ficino goes much further than any Neoplatonist, in that he defines the One both as absolutely transcendent and as the summit of the intelligible world, just as he considered that the henads were units *within* the intellectual part of the soul.

The same goes for the relation of the One and the Ideas. Ficino considers that the Ideas are not formally distinguished in the One; at this level they remain "hidden," encompassed in the unity of the first *forma totalis,* and undergo a differentiation solely at the level of the intellect:

> In fact, in the intelligible world, where the forces are varied and the modes are multiple, there can be found in some way likeness, unlikeness, equality and inequality, which constitute the most general genera to be distributed to all the realities that follow, each according to their own mode. Next, in intelligence too, their same properties shine as Ideas: the Idea of likeness, and so on. *Within the One, however, these cannot be formally distinguished, whether as genera or genera of genera, or as Ideas* [emphasis added].[92]

In this passage, Ficino seems to combine Neoplatonic and Christian modes of describing the degradation of the One into Many. Indeed, the notion of progressive distinction of multiplicity, which remains "undistinguished" and "hidden" at the higher level and becomes progressively more manifest at the lower levels, is essentially Proclean. But Proclus never applied this notion to the One. In contrast, philosophers such as Eriugena, Eckhardt, or Nicholas of Cusa had variously developed the idea that the deployment of multiplicity from God was the result of the actualization of God's potentiality, seen as a necessary stage of God's self-realization: it is in and through his Creation that God fully actualizes himself. As such, Ficino's treatment of the One and its relation with the intel-

lect represents an important moment in the assimilation of Christian and pagan theology. Although Ficino repeatedly states that the Neoplatonic triad one-intellect-soul cannot be compared with the Christian Trinity,[93] the passage above suggests that he is well aware that the Neoplatonic descriptions of the procession of being from the One were far more complicated than a subordinationist reading of Neoplatonism suggests, and could, at least in some part, be accommodated to a scholastic, and thus Christian, description of reality.

Dialectic as Poetry

Scholasticism and Platonism could be reconciled, however, only at the level of being: only Plato's divine mysteries could describe the One through negations and analogies. This is clear from Ficino's frequent associations between Parmenides' maieutic exercise and the scholastic use of abstractions, as well as the equivalence he draws between Parmenides' apparent paradoxes and the scholastic expression *signa indicativa*.[94] But Parmenides' dialectic is more than a method of preparation; it is also the highest expression of divine inspiration, comparable to poetry and prophecy. Ficino followed the Neoplatonic commentators in considering, wrongly, that Plato was presenting in the *Parmenides* the views of the historical Parmenides (early fifth century BCE), the Eleatic philosopher and author of an important metaphysical poem that has come down to us only in fragmentary form. Parmenides' *Poem* describes God in terms that differ markedly from those used in the *Parmenides* to describe the One. In this context, the Neoplatonists were particularly concerned with the extent to which one could reconcile the content of Plato's *Parmenides* with that of Parmenides' *Poem*. To resolve this conundrum, these philosophers considered that Parmenides treated of the second principle, the one being, in his *Poem*, and used it as a preliminary to the apprehension of the high-

est principle, described in the *Parmenides*. This is a position that Ficino closely follows, as illustrated by the passage below:[95]

> According to Melissus, Parmenides composed a poem about this very one being, as though it were the second principle (for the first principle is ineffable), asserting of it many things which are denied of the One in the first hypothesis, and are similarly asserted of the one being in the second hypothesis.[96]

However, as always, Ficino lays a much stronger emphasis on the mystical rather than metaphysical implications of this comparison: he attributes to the *Parmenides* the same divine powers as Parmenides' poetry, and transforms the *Parmenides'* paradoxes into poetic metaphors and allegories that initiate the reader into Plato's most divine truths. Thus Ficino argues that as a poet, Parmenides is alluding to divine mysteries in Plato's dialogue using metaphors, paradoxes, and symbols, frequently imagining the existence of things that are not, and even those that cannot be, so that "nearly every verbal surface requires an allegorical interpretation." "But what dealings do a poet and a dialectician have in common?" Ficino wonders. "Clearly almost everything. For both are alone in using their own concepts, so to speak, and their own devices; both are considered divine and both possess a form of madness."[97]

It is not the first time, as we have seen above, that Ficino invokes poetry to justify, without endorsing them, the liberties that the ancient theologians took to describe the world. Here, however, Ficino is associating Parmenides' dialectic with the "poetic madness" described in Plato's *Phaedrus*. Plato had described divine inspiration as a form of divine madness (*mania*, often rendered in Latin as *furor*), of which he believed there were four kinds: prophetic, mystic, erotic, and poetic. The notion that the poet was divinely inspired was not new. It was central in Dante's *Divine Comedy* and later developed by Albertino Mussato, Francesco Pe-

trarca, Boccaccio, Coluccio Salutati, and Leonardo Bruni, who all believed that the poet was the chosen vessel of God's inspiration and that theology was often expressed in poetic or allegorical terms.[98] Apart from Bruni, all these earlier writers were influenced by indirect traces of Platonic doctrines present in patristic and medieval literature; only Bruni had read some of Plato's dialogues in the original, and had even translated the relevant section of the *Phaedrus*. Ficino is the first to explore the doctrine in all its richness in his commentaries on Plato's *Symposium, Ion,* and *Phaedrus,* thanks to his study in the original Greek of the Neoplatonic interpretation of these texts formulated by Plotinus, Hermias, and Proclus.[99] Thus in *Platonic Theology* 13.2, he underlines the affinity between the spiritual experiences of poets, prophets, seers, and ancient philosophers, and goes as far as to compare the Neoplatonic and Christian rituals (theurgy, fasting, prayer, and abstinence) that help the soul to reach religious ecstasy. In Ficino's eyes, the poet is no longer the passive receptacle of God's inspiration described by his predecessors; he is an active agent who can intensify God's immanence by using his knowledge of medicine, magic, astrology, and philosophy; he is the poetic creator and the melancholic genius, ideas that will become commonplaces in Renaissance literature and art.[100]

By associating Parmenides' dialectic with poetry, Ficino thus restores what he believed to be the essential harmony between poetry and philosophy established by the *prisci theologi*. More specifically, Ficino wishes to show that the dialectic of the *Parmenides* is not only preparatory to the apprehension of Ideas as scholastic abstraction or Aristotelian syllogism are, but is also precisely what scholastic philosophy cannot be: a supreme form of inspiration that leads to the contemplation of Truth, comparable to the vision of the Plain of Truth described in the *Phaedrus*.[101] Just as Proclus had transformed the *Parmenides'* puzzling paradoxes and contradictions into a maieutic initiation into the theory of Ideas, Ficino

considers the text as a series of allegories that requires the interpreter's divine *afflatus* and prophetic power.

Dialectic, Astrology, and Theurgy

In Ficino's mind, the necessity for the soul to ascend toward God also implies the use of astrology and theurgy. Theurgy was a set of magical rituals used by Neoplatonic philosophers to purify the soul and achieve its deification. Despite having been condemned since Augustine as a diabolical attempt to communicate with evil spirits, theurgy was central to Ficino's work. Before undertaking the *Parmenides* commentary, Ficino had written, besides his monumental *Platonic Theology* (1482) and his commentary on Plotinus' *Enneads* (1492), three important works, all of which related in one way or another to Neoplatonic theurgy: a paraphrase/commentary on a series of Neoplatonic texts related to demonology, theurgy, and divination (1486–89); the *De Vita*, a treatise on medical, astrological, and magical practices, which drew upon Neoplatonic sources on theurgy (1489); and a commentary on Dionysius the Areopagite's treatises *On Divine Names* and *Mystical Theology* (1490–92), two texts which were themselves deeply influenced by Neoplatonic theurgy.[102] These works had a profound influence on Ficino's understanding of the *Parmenides*: in his mind the theory of the Ideas was closely associated with the notion that heaven and earth were linked magically.

Like Plotinus and Proclus, Ficino believed that the universe is structured by the existence of vertical connections between heavenly planets and earthly objects. These connections are called correspondences, and the resulting harmony between heaven and earth is called universal sympathy. As we have seen, Ficino did not wish to draw from the *Parmenides* a perfectly symmetrical metaphysical system like Proclus. However, he was fascinated by the ways in which one could exploit practically the universal sympathy

between the different levels of reality. Paraphrasing Proclus, Ficino states that each Idea communicates its power downward via a "chain" of realities, and that the intensity of the Idea's power progressively weakens as it reaches the lower degrees of reality:

> The powers that thrive yonder within the Idea of Moon in some way descend in their totality into the Moon, yet not all of them descend in the same way into the lunar demons; into lunar men on earth a smaller number of powers descend, and these in a less intense way; and even fewer and weaker powers descend into beasts, plants, metals and then into all the other things that are subject to the Idea of Moon. So the power of the architect, with its guiding wisdom, is therefore distributed in different degrees, whilst the property of the Moon under the Idea of Moon, by virtue of which this very Idea differs from the other Ideas and moonlike natures differ from solar ones, remains one (or certainly most similar to one) at all the succeeding levels of the Moon chain. [. . .] Hence the Egyptians knew the Moonlike Apis-bull and the Moonfish Selinete, which imitate the Moon's figure and movements, as well as a small stone which not only follows the power and shape of the Moon, but also its waning and waxing. Finally, if the property of the Idea of the Moon even appears at the lowest levels of the chain, it emerges to a much greater extent at the higher levels.[103]

The presence of "traces" or "tokens" (what the Greeks called *sunthemata* or *symbola,* and the Latin-speaking Christians translated by *characteres*) left by the divinities within earthly objects justifies, in Ficino's mind, the use of magic and theurgy. As he describes at length in the third book of the *De Vita,* the manipulation of material objects of a given species could have an effect on the heavenly planets of the same species. In his *Parmenides Commentary,* Ficino explicitly relates Plato's theory of Ideas—the notion that there are

connections between perfect heavenly models and earthly realities—to the notions of correspondences and universal sympathy used in magic:

> Such are indeed the series of things that the Platonists draw from the Ideas down to this world: under the Ideas of Sun, Moon and Lion are the corresponding stars, then the demons, as well as other animate beings, and the corresponding metals and stones. In addition, since the properties of Ideas and celestial things are to be found at the lowest levels, then they are necessarily even more present at the intermediate levels. Consequently, by virtue of this tightly interwoven series of cosmic components, concordance and sympathy clearly exist between the highest and the lowest levels, and vice versa. But we have sufficiently spoken about this in Book III of the *De Vita*.[104]

Similarly, Ficino mentions the Pythagorean and Neoplatonic doctrine of magical numbers, according to which numbers are seen as the archetypes of the planets and can thus carry the influences of these planets. In the commentary on the second hypothesis, Ficino explains that the second principle, the intellect, is the origin of all numbers, since all numbers derive from the dyad and the triad, which are contained in the intellect. Universal sympathy means that numbers on earth can be the symbols of divine numbers and used to invoke gods and elevate the soul to the divine. This is why, Ficino explains, the ancient priests used or invoked numbers to accomplish some magical operations, i.e., theurgy:

> There is a numerical efficacy in the divine mind and each number, proceeding from there, is destined to a particular nature, as manifested by the wondrous disposition of things within nature and the perpetual observation of numbers within highly changeable things. For this reason, the Magi,

> who observe the solar or lunar numbers and apply them to various things, often draw down the solar and lunar properties into them, and by a marvelous power they harmonize these things, which are thus in sympathy with one another. Proclus writes that the ancient priests used to employ certain numbers that possessed an ineffable power, in order to accomplish the most important operations of sacred rites — but this is Proclus' opinion.[105]

As the last sentence indicates, Ficino is careful to point out that he describes rather than fully endorses this pagan practice — a strategy of reticence that he often uses when he mentions the most delicate doctrines of pagan religion. However, given that Ficino describes in detail the way in which one can attract the divine power into numbers in the *De Vita* and devotes a whole commentary to Plato's fatal number in Book VIII of the *Republic*,[106] we can infer that he took this doctrine very seriously. Similarly, much earlier in the commentary, Ficino alludes to another important aspect of theurgy, the invocation of divine names, which carry their power upward toward superior divinities. According to this doctrine, earthly names are images (*sunthemata*) of gods, who can be conjured up by invocation:

> This is why the name that is common to the Ideas and their images is not univocal, but both the sensible object and its Idea are commonly called "man" or "horse" in the same way as the name "Socrates" in this world can either refer to a painting or to the living person. As a result, sensible things are allotted their names from the Ideas in the same way they receive their nature from them (and this nature is assuredly an image). For the first names reside in superior divinities; they are used to name intelligible realities and, in return, earthly realities; the second names reside in the souls of wise men who, after having established names by means of ideal

> concepts or concepts that are naturally known to them, first designated things that are really divine, and then, through the likeness of these, things in this world.[107]

As such, by unveiling the secret correspondences between the different degrees of being, the *Parmenides'* dialectic provides the key that ultimately leads to the deification of the soul: the poet-theologian himself becomes a god who can ascend, through the divine unity that lies in the innermost part of his soul, to God's supreme unity.

I would like to thank Stéphane Toussaint and Nigel Wilson for encouraging me, nearly ten years ago, to undertake the difficult and daunting task of translating Ficino's *Parmenides* commentary; without their continuing support and intellectual generosity I would not have persisted in a project that many considered impossible. This book would not have appeared in its present form without the skill and diligence of Martin McLaughlin, who read through the whole translation and made numerous suggestions for its improvement. I am also very grateful to Ingrid de Smet, who read the Latin text and helped me spot numerous undesirable typographical errors. I am deeply indebted to Michael J. B. Allen, Simon Gilson, and Stéphane Toussaint, whose comments and suggestions on parts of the manuscript proved invaluable. Last, but not least, I would like to express my profoundest gratitude to James Hankins, the General Editor of the I Tatti series, whose scholarship and expertise have contributed to enrich and improve considerably the final draft of this book.

In memoriam aviae dilectissimae Evelyn Menkes (1915–2011).

NOTES

1. On Porphyry's and Iamblichus' interpretations of the dialogue, which are known indirectly through Proclus and Damascius, see J. M. Dillon,

"Porphyry and Iamblichus in Proclus' Commentary on the *Parmenides*," in *Gonimos. Neoplatonic and Byzantine Studies Presented to L. G. Westerink at 75*, ed. J. Duffy and J. Peradotto (Buffalo, 1988), 21–48, and C. Steel, "Iamblichus and the Theological Interpretation of the *Parmenides*," *Syllecta Classica* 8 (1997): 15–30. The fragments of Iamblichus' interpretation have been edited by J. M. Dillon, in his *Iamblichi Chalcidensis in Platonis Dialogos Commentariorum Fragmenta* (Leiden, 1973), 206–25 and 394–403. Damascius' commentary on the second hypothesis of the *Parmenides* is also important: see *Proclus. Théologie Platonicienne*, ed. and tr. H. D. Saffrey and L. G. Westerink (Paris, 1981), lxxviii–xciv. To date, we have no evidence that Ficino read Damascius' *Parmenides* commentary. Ficino cites Damascius only once (*In Parmenidem* 38.5). However, the Medici library possessed a manuscript of Damascius's *First Principles* and *Parmenides commentary* (Laur. 86.5), which Pico might have read; see Damascius, *Traité des Premiers principes. I. De l'Ineffable et de l'Un*, ed. L. G. Westerink, trans. J. Combès (Paris, 2002), ci, and A. De Pace, *La scepsi, il sapere e l'anima. Dissonanze nella cerchia laurenziana* (Milan, 2002), 258.

2. On Neoplatonic theurgy and the Chaldean Oracles, see H. Lewy, *Chaldaean Oracles and Theurgy*, rev. ed. Michel Tardieu (Paris, 1978), and C. Van Liefferinge, *La théurgie des Oracles Chaldaïques à Proclus* (Liège, 1999).

3. See H. D. Saffrey, "Accorder entre elles les traditions théologiques: une caractéristique du néoplatonisme athénien," in *On Proclus and His Influence in Mediaeval Philosophy*, ed. E. P. Bos and P. A. Meijer (Leiden, 1992), 35–50, reprinted in H. D. Saffrey, *Le Néoplatonisme après Plotin* (Paris, 2000), 143–58.

4. On the link between the *Parmenides* and the Neoplatonic One, see Dodds, "The *Parmenides* of Plato," and H. D. Saffrey, "La philosophie néoplatonicienne."

5. With the exception of Luc Brisson, who breaks away from previous interpretations by considering "the one" as a predicate rather than a subject, all modern commentators are in one way or another influenced by the Neoplatonic interpretation of the *Parmenides*. See Plato, *Parménide*, tr. L. Brisson (Paris, 1999).

6. Proclus, *In Parmenidem* 5.1007.4–26.

7. A.-J. Festugière, "L'ordre de lecture des dialogues de Platon aux Ve/VIe siècles," *Museum Helveticum* 26 (1969): 281–96; P. Hadot, "La division des parties de la philosophie dans l'antiquité," *Museum Helveticum* 36 (1979): 201–23; L. G. Westerink, J. Trouillard, and A.-P. Segonds, *Prolégomènes à la philosophie de Platon* (Paris, 1990), xliii–lvi. On Proclus' theological interpretation of the *Sophist,* see C. Steel, "Le *Sophiste* comme texte théologique dans l'interprétation de Proclus," in *On Proclus and His Influence,* 51–64; P. Hoffmann, "What Was a Commentary in Late Antiquity? The Example of the Neoplatonic Commentators," in *A Companion to Ancient Philosophy,* ed. M. L. Gill and P. Pellegrin (Oxford, 2006), 567–622.

8. On the Plato-Aristotle controversy in antiquity, see P. Hadot, "L'harmonie des philosophies de Plotin et d'Aristote selon Porphyre dans le commentaire de Dexippe sur les *Catégories,*" in *Plotino e il Neoplatonismo in Oriente e in Occidente,* ed. E. Cerulli (Rome, 1974), 31–47; I. Hadot, "Aristote dans l'enseignement philosophique néoplatonicien: Les préfaces des commentaires sur les *Catégories,*" *Revue de Théologie et de Philosophie* 124 (1992): 407–25; F. Romano, "La défense de Platon contre Aristote par les néoplatoniciens," in *Contre Platon. I. Le platonisme dévoilé,* ed. M. Dixsaut (Paris, 1993), 175–95; R. Chiaradonna, *Sostanza, movimento, analogia: Plotino critico di Aristotele* (Naples, 1992); F. M. Najjar, "Al-Farabi's Harmonization of Plato's and Aristotle's Philosophies," *Muslim World* 94 (2004): 29–44; and G. E. Karamanolis, *Plato and Aristotle in Agreement? Platonists on Aristotle from Antiochus to Porphyry* (Oxford, 2006).

9. See C. Steel, "Proclus et Aristote sur la causalité efficiente de l'intellect divin," in *Proclus, lecteur et interprète des anciens,* ed. J. Pépin and H. D. Saffrey (Paris, 1987), 213–25.

10. There is no trace of a direct transmission of Plato's *Parmenides* in the Arabic-speaking world, although Plato's *Timaeus* and Proclus' *Elements of Theology* (misattributed to Aristotle under the title *Liber de Causis*) were very popular. See R. Walzer, "Platonism in Islamic Philosophy," in his *Greek into Arabic: Essays in Islamic Philosophy* (Cambridge, MA, 1962), 236–52, and, more recently, D. N. Hasse, "Plato arabico-latinus: Philoso-

phy, Wisdom, Literature, Occult Sciences," in Gersh and Hoenen, *The Platonic Tradition in the Middle Ages*, 31–65.

11. The direct transmission of Proclus' *Parmenides* in Byzantium occurred through George Pachymeres, who also completed Proclus' commentary by adding his own, largely Aristotelian interpretation of the rest of the text; see *George Pachymeres: Commentary on Plato's Parmenides: Anonymous Sequel to Proclus' Commentary*, ed. T. A. Gadra et al. (Paris, 1989), and *Proclus. Commentaire sur le Parménide de Platon. I. 1re Partie. Introduction générale*, ed. C. Luna and A.-P. Segonds (Paris, 2007), clvii–clxx. The indirect transmission occurred through Dionysius the Areopagite, Nicolaus of Methones' refutation of Proclus' *Elements of Theology*, Michael Psellos, and Gemistos Pletho; see K. Parry, "Reading Proclus Diadochus in Byzantium," in *Reading Plato in Antiquity*, ed. H. Tarrant and D. Baltzly (London, 2006), 223–35.

12. Klibansky, "Plato's *Parmenides*."

13. A number of sixth- and seventh-century Byzantine authors questioned the authenticity of the *Corpus Dionysiacum*, on the grounds that Dionysius the Areopagite was not mentioned by earlier ecclesiastical writers and seemed to borrow heavily from the fifth-century Neoplatonist Proclus. Maximus the Confessor and the AD 649 Council of Lateran settled the question by decreeing its apostolic origin and declaring that Proclus had actually stolen Dionysius' ideas. The debate was reopened in the Renaissance, when Lorenzo Valla demonstrated in his *Annotations to the New Testament* that the texts were a forgery. Although Ficino never openly repudiated the authenticity of the Areopagite's writings, his position remained ambiguous, oscillating between praise of Dionysius as the "foremost of all Platonists" and recognition that he might be a follower or even a usurper of the Platonists. See, for instance, Ficino, *In Parmenidem* 37.3 and 45.1.

14. On the Latin translations of the *Corpus Dionysiacum*, see *Dionysiaca: Recueil donnant l'ensemble des traductions latines des ouvrages attribués au Denys de l'Aréopage*, ed. P. Chevallier et al., 2 vols (Paris, 1937–49); S. Gersh, *From Iamblichus to Eriugena: An Investigation of the Prehistory and Evolution of the Pseudo-Dionysian Tradition* (Leiden, 1978); and P. Rorem, *Pseudo-*

Dionysius: A Commentary on the Texts and an Introduction to Their Influence (New York, 1993).

15. Proclus' commentary is preserved only until the end of the first hypothesis, the final section of which has come down to us only in the Latin translation established by the Dominican William of Moerbeke. See *Parmenides usque ad finem primae hypothesis . . . interprete Guillelmo de Moerbeka,* ed. R. Klibansky and C. Labowsky (London, 1953); Moerbeke's complete translation is in *Proclus. Commentaire sur le Parménide de Platon, traduction de Guillaume de Moerbeke,* ed. C. Steel, 2 vols. (Louvain, 1982–86). The final part of Moerbeke's translation, which is lost in the original, is now reprinted, together with a modern retroversion in Greek, in *Procli In Platonis Parmenidem Commentaria. Tomus III Libros VI–VII et indices continens,* ed. C. Steel (Oxford, 2009), 279–355. On the diffusion of Moerbeke's translation, see L. Sturlese, "Il dibattito sul Proclo latino nel Medioevo fra l'Università di Parigi e lo Studium di Colonia," in *Proclus et son influence,* ed. G. Boss and G. Seel (Zurich, 1987), 261–85, and P. O. Kristeller, "Proclus as a Reader of Plato and Plotinus and His Influence in the Middle Ages and in the Renaissance," in *Proclus, lecteur et interprète des Anciens,* 191–211.

16. Trebizond completed the translation in 1459; Bessarion published the Latin version of his pamphlet *In calumniatorem Platonis* ("Against the Slanderer of Plato") in 1469. On the *Parmenides* of Nicholas of Cusa, George of Trebizond, and Bessarion, see R. Klibansky, *Plato's Parmenides,* 24–30; J. Monfasani, *Collectanea Trapezuntiana: Texts, Documents and Bibliographies of George of Trebizond* (Binghamton, 1984); Hankins, *Plato in the Italian Renaissance,* 1: 180–92, 429–35; *Commentaire sur le Parménide de Platon: traduction de Guillaume de Moerbeke, livres V à VII et notes marginales de Nicolas de Cues,* ed. C. Steel (Leuven, 1985); I. Ruocco, *Il Platone Latino. Il Parmenide: Giorgio di Trebisonda e il cardinale Cusano* (Florence, 2003).

17. On this question, see E. N. Tigerstedt, *The Decline and Fall of the Neoplatonic Interpretation of Plato: An Outline and Some Observations* (Helsinki, 1974), 49–70; J.-L. Vieillard-Baron, *Platonisme et interprétation de Platon à l'époque moderne* (Paris, 1988); R. Bubner, "La découverte de Platon par Schelling," in *Images de Platon et lectures de ses oeuvres. Les interprétations de Platon à travers les siècles,* ed. A. Neschke-Hentschke (Paris, 1997),

257–80; W. Beierwaltes, "The Legacy of Neoplatonism in F. W. J. Schelling's Thought," *International Journal of Philosophical Studies* 10, no. 4 (2002): 393–428; and G. Varani, *Pensiero alato e modernità. Il neoplatonismo nella storiografia filosofica in Germania (1559–1807)* (Padua, 2008).

18. These are preserved in the Oxford manuscript Canon. lat. class. 163 in the Bodleian Library. See Note on the Text.

19. On Ficino's *Argumentum*, see Allen, "The Second Ficino-Pico Controversy," at 432–37; Lazzarin, "Note sull'interpretazione ficiniana del *Parmenide*," and idem, "L'*Argumentum in Parmenidem* di Marsilio Ficino."

20. H. D. Saffrey, "Notes platoniciennes de Marsile Ficin dans un manuscript de Proclus," *Bibliothèque d'Humanisme et de Renaissance* 21 (1959): 161–84, with an edition of Ficino's annotations on 168–79. In *Marsilio Ficino e il ritorno di Platone: Mostra di manoscritti, stampe e documenti*, ed. S. Gentile et al. (Florence, 1984), 35–37, no. 26, Sebastiano Gentile argues that Ficino read and annotated Ricc. 70 before 1463. Ficino also knew Balbi's translation of Proclus' *Platonic Theology* (1461–62), as shown in a famous letter to Martin Prenninger in 1489, where Ficino lists the works of Proclus available in Latin. See H. D. Saffrey, "Pietro Balbi et la première traduction latine de Proclus," in *Miscellanea codicologica F. Masai dicata*, ed. P. Cockshaw et al. (Gand, 1980), 425–37, reprinted in his *Recherches sur la tradition platonicienne au Moyen Âge et à la Renaissance* (Paris, 1987), 189–201.

21. P. O. Kristeller, *Supplementum Ficinianum. Marsilii Ficini Florentini philosophi platonici opuscula inedita et dispersa* (Florence, 1937), 1: cxx. The letters are to be found in Marsilio Ficino, *Opera quae hactenus extitere et quae in lucem nunc primum prodiere omnia* (Basel, 1576; hereafter *Op.*), 948 and 957.

22. The seven discourses, which are clearly distinguished by a separate heading, differ from the rest of the commentary in that they draw principally on Proclus' *Platonic Theology* and adopt a question-refutation structure which resembles the *disputatio* format. See my "Pico-Ficino Controversy."

23. With the exception of the commentaries on the *Timaeus* and the *Parmenides*, Ficino's Platonic commentaries have all been edited and trans-

lated by M. J. B. Allen, *Marsilio Ficino: The Philebus Commentary* (Berkeley, 1975); *Marsilio Ficino and the Phaedran Charioteer* (Berkeley, 1981), now in *Marsilio Ficino: Commentaries on Plato*, Vol. I: *Phaedrus and Ion* (Cambridge, MA, 2008); *Icastes: Marsilio Ficino's Interpretation of Plato's 'Sophist,'* and *Nuptial Arithmetic: Marsilio Ficino's Commentary on the Fatal Number in Book VIII of Plato's 'Republic'* (Berkeley, 1994).

24. Ficino wrote his commentary on Plotinus' *Enneads* between 1486 and 1490 (*Supplementum Ficinianum*, 1: cxxvi–cxxix), the commentaries on Iamblichus, Porphyry, Proclus, and Psellos between 1486 and 1489 (ibid., 1: cxxxii–cxxxv), and the commentaries on Dionysius' *Mystic Theology* and *Divine Names* in 1490–92 (ibid., 1: cxv–cxvi).

25. For a description of these two manuscripts, see Luna and Segonds, *Proclus. Commentaire sur le Parménide de Platon*, cxxiii–cxxvii and clxxxii–clxxxvi. P. Megna, "Per Ficino e Proclo," in *Laurentia laurus. Scritti offerti a Mario Martelli*, ed. F. Bausi and V. Fera (Messina 2004), 313–62, especially 351–53, has shown that for chronological and philological reasons Laur. 85.8 cannot be Ficino's main exemplar for Proclus' *Alcibiades* commentary, but she does not exclude the possibility that Ficino had access to the manuscript, which presents clear traces of horizontal transmission.

26. Ficino could have used Pierleone da Spoleto's copy, now in the Vatican Library (MS Vat. lat. 11600). On the transmission of Proclus' text, see *Procli in Platonis Parmenidem Commentaria. Tomus I Libros I–III continens*, ed. C. Steel (Oxford, 2007), vii–xlv, and Luna and Segonds, *Proclus. Commentaire sur le Parménide de Platon*, xiii–cdlxviii.

27. See P. Megna, "Marsilio Ficino e il commento al *Timeo* di Proclo," *Studi Medievali e Umanistici* 1 (2003): 93–135; idem, "Per Ficino e Proclo," 313–62; and H. D. Saffrey and A.-P. Segonds, "Ficin sur le *De Mysteriis* de Jamblique," *Humanistica* 1, no. 1–2 (2006): 117–24.

28. *Pace* Segonds' unsubstantiated claim that Ficino read Proclus in Moerbeke's version: see Luna and Segonds, *Proclus. Commentaire sur le Parménide de Platon*, cdxxi–cdxxiii.

29. On Patrizi, see M. Muccillo, *Platonismo, ermetismo e prisca theologia. Ricerche di storiografia filosofica rinascimentale* (Florence, 1996); on Scutellius, see J. Monfasani, *Nicolaus Scutellius, O.S.A., as Pseudo-Pletho: The Sixteenth-*

Century Treatise Pletho in Aristotelem *and the Scribe Michael Martinus Stella* (Florence, 2005).

30. On Ficino's indebtedness to Proclus, see Klibansky, "Plato's *Parmenides,*" 312–15; Allen, "Ficino's Theory of the Five Substances"; Beierwaltes, *Denken des Einen;* idem, "L'interpretazione ficiniana del *Parmenide* platonico"; Kristeller, "Proclus as a Reader of Plato and Plotinus"; Etienne, "Marsile Ficin"; and Malmsheimer, *Platons Parmenides und Marsilio Ficinos Parmenides Kommentar.*

31. Ficino's commentaries were produced in a nonscholastic context, in contrast with the commentaries written by Proclus. Evidence indicates, however, that Ficino taught philosophy at the University of Florence between 1466 and 1469; outside the university he also gave public lectures on Plato and had a number of pupils. See *inter alia* M. J. B. Allen, "Ficino's Lectures on the Good?," *Renaissance Quarterly* 30 (1977): 160–71; J. Hankins, "The Myth of the Platonic Academy," *Renaissance Quarterly* 44 (1991): 429–75; and J. Davies, "Marsilio Ficino: Lecturer at the Studio Fiorentino," *Renaissance Quarterly* 45 (1992): 785–90.

32. Although Ficino's interpretation of Dionysius was completed by the end of 1492, there was an overlap between the redaction of the *Parmenides* commentary and the commentaries on Dionysius, since Ficino refers to the *Parmenides* commentary in his commentaries on Dionysius (see, e.g., *Op.,* 1016, 1023, 1098) and vice versa (see, e.g., *In Parmenidem* 52.1, 57.8, 76.1, 80.2). On Ficino's interpretation of Dionysius the Areopagite, see M. Cristiani, "Dionigi dionisiaca. Marsilio Ficino e il *Corpus Dionysiacum,*" in *Il neoplatonismo nel Rinascimento,* ed. P. Prini (Rome, 1993), 185–204; D. Luscombe, "Denis the Pseudo-Areopagite in the Writings of Nicholas of Cusa, Marsilio Ficino and Pico della Mirandola," in *Néoplatonisme et philosophie médiévale: Actes du Colloque International de Corfou (6–8 octobre 1995) organisé par la Société Internationale pour l'Étude de la Philosophie Médiévale,* ed. L. G. Benakis (Turnhout, 1997), 93–107; C. Vasoli, "L'Un-Bien dans le commentaire de Ficin à la *Mystica Theologia* du Pseudo-Denys," in *Marsile Ficin. Les platonismes à la Renaissance,* ed. P. Magnard (Paris, 2001), 181–93; P. Podolak, "*Unitas apex anime.* Il commento ficiniano allo Ps. Dionigi Areopagita fra aristotelismo, platonismo e mistica medioevale," *Accademia* 11 (2009): 27–60.

33. Ficino, *In Parmenidem* 53.6–7.

34. See Proclus, *In Parmenidem* 4.1071.4–1072.11 (ed. Steel, 41–42).

35. On the Neoplatonic doctrine of the "one in the soul," see J. Rist, "Mysticism and Transcendence in Later Neoplatonism," *Hermes* 92 (1964): 213–25; W. Beierwaltes, "Der Begriff des *unum in nobis* bei Proklos," in his *Proklos: Grundzüge seiner Metaphysik* (Frankfurt, 1965), which I read in the Italian translation, *Proclo. I fondamenti della sua metafisica* (Milan, 1990), 396–411. On the reception of the doctrine in medieval mysticism, see L. Reypens, *Âme (son fond, ses puissances et sa structure d'après les mystiques)*, in *Dictionnaire de Spiritualité*, ed. M. Viller et al., (Paris, 1937), 1: 434–69; E. von Ivánka, *"Apex mentis,"* in his *Plato Christianus: Übernahme und Umgestaltung des Platonismus durch die Väter* (Einsiedeln, 1964), which I read in the French translation: *Plato Christianus: La réception critique du platonisme chez les Pères de l'Église* (Paris, 1990), 299–334. For Ficino, see Kristeller, *The Philosophy of Marsilio Ficino*, 250–51, 368; and Allen, *The Platonism of Marsilio Ficino*, 88, 124, 210–12. The concept is closely tied to the notion of the "head" of the charioteer in the mythical hymn of the *Phaedrus* 248a3; see Ficino's *In Phaedrum* 7.1–2.

36. On Proclus' doctrine of henads, see E. R. Dodds, *Proclus: Elements of Theology* (Oxford, 1933), 257–84; *Proclus. Théologie platonicienne*, ed. H. D. Saffrey and L. G. Westerink (Paris, 1978), 3: ix–lxxvii. See also J. M. Dillon, "Iamblichus and the Origin of the Doctrine of Henads," *Phronesis* 17 (1972): 102–6, and C. Steel, "Iamblichus and the Theological Interpretation of the *Parmenides*," *Syllecta Classica VIII: Iamblichus The Philosopher* (1997): 15–30.

37. Proclus, *In Parmenidem* 6.1043.30–1047.24.

38. Ficino, *In Parmenidem* 48.2.

39. See, for instance, Proclus, *In Alcibiadem* 246.21–248.4, ed. and tr. A.-P. Segonds (Paris, 1986), 2: 294–95, translated by Ficino in *Op.*, 1922, under the title *Multi gradus per quos a multitudine ad unum ascendimus contemplando*. On Ficino's translation, see Kristeller, *Supplementum Ficinianum* 1: cxxxiv–cxxxv, and P. Megna, "Per Ficino e Proclo," 313–62, who identifies Ficino's exemplar as Vatican City, Biblioteca Apostolica Vaticana MS Pal. gr. 63.

40. Ficino, *In Parmenidem* 13.1.

41. Ficino, *In Parmenidem* 15.1.

42. Allen, "The Second Ficino-Pico Controversy," and Vanhaelen, "The Pico-Ficino Controversy."

43. See, among the numerous studies on Ficino and the ideal of *prisca theologia,* D. P. Walker, *The Ancient Theology: Studies in Christian Platonism from the Fifteenth to the Eighteenth Century* (London, 1972); E. Garin, *Il ritorno dei filosofi antichi* (Naples, 1983), 67–77; Hankins, *Plato in the Italian Renaissance,* 1: 282–87, 459–64; S. Gentile, "Pletone e la sua influenza sull'umanesimo fiorentino," in *Firenze e il Concilio del 1439. Convegno di Studi (Firenze, 29 novembre–2 dicembre 1989),* ed. P. Viti (Florence 1994), 813–32; M. J. B. Allen, *Synoptic Art: Marsilio Ficino on the History of Platonic Interpretation* (Florence, 1998), 1–49; C. Vasoli, "Il mito dei *prisci theologi* come ideologia della *renovatio,*" in his *Quasi sit deus,* 11–50; B. Tambrun, "Marsile Ficin et le Commentaire de Pléthon sur les *Oracles Chaldaïques,*" *Accademia* 1 (1999): 9–48; M. Idel, "*Prisca theologia* in Marsilio Ficino and in Some Jewish Treatments," in Allen and Rees, *Marsilio Ficino,* 137–58.

44. Ficino, *In Parmenidem* 47.8.

45. See P. Hoffmann, "L'arrière-plan néoplatonicien de l'École d'Athènes de Raphaël," in *Antiquités imaginaires: La référence antique dans l'art occidental de la Renaissance à nos jours. Actes de la Table Ronde du 29 avril 1994 (École Normale Supérieure, Centre d'études anciennes),* ed. P. Hoffmann and P.-L. Rinuy (Paris, 1996), 143–58.

46. Proclus, *In Parmenidem* 1.653.4–654.10. On Ficino's conception of dialectic and its Platonic origin, see Allen, "Promethean Dialectic," in his *Synoptic Art,* 149–93.

47. Ficino, preface to *In Parmenidem,* with reference to Plato, *Republic* 7.533b and Aristotle, *Topics* 1.1.101a–b and 7.14.136a37–b13. Here Ficino follows a theory that is mentioned by Proclus (*In Parmenidem* 1.635.2–17; 1.648.14–649.2, and *Platonic Theology* 1.9, ed. Saffrey-Westerink, 35.24–36.3), although Proclus clearly differentiates the Parmenidean method from the Aristotelian (*In Parmenidem* 1.653.1). On the status of Aristotelian logic in Proclus, see J. Dillon, "Proclus and the Parmenidean Dialectic," in *Proclus. Lecteur et interprète des anciens,* 165–74; D. Buzzetti, "On

Proclus' Comparison of Aristotelian and Proclean Logic," in J. J. Cleary, *The Perennial Tradition of Neoplatonism* (Leuven, 1997), 331–44; and C. Steel, "Proclus et l'interprétation logique du *Parménide*," in *Néoplatonisme et philosophie médiévale*, 66–92.

48. Ficino, *In Parmenidem* 90.2. Here Ficino refers to a scholastic maxim (*Astrahentium non est mendacium;* see Thomas Aquinas, *Summa Theologica* 1.7.3.1) which derives from Aristotle, *Physics* 2, 193b35.

49. On this text, see F. Bausi, *Nec rhetor neque philosophus: Fonti, lingua e stile nelle prime opere latine di G. Pico della Mirandola (1484–1487)* (Florence, 1996), 13–92; L. Panizza, "Pico della Mirandola e il *De genere dicendi philosophorum* del 1485. L'encomio paradossale dei 'barbari' et la loro parodia," *I Tatti Studies: Essays in the Renaissance* 8 (1999): 69–104. The discussion between Barbaro and Pico is well documented by the first letter addressed by Barbaro to Pico (*Epistola LXVIII*, in E. Barbaro, *Epistolae, Orationes et Carmina*, ed. V. Branca [Florence, 1943], 1: 84–87), Pico's reply, the *De genere dicendi philosophorum* dating from June 3, 1485, and Barbaro's second letter to Pico. The latter are edited in both E. Garin, *Prosatori latini del Quattrocento* (Milan, 1952), 804–23 and 844–63, and F. Bausi, *E. Barbaro, G. Pico della Mirandola, Filosofia o eloquenza?* (Naples, 1998).

50. See E. Garin, *Giovanni Pico della Mirandola: De hominis dignitate, Heptaplus, De ente et uno e scritti vari* (Florence, 1942), 16–18; F. Bacchelli, *Giovanni Pico e Pier Leone da Spoleto. Tra filosofia dell'amore e tradizione cabalistica* (Florence, 2001), 103–42.

51. See *L'esprit du Quattrocento: De l'être et de l'un et Réponses à Antonio Cittadini*, ed. and tr. S. Toussaint (Paris, 1995), 166–167 (= *De ente et uno* 5). On Pico's sources and the importance of Simplicius, see De Pace, *La scepsi, il sapere e l'anima*, 255–79, especially 261–65.

52. *De ente et uno* 3–4. In the *Commento*, Pico describes divine beatitude as occurring in the soul's intellect (*Commento* 3.4 and stanzas 6–8); in the *Conclusiones* (no. 43), however, he says that it occurs in the soul's unity.

53. *De ente et uno* 2, ed. 138–42. Pico's claim differs markedly from modern logical interpretations of the dialogue, however, in that Pico's interest lies not in the need to interpret the text literally rather than mystically

but in advocating the equivalence of Plato and Aristotle (which, in itself, requires what we would now call a distorted interpretation of texts).

54. Ficino, *In Parmenidem* 49.5.

55. See Vanhaelen, "The Pico-Ficino Controversy."

56. Proclus, *Platonic Theology* 2.4 and *In Parmenidem* 6.1064.21–1066.16; Plotinus, *Ennead* 6.7.17.11. On Plotinus' doctrine of the genesis of multiplicity from the One, see M. Atkinson, *Plotinus: Ennead V 1, On the Three Principal Hypostases* (Oxford, 1983), 124–84; A. C. Lloyd, "Plotinus on the Genesis of Thought and Existence," *Oxford Studies in Ancient Philosophy* 5 (1987): 155–86; J. Bussanich, *The One and Its Relation to Intellect in Plotinus* (Leiden, 1988); C. D'Ancona, "Determinazione e indeterminazione nel sovrasensibile secondo Plotino," *Rivista di Storia della Filosofia* 45 (1990): 437–74; idem, "La doctrine de la création dans le *Liber de Causis*," *Revue des Sciences Philosophiques et Théologiques* 76 (1992): 209–33.

57. See J. Bussanich, "Non-Discursive Thought in Plotinus and Proclus," *Documenti e Studi sulla Tradizione Filosofica Medievale* 8 (1997), 190–210; idem, "Mystical Theology and Spiritual Experience," in *Proclus et la Théologie Platonicienne. Actes du Colloque International de Louvain (13–16 mai 1998) en l'honneur de H. D. Saffrey et L. G. Westerink*, ed. A.-P. Segonds and C. Steel (Leuven, 2000), 291–310.

58. Plotinus, *Ennead* 6.7.35.19, and Proclus, *In Parmenidem* 6.1071.16–19 and 6.1072.3–5.

59. Ficino, *In Parmenidem* 37.2.

60. Ficino, *In Parmenidem* 56.3 and 94.3.

61. Here Ficino is implicitly alluding to the traditional opposition (see Augustine and Thomas Aquinas) between *curiositas*, excessive desire for knowledge, sometimes associated with pagan religion, and *studiositas*, properly motivated devotion to learning. On the apologetic use of *curiositas* in Christian authors, see A. Labhardt, "*Curiositas*. Notes sur l'histoire d'un mot et d'une notion," *Museum Helveticum* 17 (1960): 206–24, especially 216–24, and P. G. Walsh, "The Rights and Wrongs of Curiosity (Plutarch to Augustine)," *Greece and Rome* 35 (1988): 73–85. It should be remembered, however, that before the seventeenth century *curiositas* was generally considered a minor vice, an unhealthy tendency to go beyond

the reach of the human intellect or to pronounce on matters where there was no certainty.

62. Ficino, *In Parmenidem* 95.2.

63. Plotinus, *Enneads* 5.3.33–44, refuted by Proclus, *Platonic Theology* 1.10 (ed. Saffrey-Westerink, p. 42.2–20). See P. Hadot, *Porphyre et Victorinus* (Paris, 1968), 1: 99–100; A. H. Armstrong, "The Background of the Doctrine 'That the Intelligibles are not outside the Intellect,'" in *Fondation Hardt. Entretiens sur l'antiquité classique. V. Les sources de Plotin* (Geneva, 1960), 391–413; J. Pépin, "Éléments pour une histoire de la relation entre l'intelligence et l'intelligible chez Platon et dans le néoplatonisme," *Revue Philosophique de la France et de l'Etranger*, 66 (1956): 34–64; C. D'Ancona, "Primo principio e mondo intelligibile nella metafisica di Proclo: problemi e soluzioni," *Elenchos* 12 (1991): 271–302. Proclus also criticizes the Plotinian conception of the soul's partial descent from the realm of the divine; see Plotinus, *Ennead* 6.8, and Proclus, *In Parmenidem* 4.948; *In Timaeum* 3.334.

64. Ficino, *In Parmenidem* 56.1. For Ficino's choice of Plotinus over Proclus in interpreting the *Phaedrus*, see Allen, *Platonism of Marsilio Ficino*, chap. 10, especially 251–55.

65. See, e.g., Ficino, *In Parmenidem* 34.4 and 78.5.

66. Ficino, *In Parmenidem* 79.6. For Ficino's conception of divinely inspired exegesis, see Hankins, *Plato in the Italian Renaissance*, 1: 314–18, and Michael Allen's forthcoming edition of Ficino's commentary on (pseudo) Dionysius the Areopagite's *Mystical Names*.

67. See Proclus, *Platonic Theology* 3.24–26; 4.28–36; 5.37–39; 6.14, 24.

68. The question as to whether the triad being-life-intelligence represents three aspects of a single reality or three successive stages in the unfolding of being from the One is tackled by Proclus in his *Elements of Theology*, prop. 103. While Plotinus considered that it was the former, Proclus thought that both were true, since each element of the triad dominates the others at some stage.

69. See Proclus, *In Parmenidem* 6.1065.15–34. See also Proclus, *Platonic Theology* 1.4 (ed. Saffrey-Westerink, p. 18.13–24). The essential link between the *Sophist* and the *Parmenides* is a fundamental point in Proclus'

metaphysics, especially in the context of his refutation of Origen the Platonist's thesis that the *Parmenides* is not theological but logical. Ficino uses Proclus' arguments against Origen to counter (in a different context) Pico's position in the *De ente et uno*.

70. Proclus, *Platonic Theology* 3.21 (ed. Saffrey-Westerink, p. 73.10–12).

71. Ficino, *In Parmenidem* 38.5. On the concept that the topic of a dialogue should correspond to the personality of its characters, see Proclus, *In Parmenidem* 1.672.

72. See Allen, "The Ficinian *Sophist* and the Controversy with Pico," in his *Icastes*, 19–22.

73. Ficino, *In Parmenidem* 53.1. See *Sophist* 243d–e, 244b–245b, and 249e–250d. See Proclus, *Platonic Theology* 2.4 (ed. Saffrey-Westerink, pp. 34.9–24 and 34.24–35.4).

74. Ficino, *In Parmenidem* 17.1, with reference to *Timaeus* 28a–c and 50b–52b; *Sophist* 239d–240b.

75. See Ficino, *In Plotinum, ad Ennead.* 3.6 (= *Op.*, 1718–19); *In Philebum* 2.1 (ed. and tr. Allen, p. 389); *In Sophistam* 46 (ed. and tr. Allen, pp. 271–77); *In Timaeum* 9 (= *Op.*, 1441–42), and *Platonic Theology* 11.4 (ed. Hankins-Allen, 3: 242–79).

76. See Plotinus, *Enneads* 3.6.6–13 and 6.7.36.6; Proclus, *In Parmenidem* 4.839–42 and 845–48.

77. On this notion, see Allen, "The Ficinian *Sophist*," 19–22.

78. The scholastic background of Ficino has been studied by P. O. Kristeller, "The Scholastic Background of Marsilio Ficino," *Traditio* 2 (1944): 257–318, reprinted in his *Studies in Renaissance Thought and Letters* (Rome, 1956), 35–98, and idem, *Le Thomisme dans la pensée italienne de la Renaissance* (Paris, 1967); A. B. Collins, *The Secular Is Sacred: Platonism and Thomism in Marsilio Ficino's Platonic Theology* (The Hague, 1967); B. P. Copenhaver, "Scholastic Philosophy and Renaissance Magic in the *De vita* of Marsilio Ficino," *Renaissance Quarterly* 37 (1984): 523–54; and J. Hankins, "Marsilio Ficino as a Critic of Scholasticism," *Vivens Homo: Rivista Teologica Fiorentina* 5 (1994): 325–34, reprinted in *Humanism and Platonism in the Renaissance*, 2: 459–69.

79. See Proclus, *In Parmenidem* 4.924. *Per reflexionem* is the scholastic expression to denote the intellect's indirect knowledge of the singular, in opposition to its direct knowledge of the universal; see Thomas Aquinas, *Summa Theologiae* 1.86.1 and 4. For the use of *consequenter* in opposition to *primo,* see *De Malo* 3.12.10.

80. Ficino, *In Parmenidem* 29.1.

81. Ficino, *In Parmenidem* 46.3. See Thomas Aquinas, *Summa Theologica* 1.5.1.3.

82. Ficino, *In Parmenidem* 58.1. Ficino here follows Proclus, *In Parmenidem* 6.1107.8–16 (ed. Steel, p. 87) and 1106.2–24 (ed. Steel, pp. 85–86). Proclus does not identify these "more ancient Platonists" (i.e., Platonists before Proclus), and Ficino's "opinion of the more ancient Platonists," below, conflates two distinct sets of opinions related by Proclus. Some modern commentators infer from similarities of language that Proclus means to refer to Iamblichus and Porphyry.

83. Lorenzo Valla, *Retractatio totius dialecticae* 1.4, ed. G. Zippel (Padua, 1982), 1: 30ff., where Valla rejects the use of the terms such as *quidditas, perseitas,* and *entitas.*

84. Pico, *De ente et uno* 5 (ed. Toussaint, pp. 160–61). On the scholastic doctrine of transcendentals according to which *ens, unum, verum,* and *bonum* are convertible, see, e.g., Albert the Great, *Summa de bono* 1.1.10, and Thomas Aquinas, *Summa theologiae* 1.6.28.

85. Ficino, *In Parmenidem* 58.2. See Proclus, *In Parmenidem* 6.1107.20–29 and 6.1109.4–14.

86. See Plotinus, *Enneads* 5.2.1. 7–9. On the difficult question of the One's absolute transcendence and omnipresence in Plotinus, see J. Bussanich, "Plotinus's Metaphysics of the One," in *The Cambridge Companion to Plotinus,* ed. L. P. Gerson (Cambridge, 1996), 38–65.

87. See Plotinus' description of the ultimate phase in the intellect's life, as described in *Enneads* 6.8.16 and commented on by J. Bussanich, *The One and Its Relation to Intellect in Plotinus: A Commentary on Selected Texts* (Leiden, 1988), 3 and 201–20, and Proclus' ambiguous statement about

the henads, which are described as *hyperousai* (above being) and thus within the One in *Elements of Theology*, prop. 115.

88. On goodness and beauty as principles that structure and limit the intelligible world, see Ficino, *Platonic Theology* 12.3, echoing Plotinus, *Enneads* 6.7.32; Proclus, *Platonic Theology* 3.28 (ed. Saffrey-Westerink, pp. 101.5–102.5) and *In Parmenidem* 4.950.39–951.7.

89. Ficino, *In Parmenidem* 84.1.

90. The notions of whole-before-parts, wholes-of-parts, and wholes-in-the-parts derive from Proclus, *Elements of Theology*, props. 67–69. See also Plotinus, *Enneads* 5.4, and Proclus, *In Timaeum* 1.177.

91. On *forma totius* and *principium formale* in medieval mereology, see Thomas Aquinas, *De ente et essentia* 2.13, *Summa contra Gentiles* 2.72, *In Aristotelis Metaphysicam* 7.17.27, and *Summa Theologica* 76.8.

92. See Ficino, *In Parmenidem* 70.1.

93. The key passages here are Ficino, *In Parmenidem* 55.2 and 94.1–2. On the relationship between the Trinity and the Neoplatonic hypostases, see M. J. B. Allen, "Marsilio Ficino on Plato, the Neoplatonists and the Christian Doctrine of the Trinity," *Renaissance Quarterly* 37 (1984): 555–84, although I consider that neither Proclus nor Plotinus adopted a proto-subordinationist model, where the second level of reality, intellect and being, was strictly separated from the One.

94. See, for instance, the title of chap. 105 (*Quomodo unum quod dicitur non ens sit natura animae, qua ratione mobilis est, de hoc non ente est scientia; huic competunt alteritas et multitudo et signa indicativa*). The scholastic expression *signa indicativa* refers to the manifest and visible signs of hidden things, in opposition to "telling signs," which are the natural accompaniments of the thing signified.

95. See, e.g., Ficino, *In Parmenidem* 55.2; 56.1; 62.1; 63.1; 66.4. See Proclus, *In Parmenidem* 6.1077–79. On the reception of Parmenides' *Poem*, see P. K. Curd, *The Legacy of Parmenides: Eleatic Monism and Later Presocratic Thought* (Princeton, 1998); J. Palmer, *Plato's Reception of Parmenides* (Oxford, 1999); and P. Thanassas, *Parmenides, Cosmos, and Being: A Philosophical Interpretation* (Milwaukee, 2007).

96. Ficino, *In Parmenidem* 55.2.

97. Ficino, *In Parmenidem* 103.1. See also Michael Allen's interpretation of this passage and of the "poetry" of the *Parmenides* in his "The Second Pico-Ficino Controversy," 445–48.

98. The best account of allegory remains that of J. Pépin, *La tradition de l'allégorie, de Philon d'Alexandrie à Dante* (Paris, 1987). On the status of poetry and philosophy in the Middle Ages and the Renaissance, see E. R. Curtius, *European Literature and the Latin Middle Ages* (Princeton, 1953), 207–13; S. Battaglia, *Dante e la teoria del poeta teologo nei secoli XIV–XV (Salutati, Bruni, Ficino, Landino)*, in *Esemplarità e antagonismo nel pensiero di Dante* (Naples, 1974), 2: 9–58; G. Ronconi, *Le origini delle dispute umanistiche sulla poesia (Petrarca e Mussato)* (Rome, 1976); R. G. Witt, "Coluccio Salutati and the Conception of the *Poeta Theologus* in the Fourteenth Century," *Renaissance Quarterly* 30 (1977): 538–63; C. Mésoniat, Poetica theologia. *La* Lucula noctis *di Giovanni Dominici e le dispute letterarie tra '300 e '400* (Rome, 1984) and *Ut philosophia poesis. Questions philosophiques dans l'oeuvre de Dante, Pétrarque et Boccace*, ed. J. Biard and F. Mariani Zini (Paris, 2008).

99. S. Gentile, "In margine all'epistola *De divino furore* di Marsilio Ficino," *Rinascimento* n.s. 23 (1983): 33–77; M. J. B. Allen, "Poetic Madness" in his *Platonism of Marsilio Ficino*, 41–67; idem, "The Soul as Rhapsode: Marsilio Ficino's Interpretation of Plato's *Ion*," in *Humanity and Divinity in Renaissance and Reformation: Essays in Honor of Charles Trinkaus*, ed. J. W. O' Malley, T. M. Izbicki, and G. Christianson (Leiden, 1993), 125–48, reprinted in M. J. B. Allen, *Plato's Third Eye: Studies in Marsilio Ficino's Metaphysics and Its Sources* (Aldershot, 1995), no. XV; idem, "Poets Outside the City," in his *Synoptic Art*, 93–123; P. Megna, *Lo Ione platonico nella Firenze Medicea* (Messina, 1999), 57–142, and, more recently, *Ficino, Commentaries on Plato I: Phaedrus and Ion*, ed. Allen, ix–lix.

100. See *inter alia* E. N. Tigerstedt, "The Poet as Creator: The Origins of a Metaphor," *Comparative Literature Studies* 5 (1968): 455–88; C. Trinkaus, *In Our Image and Likeness: Humanity and Divinity in Italian Humanist Thought* (London, 1970), 2: 683–721; S. Meltzoff, *Botticelli, Signorelli and Savonarola:* Theologia Poetica *and Painting from Boccaccio to Poliziano*

(Florence, 1987); C. Kallendorf, "From Virgil to Vida: The *Poeta Theologus* in Italian Renaissance Commentary," *Journal of the History of Ideas* 56 (1995): 41–62; N. L. Brann, *The Debate over the Origin of Genius during the Italian Renaissance* (Leiden, 2001).

101. Contrast the opposition between poetry and dialectic (in the sense of logic) in Ficino's *Argumentum* to the *Phaedrus* (ed. Allen, p. 41), where Socrates is said to distinguish different forms of love "poetically rather than dialectically" (*poetico potius quam dialectico*).

102. On the Neoplatonic sources of Ficino's *De Vita,* see B. P. Copenhaver, "Iamblichus, Synesius and the *Chaldaean Oracles* in Marsilio Ficino's *De Vita Libri Tres:* Hermetic Magic or Neoplatonic Magic?" in *Supplementum Festivum: Studies in Honor of Paul Oskar Kristeller,* ed. J. Hankins, J. Monfasani, and F. Purnell, Jr. (Binghamton, 1987), 442–45. On Ficino's translation of theurgical and demonological texts, see C. Celenza, "Late Antiquity and Florentine Platonism: The 'Post-Plotinian' Ficino," in *Marsilio Ficino: His Theology, His Philosophy, His Legacy,* 71–97, and my "L'entreprise de traduction et d'exégèse de Ficin dans les années 1486–89: Démons et prophétie à l'aube de l'ère savonarolienne," *Humanistica* 5 (2010): 125–36; on the importance of Neoplatonic theurgy in the works of Dionysius, see G. Shaw, "Neoplatonic Theurgy and Dionysius the Areopagite," *Journal of Early Christian Studies* 7, no. 4 (1999): 573–99.

103. Ficino, *In Parmenidem* 25.1. See Proclus, *In Parmenidem* 6.903–4. See also *Elements of Theology,* props. 97–102 and 110–12.

104. Ficino, *In Parmenidem* 25.2 with reference to *De Vita* 3.14. See Proclus, *In Parmenidem* 4.873–75.

105. Ficino, *In Parmenidem* 95.5. See Proclus, *Platonic Theology* 4.34 (ed. Saffrey-Westerink, p. 101.1–4).

106. See Ficino, *De Vita* 3.9–10 and 17; Allen, *Nuptial Arithmetic.*

107. *In Parmenidem* 17.4. Ficino refers to the same doctrine in his *Philebus Commentary* 11 (ed. Allen, p. 141); he relies upon Proclus, *In Parmenidem* 1.646 and 4.851–53 and *Platonic Theology* 1.29 (ed. Saffrey-Westerink, pp. 123–24).

COMMENTARIES ON PLATO

Argumentum Marsilii Ficini Florentini
in Parmenidem de uno rerum omnium principio,
ad Nicolaum Valorem prudentem optimumque civem.

1 Cum Plato per omnes eius dialogos totius sapientiae semina sparserit, in libris *De Republica* cuncta moralis philosophiae instituta collegit, omnem naturalium rerum scientiam in *Timaeo*, universam in *Parmenide* complexus est theologiam, quod quidem, ut inquit Proclus, caeteris forte incredibile videri poterit, familiaribus vero Platonis est certissimum. Cum igitur in aliis longo intervallo caeteros philosophos antecesserit, in hoc tandem seipsum superasse videtur et ex divinae mentis adytis intimoque philosophiae sacrario caeleste hoc opus divinitus deprompsisse.

2 Ad cuius sacram lectionem quisquis accedet, prius sobrietate animi mentisque libertate se praeparet, quam attrectare mysteria caelestis operis audeat. Hic enim divinus Plato de ipso uno subtilissime disputat, quemadmodum ipsum unum rerum omnium principium est, super omnia omniaque ab illo; quo pacto ipsum extra omnia sit et in omnibus omniaque ex illo, per illud atque ad illud. Ad huius quod super essentiam est unius intellegentiam gradatim ascendit, unum quippe in triplici ordine reperitur: in his quae fluunt atque sensibus subiciuntur et sensibilia nominantur; in his etiam quae semper eadem sunt et intellegibilia nuncupantur, non sensibus amplius, sed sola mente percipienda; nec in his tantum, verum etiam supra sensum et sensibilia intellectumque et intellegibilia ipsum unum existit. Quamobrem hoc in dialogo Zeno Eleates primo, Parmenidis Pythagorici discipulus, unum esse in sensibilibus probat, ostendens quod si haec multa essent,

Argument to Plato's Parmenides, *which concerns the One, principle of all things, by Marsilio Ficino the Florentine, dedicated to Niccolò Valori, wise and most virtuous citizen.*[1]

Although Plato sowed the seeds of the whole wisdom in all his dialogues, he collected in the *Republic* all the principles of moral philosophy, in the *Timaeus* all the knowledge pertaining to natural philosophy, and in the *Parmenides* he included all of theology. According to Proclus, this is something which others might perhaps find impossible to believe, but to Plato's disciples it is a fact beyond doubt.[2] Therefore, as Plato has by far surpassed all the other philosophers in the rest of his dialogues, he seems to have finally surpassed even himself in the *Parmenides*, and to have brought forth this heavenly work, with God's inspiration, from the sanctuary of the divine mind and from the innermost temple of philosophy.[3] 1

Whoever is about to undertake the sacred reading of this work should first prepare himself by tempering his soul and freeing his intellect, before daring to take up the mysteries of this heavenly work.[4] For here the divine Plato treats with the utmost subtlety of the One: how the One is principle of all things, transcends all things and is the source of all things; how the One is both outside and within all things, and how all things proceed from it, exist through it and tend toward it.[5] Plato progressively ascends toward the apprehension of the One above essence, since the One exists in three orders of realities: in the realities that are subject to flux and sense perception, and are called sensibles; in the realities that always remain the same and are called intelligibles (these are no longer perceived by the senses, but only by intelligence); and the One does not only exist in these two orders, but also beyond sense perception and the sensibles and the intellect and the intelligibles. Accordingly, the first discussant of the *Parmenides* is Zeno of Elea, the disciple of the Pythagorean Parmenides, who shows that the One exists in the sensible objects by demonstrating that many 2

nullo modo unius natura participantia, errores plurimi sequerentur. Deinde Socrates, Zenoni non repugnans quidem, sed eum altius elevans, ad considerationem unius et unitatum, quae in rebus intellegibilibus insunt, perducit, ne in hoc uno, quod sensibilibus inest, moretur. Ex hoc igitur ad ideas investigandas perveniunt, in quibus rerum unitates consistunt.

3 Postremo Parmenides ipse senior, haudquaquam Socrati contradicens, sed incohatam contemplationem eius absolvens, integram idearum explicat rationem, ubi quattuor de ideis quaestiones inducit: primam, utrum sint; secundam, quorum ideae sint et quorum minime; tertiam, quales sint quamve vim habeant; quartam, quomodo ab his quae infra se sunt participentur. Hinc iam ad unum quod super intellegibilia et ideas existit, ascendit ipse novemque de illo suppositiones adducit: quinque, si unum sit; quattuor, si non sit unum, quaerens quid utrimque sequatur. Hae vero suppositiones a triplici unius et duplici ipsius non esse partitione ducuntur, unum quippe triplex (super esse, in esse, post esse) repertum; ipsum vero non esse geminae considerationi subicitur: aut enim nullo modo esse, aut partim esse, partim non esse, quis cogitat.

4 Prima itaque suppositio tractat, si unum super esse existit, quid circa illud ad ipsum et ad alia sequitur; secunda, si unum cum esse est, id est unum ens, quomodo se habet ad seipsum atque ad alia; tertia, si unum sub esse ponitur, quid illi ad seipsum aliaque

errors would result if one supposed that these sensible objects were [only] many and did not naturally participate in the One [128A–E]. Then comes Socrates, who does not wish to contradict Zeno, but to encourage him to go beyond the sensible realm, and [thus] he leads him to consider the One and the unities that reside in the intelligibles, so as not to remain at the level of the one that resides in the sensible world [129A–E]. So it is from the One [i.e. the principle of unity] that they reach the investigation of the Ideas, because the Ideas are the unities of things.

Last comes Parmenides, who is the eldest: he does not wish to 3
contradict Socrates, but to bring the contemplation initiated by Socrates to its completion,[6] and he develops the entire doctrine of the Ideas by introducing four questions about the Ideas: firstly, whether the Ideas exist; secondly, what things have Ideas and what things have not; thirdly, what is the nature and the power of the Ideas; fourthly, how inferior realities participate in the Ideas [130A–35C].[7] Thence Parmenides ascends to the One which is above the intelligibles and the Ideas, and introduces nine hypotheses concerning the One [135C–37C]. The [first] five hypotheses postulate that the One exists; the [following] four, that the One does not exist, and they all examine the consequences that result from these two suppositions.[8] The number of hypotheses actually derives from the three different senses of the term "one" and the two different senses of the term "not-being"; for the One exists in three different ways (superior to being, united with being, and inferior to being), while not-being can be considered in two different ways—either as absolute not-being or as being in one way and not-being in another.[9]

So the first hypothesis postulates that the One superior to be- 4
ing exists and examines what the consequences are for it in relation to itself and to the others; the second, if the one united with being (i.e. the one being), exists, what the consequences are for it in relation to itself and to the others; the third examines, if the

contingit; quarta, si praeter ipsum ente superius unum sit unum in ente, quomodo se habent alia et ad se et ad unum; quinta, si est illud unum quod cum esse locatur, quid aliis ad se et ad illud accidit; sexta, si non est unum ens, ita ut partim sit, partim minime sit, qua se ratione ad sese et ad alia habeat; septima, si non est unum ens, ita ut nullo modo sit, quo pacto se habet ad seipsum atque ad alia; octava, si non est id unum, ita ut partim sit, partim non sit, quid aliis ad se et ad illud eveniat; nona, si non est hoc unum, ita ut nullo modo sit, quid alia ad sese et ad illud denique patiantur.

5 In his omnibus generatim intendit Parmenides potissimum hoc asserere, quod unum omnium principium sit, eoque posito ponantur omnia, sublato autem interimantur. Itaque in primis quinque suppositionibus quinque rerum gradus posito uno in rerum ordine tradit; in quattuor vero sequentibus inquirit quot absurda, quot errores quantaque mala ipso uno sublato sequantur. Prima ex quinque superioribus de uno supremoque deo disserit, quomodo procreat disponitque deorum sequentium ordines; secunda de singulis deorum ordinibus, quo pacto ab ipso deo proficiscuntur; tertia de divinis animis; quarta de his quae circa materiam fiunt, quomodo a supernis causis producuntur; quinta de materia prima, quemadmodum suapte natura specierum est expers et a primo uno dependet.

one inferior to being exists, what the consequences are for it in relation to itself and to the others; the fourth, if, besides the One superior to being, the one in being [i.e. the one being] exists, what the consequences are for the others in relation to themselves and to that "one"; the fifth, if the one united with being [i.e. the one being] exists, what the consequences are for the others in relation to themselves and to that "one";[10] the sixth, if the one being does not exist in the sense that it is [only] partially not-existent, what the consequences are for it in relation to itself and to the others; the seventh, if the one being does not exist in the sense that it is absolutely not-existent, what the consequences are for it in relation to itself and to the others; the eighth, if this "one" does not exist in the sense that it is partially not-existent, what the consequences are for the others in relation to themselves and to the "one"; the ninth, if this "one" does not exist, in the sense that it is absolutely not-existent, what the consequences are finally for the others in relation to themselves and the "one."[11]

5 In general, Parmenides' main purpose in all these hypotheses is to declare that the One is the principle of all things and that, when you postulate that it exists, all things exist, while when you postulate that it does not exist, all things perish.[12] So in the first five hypotheses, which posit that the One exists in the order of things, Parmenides describes the five levels of realities; in the following four he examines how many absurdities, errors and evils result from the nonexistence of the One itself.[13] Among the first five hypotheses the first treats of the One and supreme God, and of the way in which He creates and arranges the orders of the following gods; the second treats of the individual orders of gods and how they proceed from God; the third concerns the divine souls; the fourth, the forms-in-matter and how they are created by the superior causes; the fifth treats of the first matter and of the way in which it is naturally deprived of species [i.e. formless], and depends on the first One.[14]

Illud insuper advertendum est, quod in hoc dialogo, cum dicitur unum, Pythagoreorum more unaquaeque substantia a materia penitus absoluta significari potest, ut deus, mens, anima. Cum vero dicitur aliud et alia, tam materiam quam illa quae in materiam fiunt, intellegere licet.

His ergo praemissis atque servatis ad ipsum dialogum veniamus.

One must also note that in the *Parmenides* the term "one" can designate, as is customary among the Pythagoreans, any substance that is absolutely separate from matter, such as God, the intellect or the soul, while one should understand the terms "other" and "others" to designate both matter and forms-in-matter.[15]

Let us then proceed to the dialogue, bearing in mind these preliminary remarks.

<Capitula Commentarii>

<*Chapter Headings*>

Cap. xv Etiam quae per ideas ipsas non exprimuntur ad providentiam pertinent causamque divinam.

Cap. xvi Parmenides responsiones Socratis corrigit vel dirigit, non disperdit.

Cap. xvii Quomodo res nostrae participant ideas, tamquam imagines idearum, neque his atque illis est ulla ratio eadem vel natura communis.

Cap. xviii Idea non participatur corporeo more, ita ut vel tota vel pars eius aliqua capiatur.

Cap. xix Ipsa magnitudo, aequalitas, parvitas ideales non participantur conditione quadam in partes divisibili.

Cap. xx Ideas non convenire cum materialibus neque natura neque conditione.

Cap. xxi Non debemus ex qualibet multorum communione, unam illorum ideam excogitare.

Cap. xxii Oportet a speciebus quae fiunt ab anima ad species ascendere, quae naturaliter insunt animae, ab his insuper ad divinas.

Cap. xxiii Primae rerum species, quae etiam sunt principalia intellectus obiecta, intellegentias antecedunt.

Cap. xxiv Ideae non tam intellegentiae quam intellegibilia sunt atque haec intellegentias antecedunt.

Chapter 15 Even the things that are not expressed by the Ideas themselves pertain to divine providence and the divine cause.

Chapter 16 Parmenides corrects or guides Socrates' responses rather than refuting them.

Chapter 17 How earthly objects participate in Ideas as images of Ideas, and how there is no identical rational principle nor any common nature between them.

Chapter 18 The Idea is not participated in a corporeal way so that it would be taken either as whole or as part.

Chapter 19 The Ideas of greatness, equality, and smallness are not participated according to a condition that would divide them into parts.

Chapter 20 The Ideas are not aligned with material things either in nature or condition.

Chapter 21 The mere fact that an association between many things exists should not make us assume the existence of a single Idea common to them.

Chapter 22 One should ascend from the species produced by the soul up to the species that are naturally in the soul, and from these up to the divine species.

Chapter 23 The first species of things, which are also the principal objects of the intellect, precede the intelligences.

Chapter 24 The Ideas are not intelligences but intelligible objects, and they precede intelligences.

Cap. xxv Proprietas idealis una quodammodo est in tota serie, virtus autem varia.

Cap. xxvi Ideae non sunt simplices notiones quaedam, sed species naturales, vim exemplarem efficientemque habentes.

Cap. xxvii Naturales formae dicuntur quidem ideis similes, ideae vero harum similes appellari non debent.

Cap. xxviii Contra Stoicos atque Peripateticos quod ideae divinaque omnia et natura segregata sunt et virtutem habent cunctis communicabilem.

Cap. xxix Quomodo ideae a nobis cognosci non possint, item quomodo possint.

Cap. xxx Quomodo ideae non referantur vel referantur ad nostra et haec ad illas ac de dominatione illic et servitute et relationibus idearum.

Cap. xxxi Quomodo ipsa simpliciter scientia ad ipsam simpliciter veritatem refertur, scientia humana ad humanam. Quomodo ideae ignotae vel notae.

Cap. xxxii De modo divinae cogitationis atque providentiae.

Cap. xxxiii De dominatione et cogitatione divina atque de sex ordinibus idearum vel formarum.

Cap. xxxiv Nisi sint ideae penes deum et ideales in nobis formulae, peribit dialectica omnisque philosophia; non erit demonstratio vel definitio vel divisio vel resolutio.

Chapter 25 The property of the Idea in some way remains one in the whole chain, while its power varies.

Chapter 26 The Ideas are not simple notions but natural species with a paradigmatic and efficient force.

Chapter 27 The natural forms are said to be "like" the Ideas, but their Ideas should not be called "like" them.

Chapter 28 Contrary to the doctrines of the Stoics and the Peripatetics, the Ideas and all divine beings are separated from nature and at the same time have a power communicable to all things.

Chapter 29 How the Ideas cannot be known by us, and also how they can.

Chapter 30 How the Ideas relate, or not, to earthly realities, and how the latter relate to the Ideas. On mastership and slavery yonder, and on the relationships between the Ideas.

Chapter 31 How absolute knowledge is related to absolute truth and human knowledge is related to human truth. How the Ideas can or cannot be known.

Chapter 32 On the mode of divine knowledge and providence.

Chapter 33 On divine mastership and cognition, and on the six orders of Ideas or forms.

Chapter 34 If the Ideas are not within God and the ideal formulae are not within us, there will be no dialectic or philosophy; there will be no demonstration, no definition, no division, and no analysis.

Cap. XXXV De dialectica exercitatione per formas intellectuales ad species intellegibiles.

Cap. XXXVI Regulae dialecticae supponentes esse vel non esse et quot modis dicitur non ens.

Cap. XXXVII Futura disputatio dicitur ardua, quia non solum logica est, sed etiam theologica.

Cap. XXXVIII De suppositionibus *Parmenidis* et de uno bonoque quod ente et intellectu superius per verba Platonis.

Cap. XXXIX Item quomodo Plato procedit ad primum. De nomine eius. De idea boni.

Cap. XL Rursus duae Platonis ad primum viae, duo nomina primi.

Cap. XLI Sequuntur discursus Platonici probantes unum esse principium omnium et esse ipsum unum bonumque superius ente. Primus discursus.

Cap. XLII Secundus ad idem discursus.

Cap. XLIII Tertius ad idem discursus ac de simplicitate primi et ultimi.

Cap. XLIV Quartus ad idem discursus et de contemplatione boni.

Cap. XLV Quintus ad idem discursus et de appellatione primi.

Cap. XLVI Sextus ad idem discursus et quod non eligitur simpliciter esse, sed bene esse atque bonum.

Cap. XLVII Septimus ad idem discursus et quae differens ratio entis atque boni.

Cap. XLVIII Principium universi est ipsum simpliciter unum, principium in quolibet ordine quod ibi est maxime unum. De sole, natura, intellectu.

Cap. XLIX Primum rerum principium est unitas bonitasque super intellectum, vitam, essentiam.

Cap. L De unitate super essentiam, de unitatibus in essentiis, de diis, de communi intentione Parmenidis in suppositionibus suis.

Cap. LI Dispositio propositionum *Parmenidis* apud Plutarchum.

Cap. LII Quid significent in suppositionibus negationes, quid affirmationes, quae et quo ordine tractentur in eis.

Cap. LIII Intentio, veritas, ordo suppositionis primae.

Cap. LIV Ubi entium proprietates de uno negantur, significatur ipsum haec omnia antecellere atque procreare.

Cap. LV De uno ente, de ipso simpliciter uno, de intentione Parmenidis hic et in poemate, intentio et epilogus negationum.

Cap. LVI De universo ente et proprietatibus eius, et quomodo negantur de primo et quae multitudo negatur et quare negatur.

Cap. LVII Per negationem multitudinis negantur de uno partes et totum. Numerus est ante entia, omnis multitudo particeps unitatis. Idem est prima essentia, vita, mens.

Cap. LVIII Opinio affirmans abstractorum abstracta de deo. Item tutiores sunt negationes relationesque circa deum.

Cap. LIX Si unum non habet partes, consequenter nec habet principium vel finem aut medium.

Cap. LX Quomodo ipsum unum dicatur infinitum omniumque finis.

Cap. LXI Quomodo negatur de uno figura et rectum atque rotundum.

Cap. LXII Ipsum unum nusquam est quia nec est in seipso nec in alio. Item quomodo separata dicuntur ex seipsis existere vel produci.

Cap. LXIII Quomodo unum neque moveri neque stare dicatur, et quomodo sit motus et status in omnibus praeter primum.

Cap. LXIV	Unum neque circulo movetur nec in rectum.
Cap. LXV	Quomodo negatur de uno status.
Cap. LXVI	Quinque genera entis. Tres negationum gradus. Decem praedicamenta negata. De eodem alteroque nonnihil.
Cap. LXVII	Unum nec a seipso alterum est nec idem alteri et ab omnibus conditionibus est absolutum.
Cap. LXVIII	Unum non est ab aliis alterum.
Cap. LXIX	Unum non est sibi ipsi idem.
Cap. LXX	Unum nec est simile neque dissimile vel sibi vel cuiquam.
Cap. LXXI	Unum nec sibi nec aliis est aequale vel inaequale.
Cap. LXXII	Confirmatio superiorum.
Cap. LXXIII	Unum neque iunius neque senius neque coaetaneum vel ad se vel ad alia esse potest.
Cap. LXXIV	Ipsum unum super aeternitatem et tempus et motum est, nec ulla ratione esse in tempore dici potest.
Cap. LXXV	Relativorum regula cum confirmatione quadam superiorum.
Cap. LXXVI	Cum unum sit supra tempus consequenter conditiones temporis temporaliumque excedit.

Cap. LXXVII Ipsum unum nec est essentiae particeps nec ipsa essentia nec ipsum esse, sed longe superius.

Cap. LXXVIII Qua conditione negatur essentia vel esse de uno. Item quare cognosci vel nominari non possit.

Cap. LXXIX De firmitate suppositionis primae et quod unum ente superius.

Cap. LXXX Secundae suppositionis intentio.

Cap. LXXXI Quomodo in uno ente alia sit ratio unius, alia entis sit, totum partes habeat et multitudinem infinitam.

Cap. LXXXII In uno ente per binarium et ternarium omnes numeri continentur. Qui numeri distributionem entis unius in entia multa praecedunt.

Cap. LXXXIII Quomodo in mundo intellegibili dividatur essentia simul et unum multitudoque finita vel infinita sit.

Cap. LXXXIV Quomodo in mundo intellegibili partium multitudo sub gemina totius forma concluditur. Quomodo terminos mediumque habet atque figuras.

Cap. LXXXV Quomodo unum ens in seipso sit et in alio.

Cap. LXXXVI Quomodo unum ens stet semper atque moveatur.

Cap. LXXXVII Unum ens est sibimet idem atque alterum. Item caeteris idem atque alterum.

Cap. LXXXVIII Unum ens et ad seipsum et ad alia simile est atque dissimile.

Cap. LXXXIX Quomodo unum ens tangit et tangitur neque tangit neque tangitur quantum ad se et ad alia pertinet.

Cap. XC Quomodo unum ens sit aequale vel inaequale sibi vel aliis.

Cap. XCI Quomodo unum ens sit numero par et plus et minus ad seipsum atque caetera.

Cap. XCII Quomodo unum ens dicatur senius et iunius atque coaetaneum ad seipsum atque caetera.

Cap. XCIII Quomodo distinguatur senius iuniusve fieri rursumque senius iuniusve esse. Ac de uno ente conclusio.

Cap. XCIV Summa vel epilogus suppositionis secundae. De distinctionibus divinorum.

Cap. XCV Summae huius vel epilogi distinctiones. De uno ente, multitudine, numero infinito ordinibusque deorum.

Cap. XCVI Tertia suppositio. Intentio suppositionis. Quomodo anima ens dicatur atque non ens, de motu et tempore in anima. Item de quodam eius aeterno. Rursus quomodo commutatione quadam sui ipsius omnia repraesentet.

Chapter 87 The one being is the same as, and different from, itself. Similarly, it is the same as, and different from, the others.

Chapter 88 The one being is like and unlike itself and the others.

Chapter 89 How the one being has, and has not, contact with itself and with the others.

Chapter 90 How the one being is equal and unequal to itself and to the others.

Chapter 91 How the one being is equal, superior, and inferior in number in relation to itself and to the others.

Chapter 92 How the one being is said to be older, younger, and equal in age, in relation to itself and the others.

Chapter 93 How to distinguish between becoming older and younger and being older and younger. Conclusion on the one being.

Chapter 94 Summary or epilogue of the second hypothesis. Regarding the distinctions of divine realities.

Chapter 95 Distinctions in this summary or epilogue. On the one being, multitude, infinite number, and the orders of gods.

Chapter 96 Third hypothesis. The purpose of the hypothesis. The way in which the soul is called being and not-being. On motion and time within the soul. On a certain eternal thing belonging to it. Again, how by a kind of sharing of itself it represents all things.

Cap. XCVII Qua ratione caelestis anima circa mentem stabilem moveatur agatque circuitum. Quot sint motus animae. Quot motus et quies in tempore, et de medio inter motus.

Cap. XCVIII Summa suppositionis tertiae vel epilogus. De uno, multitudine, ente, non ente, motu, statu, momento, tempore, oppositione. Motus ad motum atque statum.

Cap. XCIX Suppositio quarta. Quartae suppositionis intentio. Totum ante partes, totum post partes, res divinae, res naturales, relatio partium ad totum.

Cap. C De multitudine quomodo se habeat ad unum, de infinito et termino entium elementis, de caeteris inter se oppositis.

Cap. CI Suppositio quinta. Quintae suppositionis intentio. De uno, de aliis ab uno, utrum unum cum his conveniat, de omniformi ente, de informi materia.

Cap. CII Confirmatio superiorum et quomodo materia formales in se conditiones nullas habeat. Item unde sit vel formetur vel moveatur.

Prooemium Marsilii Ficini
in commentarium suum in Parmenidem:
materia quidem Parmenidis plurimum theologica,
forma vero dialectica.

1 Pythagorae Socratisque et Platonis mos erat ubique divina mysteria figuris involucrisque obtegere, sapientiam suam contra sophistarum iactantiam modeste dissimulare, iocari serio et studiosissime ludere. Itaque in *Parmenide* sub ludo quodam dialectico et quasi logico, exercitaturo videlicet ingenium ad divina dogmata, passim theologica multa significat. Praeterea consuetudo fuit Pythagoreorum Platonisque plures invicem materias, partim more naturae, partim ratione gratiae, opportune miscere. In *Phaedro* conflat cum theologia oratoriam et poesim, in *Timaeo* physicis inserit mathematica. Disserendi artem cum divinis vel etiam cum moralibus saepe coniungit, divisivam quidem et definitivam in *Philebo* et *Politico* atque *Sophiste*, demonstrativam in *Parmenide* similiter copulat cum divinis, ne forte si sola logica tradiderit rudimenta, tamquam paedagogus quidam erudire pueros videatur. Quemadmodum vero demonstrativa divisivam et definitivam antecellit tamquam finis, sic eam in materia quadam diviniore traditam arbitrantur. Aristoteles quinetiam dialecticam summam—malo enim dialecticam dicere quam *dialecticen*—miscuit cum divinis, Platonem, ut arbitror,

Marsilio Ficino's preface
to his commentary on the Parmenides.
The subject of the Parmenides *is for the most part theological,*
but the form is dialectical.

1 It was the custom of Pythagoras, Socrates and Plato to conceal divine mysteries everywhere beneath figures and veils, to modestly dissimulate their wisdom, in contrast to the sophists' arrogance, to jest in seriousness and to joke in the greatest earnest. For this reason, at many points in the *Parmenides* Plato alludes to a number of theological issues in the guise of a dialectical and almost logical game, in order to exercise the mind continuously in the apprehension of divine dogmas. In addition, the Pythagoreans and Plato used suitably to blend together a large number of topics, partly after the manner of nature and partly following the pattern of Grace.[1] In the *Phaedrus* Plato blends oratory and poetry with theology, in the *Timaeus* he mingles mathematics with physics. He frequently unites the art of debating with divine or even ethical matters. In the *Philebus, Statesman,* and *Sophist* Plato combines the consideration of divine matters with the methods of division and definition; likewise in the *Parmenides* he combines it with the method of demonstration. This was perhaps done to prevent the impression that Parmenides is teaching solely elementary principles of logic like a schoolmaster.[2] Just as the method of demonstration surpasses, as an end, the methods of division and definition, so, they believed, it should be imparted in the case of any given material that contains divine truths. Aristotle himself blended the highest form of dialectic (I prefer the Latin word *dialectica* to the Greekish *dialektikè*)[3] with divine matters, in imitation, I believe, of Plato, who used the term "dialectic" to designate theol-

imitatus theologiam in *Republica* sub dialectico nomine designantem. Materia igitur *Parmenidis* huius potissimum theologica est, forma vero praecipue logica. Qualem utique dispositionem ordinemque libri Proclus eiusque sectatores existimaverint, narravimus in principio; qualem vero ipse putem et quatenus sequar illos, paulatim in sequentibus declarabo.

ogy in the *Republic*.[4] In other words, the subject of the *Parmenides* is theological above all, yet its form is particularly logical. We have first [in the *argumentum* to the *Parmenides*] described what Proclus and his successors thought about the book's arrangement and order; what I think about that, and to what extent I follow these philosophers, I shall gradually explain in the following commentary.

COMMENTARY ON THE *PARMENIDES*

: I :

Dispositio ad dialogum Parmenidem.

1 Cephalus et socii rogant Adimantum et Glauconem Platonis fratres ex patre simul atque matre ut persuadeant Antiphoni eorum non ex patre fratri, sed ex matre germano, ut narret illis disputationem illam quam acceperat a Pythodoro, qui quondam interfuerat quando Parmenides Zenoque, Pythagorici et Socrates invicem disputabant.

: II :

Quomodo omne ens sit unum, ipsum vero unum super ens.

1 Parmenides argumentis plurimis in poemate confirmavit universum vel omne ens esse unum. 'Universum' vero 'sive omne' tribus his modis accipitur, singulatim, congregatim, summatim. Primo itaque pacto ens quodlibet et hoc seorsum et istud et illud est aliquid in se unum, ab aliis singulari quadam proprietate distinctum. Secundo vero cuncta simul entium amplitudo ita unum est ut quoquomodo cuncta invicem in essendo conveniant, ab eodem interim principio ducta, et ad eundem finem communem, postremo redacta invicemque motu quodam actionibusque et passionibus conspirantia. Tertio denique ipsum inter entia primum et unum est et omne. Unum quidem, quoniam sicut entia naturalia ad naturam unam et corporea ad corpus unum, sic omnia simpliciter entia ad ens tandem unicum referuntur. Omne rursus, quoniam sicut omnium naturarum corporumve vires in prima na-

: I :

The arrangement of the Parmenides.

Cephalus and his friends ask Plato's brothers, Adeimantus and Glaucon, to persuade Antiphon, their brother on their mother's side, to recount for them the discussion that Antiphon had heard from Pythodorus, who was present the day Parmenides, Zeno, the Pythagoreans and Socrates had a philosophical debate [126A–27A]. 1

: II :

How every being is one, but the One itself is above being.

In his poem Parmenides used many arguments to establish that "universal or all being is one" [128A–B]. The expression "universal or all" is used in three senses: individually, collectively, or as a whole. So according to the first sense, any indeterminate being taken separately is one in itself, and distinct from the rest of beings by an individual property. According to the second sense, the whole extent of beings is collectively one, since beings are in some way all in accordance by virtue of "being": they originate from the same principle, they are ultimately brought back to the same end, and they all undergo motion, actions and passions. Finally, according to the third sense, the first among the beings is both one and all. It is "one" because, just as natural beings are related to one nature and corporeal beings to one body, so all the simple beings are ultimately related to one unique being. It is "all" because, just as the forces of all the natures and bodies are contained in the first 1

tura et primo corpore continentur, sic in uno primo ente entia omnia comprehenduntur, quem mundum intellegibilem nominamus.

2 Neque vero Peripateticorum quorundam recipiendae sunt calumniae, quibus suspicemur Parmenidem, ubi dicit omne ens unum esse, omnem penitus ex universo multitudinem auferre, alioquin Plato in *Theaeteto* ubi de uno immobili ente fit mentio, Parmenidem non reveritus quidem esset, sed potius insecutus. Enimvero Plato una cum Pythagoricis multitudinem etiam in primo ente ponit, scilicet oppositorum generum et idearum varietatem omnemque prorsus originem numerorum. Sed illud interea, una cum numero, usque adeo unum esse vult, ut post primum aliquid magis unum cogitari non possit.

3 Hactenus[1] Parmenides ter unum nominans intellegit participatione unum. Primo quidem et secundo modo participatio unitatis est imperfecta, tertio vero perfecta. Sed praeter unitatem illam intellegibili mundo perfecte participatam, eminentissimam excogitat unitatem universo ente uno excelsiorem. Alia enim ipsius entis, alia unitatis ipsius ratio est, entis siquidem rationi multitudo et compositio non repugnat, unitatis autem rationi repugnat. Illi praeterea non ens, huic non unum est oppositum. Dicere vero non ens non est prorsus idem atque non unum dicere, siquidem non unum non necessario nihilum significat, sed diversam etiam multitudinem. Unum igitur ens non est ipsum simpliciter unum, sed quoquomodo compositum multitudinique permixtum. Quemadmodum vero a calore vel lumine mixto frigori aut tenebris, ad calorem lumenque purissimum perveniendum ratio naturaque docet, et a substantia incorporea quidem, sed coniuncta corpori, ad incorpoream substantiam a corpore separatam, item ab ente temporali quod quodammodo est non enti permixtum, ad ens aeter-

nature and the first body, so all beings are contained in the first and one being, which we call the intelligible realm.

Let us not pay attention to the calumnies of some Peripatetics, who try to make us believe that when Parmenides says that "all being is one" he abolishes all multitude from the universe [128B–E].[1] If this were the case, Plato would not express reverence but hostility toward Parmenides in the passage of the *Theaetetus* where he mentions the motionless one being.[2] Assuredly Plato, like the Pythagoreans, places multitude (namely, the variety of opposite genera and Ideas and indeed the very principle of numbers) even in the first being. Yet he considers that the first being, as well as number, is "one" to such an extent that, with the exception of the first principle, nothing can be conceived of as more "one" than that. 2

Thus far, when Parmenides refers to the three senses of the term "one," he considers a reality that is one by participation. According to the first two modes, participation in unity is imperfect; according to the third mode, it is perfect. But beyond the unity that is perfectly participated in by the intelligible world, Parmenides conceives an absolutely transcendent unity that is superior to the universal one being. For the rational principle of being is different from that of unity, since the former does not reject multitude and composition, while the latter does; in addition, the opposite of being is not-being, while the opposite of one is not-one. Not-being is completely different from not-one, since "not-one" does not necessarily mean "nothing," but can also refer to the multitude that is distinct from unity. The one being, therefore, is not the absolute One, but is in some way a composite and is mixed with multitude. Just as reason and nature teach us to reach the purest forms of heat and light, starting from heat or light that are mixed with cold and darkness, and the incorporeal substance that is separate from the body, starting from the substance that is incorporeal but joined to the body (and similarly, how to reach eternal being, starting from the temporal being that in some way is 3

num, sic ab unitate cum essentia iuncta ad unitatem ab essentia penitus absolutam. Quae quidem, qua ratione est simplicior quam essentia, eadem est necessitate superior. Hoc nomine rerum principium finemque omnium propter summam simplicitatem virtutemque unitate significatam Parmenides nuncupavit.

: III :

Omnis multitudo est particeps[2] unitatis.

1 Positionem vero Parmenidis qua omne ens esse unum, id est particeps unius, asseritur, Zeno discipulus alia positione confirmat, qua probat ens non esse multa, id est solum multa, sed praeter multitudinem esse particeps[3] unitatis. Nisi enim in tanto diversorum entium numero aliqua unitatis participatio foret, essent inter se penitus dissimilia[4] nec invicem vel ordine vel alio quopiam convenirent, quod patet unicuique falsum. Item qua ratione ita essent inter se dissimillima, eadem quoque similia forent, quod dictu stultum, siquidem in hoc similiter invicem se haberent, quod, sicut hoc discrepat prorsus ab illo, ita vicissim et ab hoc illud penitus discreparet, par pari, ut dicitur, invicem referentia. Quatenus ergo nullum haberent unum, dissimillima forent—similitudo enim in quadam unione consistit—eadem quoque ratione similia, siquidem hoc ipsum commune saltem inter se haberent, quod fingebamus, unum videlicet, non habere. Item neque similia neque dissimilia forent: non quidem similia, si privarentur uno omnis

mixed with not-being), so they teach us how to reach, starting from the unity that is joined to essence, the unity that is totally separated from essence. This unity is necessarily superior to essence, for the very reason that it is simpler than essence. Parmenides named "unity" the principle and end of all things, because this word expresses the highest simplicity and power [of the first principle].

: III :

Every multitude participates in unity.

1 According to Parmenides, the universal being is one, which means that it participates in the One. This is confirmed by another position formulated by Parmenides' disciple Zeno, who demonstrates that being is not many, that is to say, being is *not only* many, but besides multitude it also participates in unity [128A–E]. For if so many different beings did not participate in unity, they would be totally unlike one another, and would not be in accordance with each other in any order or anything else, which is evidently false. Similarly, by virtue of being completely unlike one another, they would also be like one another, which is a foolish thing to say. For these beings would be like one another in their disposition, by virtue of the fact that, just as one totally differs from the other, so the latter totally differs from the former, in a relation of like to like, so to speak. Therefore, inasmuch as they would possess no unity they would be completely unlike (for likeness consists in union), and for the same reason they would also be like, since they would have in common at least the very thing we imagined—the fact of not possessing unity. Similarly, they would be neither like nor unlike. They would not be like, since they would be deprived

similitudinis auctore; non etiam dissimilia, dum similiter in hac ipsa privatione congruerent. Haec utique sequentur absurda caeteraque permulta, quae alibi diximus et dicemus, si quis multitudinem rerum finxerit unitatis expertem. Sequentur itidem, si plura rerum principia prima: sive enim unius eiusdemque participia sint, sub illo uno tamquam principio ipsa iam non principia locabuntur, sive nullum commune unum habuerint, iam neque communiter principia erunt neque inter se similia, rursus neque penitus dissimilia, siquidem communem unius absentiam patiantur. Denique eadem iterum ratione cum dissimilia, tum similia probabuntur.

: IV :

Ideas esse et quales.

1 Hanc de multitudine unionis participe disputationem Zenonicam transfert Socrates ad ideas, ipse videlicet idearum semper amicus cum Pythagoricis in praesentia disputans, ut Plato in *Sophiste* testatur, amatoribus idearum. Rationes equidem confirmantes ideas in *Theologia* et in Plotino sum latius prosecutus. Socrates in praesentia eiusmodi nititur probatione: specialis quaelibet singularium multitudo in unaquadam proprietate naturaque convenit speciali, ut homines in una humanitate multi. Id vero commune unum neque dependet a multis, qua ratione multa sunt et varia, neque a

of the One, which is the cause of all likeness; neither would they be unlike, since they would share the fact that they are deprived of the same thing. Such are, assuredly, the absurdities that will follow, as well as many others, which we have mentioned elsewhere and will mention again, if we imagine that the multitude of things is deprived of unity.[3] The same absurdities will follow if we imagine that there is more than one first principle. For either these many principles participate in a unique and identical principle, and will thus be placed under that one principle and cease to be themselves principles, or they have no unity in common, and will then cease to share the fact of being principles and will no longer be like one another; they will no longer be totally unlike either, since they will undergo the same absence of unity. Finally, according to the same reasoning they will be shown to be both dissimilar and similar.[4]

: IV :

Existence and nature of Ideas.

1 Socrates leads the discussion with Zeno away from the participation of multitude in unity, to the Ideas [129A–E]. Socrates, the eternal friend of Ideas, is presently discussing the question with the Pythagoreans who, according to Plato's *Sophist,* are the "lovers of Ideas."[5] I have myself described at length the reasons confirming the existence of Ideas in my *Theology* and in my commentary on Plotinus.[6] Now Socrates tries to prove their existence with the following demonstration: any multitude corresponding to an individual species shares each property and nature of that species — for instance, the multitude of human beings have in common humanity, which is one. Yet this "one" they have in common does not depend on the many, since the many are many and differ-

quolibet multorum, qua ratione proprium est quodlibet atque differens, neque per se et ex se existit, quandoquidem nec in seipso manet, sed in multitudine iacet, neque purum perfectumque unum est, siquidem est particeps multitudinis, neque perfecta natura, quandoquidem alienis mixta conditionibus atque mutabilis. Haec igitur, tamquam in his multis una, ab una tandem perfecta dependet his multis longe superiore, scilicet ab idea hominis, humana natura; ab idea ignis ignea quoque natura. Humana profecto species, quod sempiterna sit, non habet nisi a causa quadam immobili; item quod universalis non habet a particulari causa, sed tantum universali. Causa vero immobilis simul universalisque necessario est intellectus et intellectualis idea.

2 Definitiones scientiasque naturarum ad has ipsas ideas existimat Socrates pertinere, si modo quod definitur atque scitur absolutum sit neque possit aliter se habere atque ita intrinsecus moveat intellectum quod revera intellegibile est, quemadmodum quod revera sensibile extrinsecus movet sensum. Ideae rursus multae sunt, quot saltem rerum species naturalium, et unaquaeque unitas appellatur, unitas inquam non simpliciter, immo quaedam. Nempe idea hominis non unum ipsum est absolutum, sed unum aliquid, id est humanum, nec ad quaslibet rerum multitudines, sed ad multitudinem hominum habet imperium; similiter ideae reliquae ad suas quaelibet multitudines definitae. Quamobrem super ideales unitates exstat ipsum simpliciter unum per quaslibet multitudines latissime regnans.

3 Iam vero ideae non solum sub ipso uno sunt, ut diximus, primae intellegentiae patre, sed etiam in uno quodam sunt, id est intellectu primo primaque forma. Sicut enim formae naturales, quamvis diversissimae, in una tamen materia sunt, ita et ideales in una eademque mentis forma, quae, quoniam est omniformis, a

ent, nor on any individual among the many, since any given individual is particular and different, nor does this "one" exist by itself (*per se*) and of itself (*ex se*)—since it does not remain within itself, but lies in multitude. Nor is this "one" a pure and perfect one, since it participates in multitude, nor is it a perfect nature, since its own nature is a mixture of alien conditions and is changeable. Thus human nature, which is one within many, ultimately depends on a unity that is perfect and by far superior to these many, namely on the Idea of man—and fiery nature depends on the Idea of fire. Certainly the human species, which is eternal, derives its existence solely from a cause that is motionless; likewise what is universal does not depend on a particular cause, but solely on a universal one. Yet the cause that is both motionless and universal is necessarily the intellect and the intellectual Idea.

Socrates considers that the definitions and sciences used to de- 2
scribe natures pertain to these intellectual Ideas, since what is defined and known is absolute, cannot be altered, and what is truly intelligible moves the intellect from the inside, just as what is truly sensible moves the sense from the outside. In turn, there are many Ideas, at least as many as the species of natural things, and each is called a unity (and by this I do not mean absolute unity, but a particular unity). Surely the Idea of man is not the absolute One, but a particular "one," the human "one," which does not govern any given multitudes of things, but the multitude of men; similarly the other Ideas only govern their own individual multitudes. Therefore, the absolute One transcends the ideal unities and reigns most extensively over the individual multitudes.

In addition, the Ideas are not only located under the One, 3
which, as we have said, is the father of the first intelligence, but are also contained within a particular "one," that is the first intellect and the first form. For, just as the natural forms, despite being highly differentiated from one another, reside in matter, which is one, so the ideal forms too reside within a unique and identical

superiore dependet simplicissimo penitus et, ut ita dixerim, uniformi. Formae quidem in materia, quoniam sunt in malo, partim quidem pugnant invicem, partim etiam confunduntur. Ideae vero, quoniam sub ipso bono statim sunt in optimo, neque mutuo confunduntur neque etiam adversantur. Ignis illic cum aqua, natura humana cum bruta neque confluit nec ulla violentia dissidet, sicut et in natura caelesti, tamquam et ipsa divina, virtutes contrariarum apud nos qualitatum, immo et motiones oppositae sine iniuria simul esse possunt. Appellat ergo Socrates ideas aliquas inter se contrarias, non quoniam inter se dissideant, sed quoniam apud nos contraria faciant et ipse deus per illas contraria videat atque agat.

4 Si desideras quales illic ideae sint planius intueri, cogita naturalium rerum rationes seminales in ipsa natura, animadverte rursus artificiorum formas in arte, sed in natura quidem seminariae rationes vim ad faciendum habent, non autem ad cognoscendum; formae vero in arte ipsae cognoscendi quidem et iudicandi rationes sunt, seipsis vero nihil agunt nisi motrix praeterea virtus accesserit et instrumenta quaedam coniuncta pariter et seiuncta. Sed quoniam intellectus ille divinus munera haec apud nos separata mirabiliter in seipso coniungit, ideae penes ipsum tum contemplandi, tum agendi principia sunt, atque rursus quoniam ille non argumentatione, non casu, sed natura sua et hac quidem intellectuali perficit universum sibique reddit simile, necessario vires formasque omnium intellectuali simul atque naturali ratione distinctas possidet in seipso.

5 Ideas vero alias quidem communissimas arbitrantur, ut essentiam, identitatem, alteritatem, statum, motum, alias specialissimas,

form of mind, which, because it is multiform, depends on a superior principle that is absolutely simple and, so to speak, uniform. The material forms, since they are located in evil, are partly opposed to one another and partly mixed with one another. But the Ideas, since they are in the best position, being located right from the start under the Good, are neither mixed with nor opposed to one another. In the realm of Ideas, fire is neither mixed with nor strongly opposed to water, nor is human nature with that of the beast, just as in celestial nature, which is also divine in itself, the powers of the qualities that in our world are opposed to one another, and even opposite motions, can coexist without harm. Socrates, therefore, does not say that some Ideas are contrary to one other [129A] because they are opposed to one another, but because they produce things that are contrary in our world, and because through them God sees and governs contraries.

If you wish to see more clearly the way in which the Ideas are disposed in the intelligible world, consider the seminal reasons of natural things in nature, pay attention to the forms of artistic objects in art—bearing in mind that seminal reasons in nature have the power of creating, not of knowing, while the forms in art are the rational principles for knowing and judging, but do not create anything by themselves without the addition of a moving force and some tools that are both linked with this force and separate from it.[7] But since the divine intellect admirably unites within itself gifts that are separate in our world, the Ideas, which reside in the intellect, are the principles of both contemplation and action, and in turn, because the intellect perfects the universe and makes it in its own image by its nature (which is intellectual) rather than by deliberation or by chance, it necessarily possesses within itself the forces and forms of all things, and these are distinct both intellectually and naturally. 4

Some Ideas are considered to be very general, such as essence, sameness, otherness, rest, motion; others are considered to be very 5

ut hominem atque equum, alias vero medias, ut pulchrum, iustum, magnum, parvum, simile vel dissimile. Socrates ergo putat multa quidem in una idea communicare atque etiam ex participationibus idearum plurium commisceri, ideam vero nullam cum idea confundi, etsi penes unius divinae mentis intellegentiam cunctae consistunt. Aliter quidem cum ideis suis communicant intellectus ipsi intellectualesque animae atque rationales, aliter vero res corporeae vitaeque addictae corporibus. Illa namque sunt velut quaedam progenies vel propagines idearum, quamvis quodammodo inde degenerantes. Haec autem sunt dumtaxat imagines nullam idealem naturam in se habentes, sed illas speculari quadam similitudine referentes.

: V :

Quomodo ideae inter se differant et conveniant.

1 Neque vero putandum est quas ideas excogitamus nihilo re ipsa inter se differre, alioquin unica erit idea et quod in ordine rerum est secundum simplicissimum erit sicut primum, et distinctio[5] in sequentibus casu quodam forte continget. Neque rursus existimandum ideas adeo inter se discretas ut nulla illic aliquid habeat aliarum, alioquin mundus ille primus diversior erit quam secundus, primusque unitatis divinae fetus unionem forte nullam in se habebit, nulla in sequentibus erit unio, nullus ordo. Unaquaeque

specific, such as the Ideas of man and horse; some are intermediate, such as the Ideas of beautiful, just, great, small, like and unlike. So Socrates considers that the many [entities] have one Idea in common, and that together these entities can also participate in many different Ideas, but that no Idea is mixed with another, although all the Ideas coexist in the unity of the divine mind's intelligence. The intellects themselves and the intellectual and rational souls communicate with their Ideas in a way that differs from the way in which the corporeal beings and lives bound to bodies do. For the former are like the offspring or progenies of the Ideas, although they are in a sense inferior to them; the latter are only their images: they possess no ideal nature, but relate to the Ideas as if they were their mirror reflections.

: V :

How Ideas differ from, and are in accordance with, one another.

Let us not think, however, that the Ideas, as we conceive them, in no way really differ from one another. Otherwise, there will only be one Idea, and what comes second in the order of things will have the same degree of simplicity as that of the first principle, and the differentiation between things at the following levels will occur by chance. Conversely let us not consider that the Ideas are so distinct from one another that in the intelligible realm none of them possesses any property derived from the others. Otherwise the first [divine] realm will be more differentiated than the second [earthly] realm, the first offspring of the divine unity will possess no union within itself, and there will be neither union nor order at the following levels. Each Idea, therefore, has its own na- 1

igitur idea naturam quandam atque vim habet propriam ab aliis revera distinctam et accipit interim nonnihil a caeteris traditque vicissim, suntque coniunctae invicem cum praesentia tum communione mirabili, et interim mirifice sua quadam proprietate distinctae[6]—coniunctae, inquam, absque confusione, distinctae rursus absque disiunctione.

2 Cum enim in mundo corporeo tria consideremus, materiam dimensionesque et corporeas qualitates, materiam quidem esse deprehendimus commutationis et confusionis originem, dimensiones autem distantiae causam, qualitates denique causam repugnantiae. Quo fit ut corpora formaeque corporeae, cum propter dimensiones et qualitates inter se distent atque dissideant nec in unum facile conciliari queant, tum etiam propter materiam, si quo forte congrediantur[7] impetu, commisceantur tandem atque invicem confundantur. Verum ideales illae formae eiusmodi conditionibus nullis obnoxiae et simul semper sunt cunctae penitus in eodem prorsus indivisibili, communionem maximam conservantes et interim ita inter se proprietate distinctae, ut nulla puritatem proprietatemque suam ex aliarum commercio amittere vel remittere possit.

3 Radiales visibilium species, quoniam magis a materia distant quam voces odoresque et sapores atque tactiles qualitates, ferme similiter atque ideae se habent. In eodem enim impartibili cunctae sunt simul semelque totae neque se invicem ullo pacto confundunt, aliquanto minus id voces possunt, minus[8] odores, caetera vero minime. Hinc iam profectus ad animam cognosces et rationes seminales in vegetali natura et artificiosas rationes in arte atque in ipsa scientia rationes esse simillimas idearum, servantes videlicet

ture and power, which are really distinct from the other Ideas, while it also receives something from the other Ideas and gives something back to them in turn. The Ideas are joined to one another by both their presence and their marvelous communion while remaining wonderfully separate from one another by virtue of some property of their own—in other words, they are joined without confusion and distinct without separation.

Considering the three components of the corporeal world (mat- 2
ter, dimensions and corporeal qualities), we observe that matter is the origin of change and confusion, dimensions are the causes of distance, and finally qualities are the causes of opposition. As a result, on account of dimensions and qualities, bodies and corporeal forms differ and are opposed to one another, and cannot easily be reconciled into one; on account of matter, if perchance bodies and corporeal forms come together through a sudden motion, they also end up being mixed up and confused. By contrast, the ideal forms are not subject to any of the conditions mentioned above; they are all at once and always absolutely together within the same and absolutely indivisible principle, preserving the highest degree of community with one another while being so distinct in their own properties, that no Idea can lose or give away its own purity and property because of its relation with the others.

The radial species[8] of visible objects, which are more distant 3
from matter than voices, smells, savors and tactile qualities, are disposed in almost the same way as the Ideas. For they are altogether and all at once in the same indivisible subject, without any confusion whatsoever; voices are similarly disposed, but to a slightly smaller extent; odors, to a smaller extent and the rest to the smallest extent. If you ascend from there up to soul, you will realize that the seminal rational principles in vegetal nature, the artificially made rational principles in art, and even the rational principles within wisdom itself, are very much like the Ideas: they admirably retain their individual character while preserving an

una cum individua quadam communione distinctionem quoque mirificam. Admonuimus autem supra naturam cum intellectu coniungere naturamque intellectualem simul et intellegentiam naturalem excogitare, in qua unaquaeque ratio, seu vis seu forma, sicut est notio et contemplatio quaedam, ita et quaedam sit natura, rursusque si est natura, pariter sit et notio. Eiusmodi est idea quaelibet cognitionis pariter generationisque fundamentum.

4 Illic est igitur ipse status, ipse motus, quibus status omnes resque stabiles, item motus omnes resque mobiles et cognoscuntur et fiunt. Identitas illic similiter et alteritas speciesque reliquae. Status ipse nec est ipse motus neque umquam minus status evadit neque, qua ratione status est, ullo pacto mobilis iudicari potest. Participat tamen ipsum motum. Omnes enim ideae invicem quoquomodo participant et quatenus participat ipsum motum, scilicet idealem, in effectibus ipsius motus quoquomodo conspirat. Item identitas nec est alteritas nec, qua ratione identitas est, eadem est et altera. Participatione tamen alteritatis habet ut altera sit ab aliis. De caeteris similiter iudicandum.

5 Ideae cum sint aeternae et ad puritatis summum intellectuales, effectus procreant, in eadem sub ipsis serie, stabiles atque puros priusquam mobiles et impuros. Ita sub ideis elementorum, elementa immaterialia sunt in caelis ante materialia quae sub caelo (leo et equus et arbor quaelibet caelestis, deinceps elementalis; sub homine ideali, homo primo caelestis subinde aerius et terrenus), et sicut quilibet intellectus omnia intellectuali et intellegibili ratione comprehendit (intellectus sane circuli quidam sunt atque mundi), ita sphaera quaelibet omnia, non[9] corporali quidem conditione, sed sua quadam proprietate complectitur.

indivisible communion with one another. As suggested above, however, we must unite nature with intellect and conceive at once both intellectual nature and natural intelligence, where each rational principle, whether a force or a form, is a certain nature inasmuch as it is a certain notion and contemplation; conversely, it is also a notion inasmuch as it is a nature. Any Idea of this kind is a principle of both cognition and generation.

In the intelligible realm, therefore, rest and motion in themselves are the principles whereby all states of rest, and all things at rest, as well as all motions and all things in motion, are known and come to be. The same goes for sameness and otherness there, as well as all the other species. Rest itself is not motion itself, and it never becomes rest to a lesser degree, and under the description of rest it can by no means be considered in motion. Yet it participates in motion itself, for all the Ideas in some way participate in one another, and inasmuch as it participates in motion itself (that is, in ideal motion), it acts in some way in harmony with the effects of motion. Likewise, sameness is not otherness nor, under the description of sameness, is it the same and the other. Yet through its participation in otherness it is disposed so as to be distinct from others. The same must be true of all the other Ideas.[9] 4

Since the Ideas are eternal and intellectual to the highest degree of purity, they first create, within the same series which derives from them, effects that are at rest and pure, before creating those that are in motion and impure. So, under the Ideas of elements the immaterial elements in heaven occur before the material elements in the sublunar world: celestial lion, horse and tree, then elemental ones; under the Idea of man the celestial man comes first, then the aerial and terrestrial ones. And just as any intellect embraces everything in an intellectual and intelligible way (for the intellects are circles and worlds), so any sphere embraces everything, not by virtue of its corporeal condition, but by virtue of its own property.[10] 5

: VI :

Quorum sint ideae, quorum non sint. Quot sunt rationales animae, totidem earum sunt ideae.

1 Animae rationales, ut inquit Proclus, cum neque per ipsam materiam neque per materiales conditiones inter se distingui possint (sunt enim separabiles a materia), per formales specialesque distinguuntur proprietates. Quot ergo sunt animae, tot species totidemque animarum rationalium sunt ideae. Irrationales autem cum a causis mobilibus, id est diis inferioribus simul et animabus rationalibus dependeant, ideoque sint mutabiles per essentiam et circa corpora dividantur, tamquam singulatim mortales, solam speciem sempiternam habent. Quae quidem species perpetuitatem sortita est ab immobili causa, id est idea. Idcirco et unius communiter speciei una est idea. Quot insuper species naturarum corporumque sunt in mundo, totidem horum in conditore sunt ideae.

: VII :

Nulla est idea materiae.

1 Materiae vero, quae omni penitus specie caret, nulla est idea, siquidem idea species est. Species autem non potest rei omni specie carentis exemplar esse. Habet ergo informis materia causam qui-

: VI :

What things have Ideas, what things have not. There are as many Ideas of rational souls as there are rational souls.

According to Proclus, rational souls cannot be distinguished from one another by virtue of matter or material conditions (for they are separate from matter), and are thus distinct by virtue of formal and specific characters. Therefore, there are as many species as there are souls, and the same number again of Ideas of rational souls. As to the irrational souls, since they depend on causes that are in motion (that is, on both inferior gods and rational souls) and thus are subject to change in their essence and are divided in their bodies (since they are individually mortal), they possess one unique and eternal species. This species has been granted eternity by a motionless cause, that is, an Idea. For this reason there is one common Idea for the species, which is also one. Moreover, there are as many Ideas of species in the Creator as there are species of natures and bodies in this world.[11] 1

: VII :

There is no Idea of matter.

Of matter, which is totally deprived of all species, there is no Idea, 1
since an Idea is a species. A species cannot be the paradigm of a thing deprived of all species. Thus formless matter has a divine

dem apud superos divinam, exemplar vero non habet. Materia vero caeli propria, si quam sibi speciem propriam inseparabilemque vendicat—quod est probabile, ut super imperfectam materiam sit perfecta—proprium habet exemplar, si Procli sententiam sequimur.

: VIII :

Singularium non sunt[10] *ideae.*

1 Non sunt autem ideae quaedam propriae singularium corporum, qua ratione singularia sunt. Idea enim causa est prorsus immobilis; quod autem ab eiusmodi causa fit, est immutabile per essentiam. Singula vero corpora non sunt talia. Item si singulorum mutabilium successione innumerabilium iam actu sunt ideae, duo sequuntur absurda, primum quod idea nunc quidem erit exemplar imagine videlicet existente, nunc vero non erit exemplar, imagine desinente; secundum quod innumerabiles ideae forent et multitudo illa intellegibilis unitati proxima, quoniam infinita erit, erit et minime una. Differentia vero est inter exemplar et causam. Nam exemplar quidem illud intellegibile causa est, non tamen omnis causa est exemplar. Singularia igitur, etsi non secundum[11] proprium quoddam[12] exemplar fiunt, efficiuntur tamen secundum causam, immo causas, et has quidem proprias atque particulares, scilicet differentes mundi motus, naturas particulares, varietates temporum atque locorum.

cause among the superior beings, but does not have a paradigmatic cause. The matter that is proper to the heavens (if it is entitled to a proper and inseparable species, which is probable, since there is, above imperfect matter, a matter that is perfect) has its own paradigm, if we follow Proclus' opinion.[12]

: VIII :

There are no Ideas of particulars.

There are no individual Ideas of particular bodies, precisely be- 1
cause these bodies are particular. For the Idea is a cause that is completely motionless, and what is created by such a cause is unchangeable in its essence. Yet particular bodies are not disposed in this way. Similarly, if we suppose the existence of actualized Ideas for the infinite succession of changeable particulars, there follow two absurdities: firstly, the Idea will be at one time a paradigm, when its image exists, and at another time not, when the image ceases to exist; secondly, there would be an infinite number of Ideas, in which case this intelligible multitude, while being the closest to unity, will also be the least "one," since it is infinite. But there is a difference between paradigm and cause: an intelligible paradigm is a cause, while every cause is not a paradigm. Therefore, even if particulars do not receive their existence from their own paradigm, they are nevertheless produced by virtue of a cause, or rather several causes, which are individual and particular: these are the various movements of the heavens, the particular natures, the changes of seasons and of regions.[13]

: IX :

Partium non sunt ideae.

1 Ignis quidem totius illic est idea, eius vero partium nulla; humani corporis totius est idea, non autem capitis, manus, pedis propriae sunt ideae. Nam penes multitudinem illam intellegibilem unitati quam proximam, unum antecedit multitudinem, impartibile partita, totum partes, et sub illorum ratione continentur et ista. Penes vero naturam vegetalem minus unitam,[13] propriae iam rationes sunt singulorum membrorum seminales: oculi, digiti, pedes[14] atque manus.

: X :

Quomodo accidentium sint ideae.

1 Quae accidentales apud nos qualitates alicubi nominantur, si omnes aliquibus speciebus generibusve substantiarum propriae sunt atque ibi essentias necessario complent atque perficiunt, nimirum omnes in ipsis substantiarum[15] ideis exemplariter comprehenduntur. Si quae vero forte sunt nullis speciebus propriae, sed passim per singularia contingentes, causas quidem remotas habent hae quoque apud ideas, exemplaria vero nequaquam, causas vero propinquas, non solum in complexionibus corporum, sed in ipsis quoque naturis, in quibus talium insuper rationes quaedam sunt seminales.

: IX :

There are no Ideas of parts.

In the intelligible realm there is an Idea of fire as a whole, but no ideas of its parts; there is an Idea of the whole human body, but no individual Ideas for the head, the hand, the foot. For within the intelligible multitude, which is the closest to unity, the One precedes the multitude, the indivisible precedes the divided, the whole precedes the parts, and the latter are contained under the rational principle of the former. In vegetal nature, which contains less unity, there are individual seminal reasons for each member: the eyes, the fingers, the feet and the hands.[14] I

: X :

How there are Ideas of accidents.

Let us consider what we call elsewhere accidental qualities in the sensible world. If all the accidental qualities are proper to the species and genera of substances and thus necessarily complete and perfect their essences, surely they are all comprehended in the Ideas of the substances in a paradigmatic way. By contrast, the accidents that are not proper to species, but are randomly present in particulars, do not have Ideas as paradigmatic causes, but as remote causes; their proximate causes reside in both the bodies' complexions and the natures themselves, in which the seminal reasons of these accidental qualities also reside.[15] I

: XI :

Artificiorum non sunt ideae.

1 Artificiorum ideas Plato in decimo *De Republica* videtur asserere, non quia ideas lecti et mensae intellectus divinus aut noster naturaliter habeat, sed quoniam intellectus noster et artificiosam industriam divinitus habet et per hanc quasi ideas quasdam artificiosorum in se machinatur. Totum vero illud exempli cuiusdam gratia apud Platonem Socrates illic adduxit. Ideales profecto rationes cuicumque[16] intellectui naturaliter insunt, sive divino, sive nostro, non aliter quam per mediam naturam viventem et inde formatam transeunt in materiam, in qua et viventia generant. Artificiosa vero neque per mediam naturam ab intellectu procedunt neque vivunt. Nusquam igitur naturalem habent ideam.

2 Haec et superiora confirmat Xenocrates, Proclo teste, ideas ita definiens: ideae sunt causae exemplares eorum quae secundum naturam semper consistunt. Dixit 'exemplares' quidem, quoniam finalis causa est superior, id est ipsum bonum, causa vero proprie efficiens quodammodo est inferior, ipse scilicet artifex intellectus exemplar ideale suspiciens quod insuper est et efficax. Adiunxit 'eorum quae secundum naturam,' quia eorum quae vel praeter naturam, vel per artem fiunt ideae non extant. Addidit 'eorum quae semper consistunt,' quia singulorum mutabilium non sunt ideae. Haec de Xenocratis definitione satis, pergamus ad reliqua.

: XI :

There are no Ideas of artificial objects.

When Plato appears to say in Book X of the *Republic* that there are Ideas of artificial objects, he does not mean that the divine or the human intellect naturally possesses the Ideas of bed and table, but that the human intellect possesses by divine inspiration the skill to produce them, and through this skill produces in itself quasi-Ideas, so to speak, of artificial objects.[16] Socrates used this whole image in that passage of Plato's *Republic* as an example. Certainly the rational principles of the Ideas naturally reside in every intellect, whether divine or human, and it is precisely through the medium of nature, which is alive and formed by them, that the intellects enter into matter, where they also generate living beings. By contrast, the artificial objects do not proceed from the intellect, nor do they live through the medium of nature. Thus they never possess a natural Idea.[17] 1

This, as well as what has been said above, is confirmed by Xenocrates, who, according to Proclus' testimony, defines the Ideas as follows: "The Ideas are the paradigmatic causes of the things that always are composed in accordance with nature." By "paradigmatic" Xenocrates meant that the final cause, that is, the Good, is superior in a sense to the properly efficient cause, that is, the intellect artisan, who is looking up at the ideal Paradigm, which is also efficient. He added "of things that are according to nature," because the things that receive their existence independently of nature or are produced by art do not have Ideas. He added "of the things that always are composed" because the changeable particulars do not have Ideas. This suffices for Xenocrates' definition, so let us proceed.[18] 2

: XII :

Scientiarum solum speculativarum sunt ideae.

1 Scientiarum, quae animam ad materialia deducunt humanaque curant, nulla est idea, sed harum facultas primo quidem est in daemonibus, ut medicina in quodam Phoebo, agricultura in Cerere, aeraria fabrica in Vulcano, textilis in Minerva, secundo illinc est in nobis, sed in illis alia ratione atque admodum excellentius. Scientiarum vero contemplativarum, quae animum ad intellegibilia revocant, generales quaedam quodammodo sunt ideae, similiter moralium virtutum, non civilium inquam, sed excellentiorum quae purgantes animam ad intellegibilia ducunt.

: XIII :

Non sunt ideae malorum.

1 Mala exemplar ideale nullum habent proprium penes deum, alioquin aut illud foret malum aut bonum. Non autem malum, quia in ipso optimo non est malum. Item illud neque bonum est, faceret enim pro natura sua bonum, nullum vero malum. Denique si penes deum sit idea mali, facit deus mala. Idea enim ultra exemplar causa insuper est efficiens. Immo deus esset malus, si propriam mali haberet ideam, quaelibet enim idea est ipse deus. Iam vero ubi Plato dicit architectum mundi velle sibi omnia quam si-

: XII :

There are only Ideas of speculative sciences.

1 There is no Idea for the sciences that lead the soul downward into the material objects and concern human things; these sciences are initially in the hands of demons (for instance, medicine is protected by some demonic Phoebus, agriculture by Ceres, the art of bronze-working by Vulcan, the art of weaving by Athena) and thence come subsequently into our hands, although demons possess this faculty in a different and much more excellent way. Of the contemplative sciences, which summon the soul back to the intelligible realities, there are some general Ideas, as it were, as well as of moral virtues — and by moral virtues I do not mean the civil virtues, but the excellent virtues that purify the soul and lead it up to the intelligible realities.[19]

: XIII :

There are no Ideas of evils.

1 There are no proper paradigmatic Ideas of evils within God. If that were the case, this paradigm would be either good or bad. It could not be bad, since no evil exists in what is best; it could not be good either, for it would then naturally produce what is good, and not what is evil. Finally, if there exists an Idea of evil within God, God produces evil things. For the Idea, besides being a paradigmatic cause, is also an efficient cause. Moreover, God would be evil if He had a proper Idea of evil, for any Idea is God itself. Indeed when Plato says that the artisan of the world desires to make

millima facere, nullum vero malum, sed bona pro viribus omnia, plane declarat nullum penes deum malorum exemplar existere.

: XIV :

Sordium non sunt ideae.

1 Non sunt ideae penes conditorem propriae, nisi eorum quae ipse facit et perficit. Non sunt igitur ideae sordium, id est degenerationum et detrimentorum atque malorum, quae vel divulsarum confluentia causarum, vel nostris actionibus et passionibus accidunt, nec distincta idea pilorum, sed corporis semel totius, non partium particularumve seorsum. Cognoscit autem ille privationes, informia, mala, per ideas habituum et formarum atque bonorum. Non est idea luti, sed aquae terraeque idea. Lutum vero non est adhuc species ulla ad aliquid naturaliter absoluta, qualis ad ideam attinere solet, contingit autem vel sorte vel arte.

: XV :

Etiam quae per ideas ipsas non exprimuntur ad providentiam pertinent causamque divinam.

1 Socrates horum quae modo dicta sunt infimorum defectum considerans, in suspiciones geminas incidit, primam quidem ne praeter ideas fierent, secundam ne forte etiam praeter omnem divinam

all things as similar as possible to himself[20] (nothing evil, but all things as good as he can), he clearly indicates that there is no paradigm of evil within God.[21]

: XIV :

There are no Ideas of vile things.

Within the Creator there are only Ideas of things that are made and perfected by Him. Thus there are no Ideas of vile things, that is, of degenerations, damages and evils, which occur either through the confluence of opposite causes or through human actions and passions. There is no distinct Idea of hair; there is an Idea of the body as a whole, but not of separate parts or particles. God knows, however, privations, absences of forms and evils through the Ideas of dispositions, forms and good things. There is no Idea of mud, but there is an Idea of water and earth. Mud is not yet a naturally separate species that tends toward something, as a species usually tends toward its Idea, but occurs by chance or by being produced artificially.[22] 1

: XV :

Even the things that are not expressed by the Ideas themselves pertain to divine providence and the divine cause.

When Socrates realizes that there are no Ideas for the defective things that have been mentioned above, he is seized by two doubts: first, might it be that these things exist independently from the 1

causam providentiamque contingerent. Primam quidem suspicionem non corrigit Parmenides, sed secundam, cognoscens videlicet nihil esse in mundo sapientissime et pulcherrime optimeque disposito, tam deforme, tam abiectum, quod non et ad pulchritudinem redigatur universalem et alicuius boni sit particeps. Ipsas quinetiam particulas animalis ad finem certum institutas totique necessarias; informem quoque materiam divino huic opificio necessariam nemo dubitat. Omnia igitur eiuscemodi et a providentia proculdubio comprehenduntur et saltem a prima causa, ipso videlicet bono, dependent, ad quod sane pertinet unitatem, bonitatem, essentiam omnibus impartiri; ad intellectum vero per ideas omnia formis insuper exornare.

2 Quae igitur deformia et informia sunt, etsi praeter speciosissimum illud exemplar eveniunt, non tamen vel praeter omnem mentis illius intuitum, vel praeter actionem ipsius boni proficiscuntur. Articulorum quoque corporis animati seminariae rationes quoquomodo divinae in vivente quadam natura consistunt et quae formas sortiuntur ab arte nostra, haec ab intellectu divino nanciscuntur essentiam, quemadmodum quae ab illo formarum varietatem habent, antiquiorem habent ab ipso bono substantiam.

: XVI :

Parmenides responsiones Socratis corrigit vel dirigit, non disperdit.

1 Quemadmodum Socrates obstetricis filius erga pueros adolescentesque passim obstetricis munere fungitur idque prae caeteris profitetur, ita Parmenides iam senex Socratem adhuc adolescen-

Ideas? Secondly, might they even exist independently from the divine cause and providence [130D–E]? Parmenides does not question the validity of Socrates' first doubt, but that of the second: he knows that in a world that is disposed in the wisest, most beautiful and best way, nothing can be so ugly and abject that it cannot be referred to universal beauty and participate in something good. Moreover, nobody doubts that even the smallest parts of an animate being exist for some fixed end and are necessary to the whole—even formless matter is necessary for the divine artisan. All these things, therefore, are undoubtedly comprehended by divine providence and depend at least on the first cause, which is the Good. It pertains to the Good to impart unity, goodness and essence to all things, while it pertains to the intellect also to adorn all things with forms through the intermediary of Ideas.

Therefore, even if deformed and formless things occur without 2
the agency of a very specific paradigmatic cause, they do not proceed without benefiting from the whole gaze of the intellect or the action of the Good. The limbs of an animated body have somehow divine seminal reasons that reside in some living nature; the things that obtain their forms from human art receive their essence from the divine intellect, just as those who obtain a variety of forms from the intellect first receive their substance from the Good.[23]

: XVI :

Parmenides corrects or guides Socrates' responses rather than refuting them.

Just as Socrates, who is the son of a midwife, always plays the role 1
of a midwife toward children and youth (and he claims to be so above anything else),[24] so Parmenides, who is already an elderly

tem miris quibusdam ac ferme divinis opinionibus gravidum propemodumque parturientem, piae cuiusdam obstetricis more, provocat adiuvatque ad partum. Nascentes praeterea fetus vel minus formosos non respuit quidem vel disperdit, immo suscipit fovetque mirifice. Teneriores confirmat, obliquos dirigit, conformat informes, perficit imperfectos. Nemo itaque suspicetur Parmenidem Pythagoricum suorum more idearum amicum ipsiusque entis a sensibilibus separati atque ipsius unius ente superioris asseveratorem, opiniones eiusmodi reprobare, sed meminerit unusquisque Platonicus Socratem a Parmenide in dialecticis diligentius exerceri, ut in divinis mysteriis sit admodum observantior, incedat cautius tutiusque perveniat.

: XVII :

Quomodo res nostrae participant ideas, tamquam imagines idearum, neque his atque illis est ulla ratio eadem vel natura communis.

1 Etsi modus quo materia fit particeps idearum cum modis apud nos consuetis conferri omnino non potest, tripliciter tamen hunc pro viribus comparare fas est. Tres enim Plato partim in *Timaeo*, partim in *Sophiste* significat. Itaque tres merito Platonici prosequuntur, nempe contemplari licet cum mundani architecti virtutem, tum etiam formabilem materiae facilitatem simplicitatemque

man, encourages and assists like a pious midwife the still young Socrates to give birth to admirable and almost divine opinions, which Socrates is bearing and about to produce as if they were his offspring. In addition, Parmenides does not spurn or destroy the thoughts that are about to be born, even the ones that are less beautiful, but he rather embraces them and cherishes them in an admirable way: he strengthens those which are fragile, he straightens out those which are crooked, gives form to the formless ones and perfects the imperfect ones. Let no one, therefore, suspect that Parmenides reproves opinions of this kind, since he is, like his Pythagorean colleagues, a friend of the Ideas, the defender of being itself, separate from sensible things and of the One itself, superior to being. Every Platonist should rather remember that Socrates is being carefully trained by Parmenides in the art of dialectic, to become more heedful of divine mysteries, to approach them with more caution and reach them more securely.[25]

: XVII :

How earthly objects participate in Ideas as images of Ideas, and how there is no identical rational principle nor any common nature between them.

We cannot really compare the way in which matter participates in the Ideas with the way in which objects familiar to us participate in them. However, we can (as far as this is humanly possible) establish this comparison in three ways. Indeed Plato develops three doctrines, partly in the *Timaeus* and partly in the *Sophist,* on the basis of which the Platonists rightly establish three contemplative truths: the power of the world's architect, matter's readiness to be formed and its eternal simplicity, and, finally, the somewhat insub- 1

perpetuam, tum denique rerum naturalium, si cum divinis conferantur, ut ita loquar, exilitatem atque vanitatem. Si igitur participationem idearum in materia similem dixeris vel signorum impressionibus ex sigillo, vel simulacris per aquam et speculum apparentibus, vel picturis, et proprie, quantum fas est, comparaveris et cum Plotino Platonicisque consenseris.

2 Ideales utique rationes et in conditore sunt intellectu et in ipsa mundi anima et in universali natura, item per officia supercaelestium deorum et caelestium et subcaelestium perveniunt in materiam. Si horum illorumve trium prima consideres, picturam quodammodo finges, si secunda, idolum merito speculare,[17] si tertia, iure signum impressum.[18] Materiam quidem ipsam ex antiquissima causa, unde et intellectum primum plerique deducunt. Itaque ab ipso bono tam mentem quam materiam boni unionisque avidam esse factam et illam quidem efficacissimam et promptissimam ad formandum, hanc autem facillimam proclivissimamque formatu. Hinc ergo formationem facilem admodum perpetuamque provenire.

3 Quae apud nos haec denominantur aut illa non sunt vere perfecteque talia; mixta enim sunt aut oppositis aut conditionibus alienis: sic calida frigus habent, aequalia inaequalitatem, levia pondus, formosa deforme nonnihil, homo brutum, ac semel per unicam formam homo est, per partes autem plurimas articulatim non est homo; in motu, in tempore est aliquid quod non est motus, quod non tempus. Quid plura? Ipse quinetiam ignis, qui putatur mixtionis impatiens, apud nos nescio quid crassum habet et iners atque fuscum; in caelestibus etiam motus et oppositum motum

stantial and illusory character of natural things when compared to divine realities.[26] Thus if you say that the participation in Ideas by matter is like impressions made by a seal upon wax, or like reflections on the surface of water or of a mirror, or like paintings, you will have established a comparison that is appropriate (as far as this is right) and in agreement with Plotinus and the [other] Platonists.[27]

In any case, the rational principles of the Ideas reside within the Creator's intellect, in the world soul, and in universal nature. Similarly, it is through the offices of the supercelestial, celestial and subcelestial gods that they reach matter. If one takes the first element of each of these triads, one will imagine a painting of some sort; if one takes the second element of each triad, one will rightly imagine a mirror reflection; if one takes the third element, it will certainly be described as an impression.[28] Most Platonists infer that matter derives its existence from the most primitive cause, whence they also deduce the existence of a first intellect. This is why, they argue, both the intellect and matter are created by the Good itself and are full of desire for goodness and union, the former being utterly efficient and ready to form, the latter utterly ready and inclined to be formed—hence the notion of "ready and eternal formation."[29] 2

The things that are given a name in this world exist as such in a way that is neither true nor perfect, for they result from the combination of opposite or alien conditions. For instance, warm things contain something cold, equal things contain inequality, light things contain weight, beautiful things have something ugly, man contains something beastly, and as a whole he is man through his one form, but limb by limb through his many parts he is not man; in movement, in time, there is something that is not movement, not time. Indeed, even fire itself, which is thought to be exempt from mingling, possesses in this world some density, sluggishness, and even opacity. Among celestial beings even motion 3

tolerat atque statum. Neque quicquid est in sole est sol ipse totus et compositio dimensioque caelestium non per se prorsus indissolubilis neque motus per se stabilis in aeternum. Plurima in hanc sententiam in *Theologia* iam diximus. Et Plato in *Timaeo* septimoque *De Republica* manifeste declarat substantias quidem veras ideas existere, res vero nostras rerum verarum, id est idearum, imagines esse.

4 Quamobrem nulla his communiter atque illis denominatio est univoca, sed hic et ille ita communiter homo dicitur aut equus, quemadmodum apud nos pictus Socrates atque vivens. Proinde sicut haec inde naturam habent, et hanc quidem imaginariam, ita denominationem sortiuntur inde. Prima enim nomina sunt apud superos quibus mutuo sua cognominant atque nostra. Secunda vero apud animos sapientum, qui per conceptus ideales vel naturaliter sibi notos constituentes nomina, res quidem divinas primo revera, deinde ad illorum similitudinem nostras nominaverunt.

: XVIII :

Idea non participatur corporeo more, ita ut vel tota vel pars eius aliqua capiatur.

1 Aliter quidem corpus hoc participat illud, aliter autem corpus animam, aliter rursus anima mentem, aliter mens nostra vel universa deum. Parmenides igitur Socratem instructurus, vel potius

tolerates a motion that is opposite to it, and even rest.[30] Everything that exists in the sun is not entirely the sun itself, the composition and dimension of the heavens are not intrinsically and entirely indissoluble, nor is motion intrinsically at rest for eternity. Numerous arguments in the *Platonic Theology* confirm this doctrine.[31] Plato clearly states in the *Timaeus* and in Book VII of the *Republic* that true substances are Ideas, while things in this world are the images of true things, that is, the Ideas.[32]

This is why the name that is common to the Ideas and their images is not univocal, but both the sensible object and its Idea are commonly called "man" or "horse" in the same way as the name "Socrates" in this world can either refer to a painting or to the living person. As a result, sensible things are allotted their names from the Ideas in the same way they receive their nature from them (and this nature is assuredly an image). For the first names reside in superior divinities; they are used to name intelligible realities and, in return, earthly realities; the second names reside in the souls of wise men who, after having established names by means of ideal concepts or concepts that are naturally known to them, first designated things that are really divine, and then, through the likeness of these, things in this world.[33] 4

: XVIII :

The Idea is not participated in a corporeal way so that it would be taken either as whole or as part.

A body participates in another body in one way, a body participates in a soul in another, a soul participates in an intellect in yet another, and an intellect, whether human or universal, participates in God in another way still. So Parmenides, who wishes to in- 1

provocaturus ad contemplandum verum illum participationis modum, quo ab inferioribus ideae percipiuntur, modos paulatim non legitimos reprobat, maxime vero corpoream participandi conditionem. Si corpus aliquod accipis, aut totum assumis, sicut escam, aut partem, quemadmodum elementum; si aquam bibis, aut totam, aut partem. Probat igitur non eiusmodi conditione corporea ideas accipi posse, ut ita vel tota quaevis idea vel quaedam dumtaxat portio capiatur, ut Socrates admoneatur incorporeum quendam, immo divinum, perceptionis morem excogitare.

2 Aut enim virtutem ideae aut proprietatem consideramus. Nulla quidem rerum nostrarum totam capit ideae virtutem, scilicet aeternam illam efficaciam, individuam prorsus essentiam, vitam intellegentiamque perfectam. Quaecumque in eadem specie sunt, idealem proprietatem illi speciei concessam aeque capiunt. Sic ergo non corporali quidem modo, sed alia ratione idea est tota in quolibet et non tota. Item, cum in seipsa consistat, potest per praesentiam tota simul multis inter se disiunctis adesse, quod sane neque corpori certum deinceps locum requirenti neque virtuti corporali, quae certo cuidam subiecto est addita, competere potest.

3 Socrates igitur, tamquam ad idearum contemplationem naturaliter aptus, vere quidem putat totam multis ideam quoquomodo simul adesse posse atque ad modum quendam praesentiae incorporeum adnititur, sed non prorsus assequitur. Praeterea ideam diurno lumini comparans recte vaticinatur, sed suspicans lumen ita per aerem extendi sicut calor et sicut velum extensum super multorum capita similiterque ideam multis adesse, redarguitur a Par-

struct Socrates, or rather to encourage him to contemplate the true mode of participation, whereby Ideas are perceived by inferior beings, gradually rejects the modes that are not appropriate, especially the corporeal mode of participation. For instance, a body can be considered as a whole, like food, or as a part, like an element: when you drink water, you absorb it either entirely or partially.[34] Parmenides demonstrates, therefore, that Ideas cannot be understood according to a corporeal condition of this kind, whereby a given Idea would be received either as a whole or only as a part. As a result, Socrates is invited to envisage a noncorporeal, or rather divine, way of conceiving participation [131A–E].

For the fact is, we consider either the power or the property of 2
the Idea. None of the things in this world captures the power of an Idea in its totality, that is, its eternal efficiency, its completely indivisible essence, its perfect life and intelligence. All the things that reside in the same species receive to an equal extent the property of the Idea that is allowed to that species. As a result, then, it is not in a corporeal way, but in accordance with another principle that the Idea resides in each thing, both as a whole and not as a whole. Similarly, since the Idea remains within itself, it can by its presence be totally and simultaneously present to many different things. This assuredly cannot be the case for a body, which always requires a particular place, or for a corporeal power, which is added to a certain subject.

So Socrates, as someone naturally gifted at contemplating the 3
Ideas, does actually think that the Idea can somehow be present totally and simultaneously in many things. He seeks, therefore, to find a way to describe the noncorporeal presence of the Ideas, but does not quite succeed. He has a correct intuition when comparing the Idea to the light of the day, but when he compares the Idea's presence in many things with light extended through air like heat and with a sail that is extended above the heads of several people, he is refuted by Parmenides: for in this

menide dicente sic ideam non totam cuique, sed per partes sui alias aliis rerum partibus adfuturam, ut compellat adolescentem accuratius respondere.

: XIX :

Ipsa magnitudo, aequalitas, parvitas ideales non participantur conditione quadam in partes divisibili.

1 Divisio passio quaedam est non qualitatis vel virtutis proprie, sed quantitatis. Postquam ergo divisisti corpus uniforme, vides partes semper inaequales toti nec inter se semper aequales, qualitate tamen et virtute consimiles. Ipsa magnitudo, aequalitas, parvitas ideales ad quantitatem pertinere videntur. Quantitatis enim notionem necessario secum afferunt, neque tamen sunt conditione corporea divisibiles. Itaque multo minus ideae reliquae sunt partibiles. Sit autem, si vis, ipsa magnitudo idealis ita partibilis participabilisque per partes, sicut moles quaedam cuius partes sint toto minores atque parvae: duo statim sequentur absurda. Primum quidem quod ipsa ratio magnitudinis ex oppositis parvisque constabit, perinde ac si calor ipse igneus confletur ex frigidis. Secundum quod haec multa, quae apud nos magna per participationem ipsius magnitudinis denominari solent, facta iam eiusmodi sectione magnitudinis illius in partes parvas, certe per parvitatem quandam quaelibet potius quam per magnitudinem, magna inepte nuncupabuntur.

case the whole Idea would not be present in each thing, but different parts of the Idea would be present in different parts of things [131B–C]. So the young Socrates is compelled to find a more precise answer.[35]

: XIX :

The Ideas of greatness, equality, and smallness are not participated according to a condition that would divide them into parts.

Division is an effect that does not properly pertain to quality or power, but to quantity. Thus when we divide a body, which is uniform, we can see that the parts are always unequal to the whole and are not always equal among themselves; yet they are entirely similar in quality and power. The Ideas of greatness, equality, and smallness seem to concern quantity. For they necessarily imply the notion of quantity, yet they are not subject to a corporeal type of divisibility. For this reason, the rest of the Ideas are even less divisible. Let us postulate, if you wish, that the Idea of greatness is divisible, and that its parts may be subject to participation, like the parts of a mass, which are both smaller than the whole, and small. Two absurdities will immediately follow. Firstly, the very rational principle of greatness will be composed of parts that are small and opposed to greatness, as if heat, which is made of fire, was composed of parts that are cold. Secondly, if the multitude of things that are usually called "great" in this world by virtue of their participation in greatness, are actually so by virtue of a division of greatness into small parts (thus by virtue of some smallness rather than greatness), then they will be improperly designated by the term "great." 1

2 Sed profecto idealis illa magnitudo non molem primo solumque decernit, sed excellentiam, et hanc quidem communissimam, qua et incorporea se invicem virtutibus superant eisdemque corporea prorsus excedunt, qua rursus et haec inter se corporalia non virtutibus solum, sed dimensionibus quoque superant. In idea quidem illa non partes multae sunt, sed vires. In cunctis viribus proprietas eadem, quae quidem ipsa magnitudo vocatur, vires quidem sequentibus deinceps factis inde magnis, gradatim aliis distribuit alias, idealem vero proprietatem consimilem et eandem.

3 Post magnitudinem idealem consideramus idealem aequalitatem, scilicet rationem quandam intellectualem tam exemplarem quam conciliatricem, universae congruitatis et proportionis harmonicae aequalitatisque cuiuslibet. Quae quidem ratio idealis secundum totam proprietatem suam, quamvis non secundum virtutes omnes in omnibus aequalibus invenitur. Si fingas ipsam quasi molem aliquam in duas dividi partes inaequales toti, quando participatur a duobus aequalibus, absurde confiteri cogeris aequalitatem ipsam per inaequalitatem quandam, aequalia facere, quandoquidem in duo membra inaequalia toti dividitur necessario, ut caetera per ipsius participationem inter se reddantur aequalia. Post aequalitatem Parmenides circa parvitatem exercet adolescentem, non tam quia existimet esse propriam parvitatis ideam, quae forte sub magnitudine clauditur, quam ut passim ostendat non posse ideam ullam per divisionem in partes suas more quodam molis alicuius participari. Sunt vero qui putent parvitatis idea significari quicquid est in universo collectum, vel individuum, vel unificum. Haec illi viderint.

Yet surely the Idea of greatness does not primarily and solely designate mass, but excellence; this excellence is the most universal one. It is thanks to this excellence that incorporeal realities are superior to one another by virtue of their powers, and by virtue of the same powers they are superior to corporeal things; in turn, corporeal things are also superior to one another, not only by virtue of their powers, but also because of their dimensions. It is not the parts that are multiple in the Idea of greatness, but its powers. In all these powers the same property, called greatness, progressively distributes various powers among the various things posterior to it (these in turn becoming great as a result), but distributes an ideal property which is similar and the same. 2

After the Idea of greatness let us consider the Idea of equality, which is a rational principle belonging to the intellectual order; it is both paradigmatic and conciliatory, responsible for universal congruency and harmonious proportion as well as for any equality. The rational principle of the Idea of equality is to be found in all equal things in the totality of its property, but not in the totality of its powers. If one imagines that equality is divided, as if it were a mass, into two parts that are unequal to the whole, then, when it comes to be participated in by two equal things, one will have to concede that equality creates equal things by virtue of some inequality (which is absurd), since it is necessarily divided into two components that are unequal to the whole, in order for the other things to be made equal among themselves through their participation in equality. After equality Parmenides subjects the young Socrates to the same exercise with smallness, not so much because he thinks that there is a proper "Idea" of smallness, which is probably comprehended in the Idea of greatness, as because he wishes to demonstrate that no Idea can ever be participated in through the division of its part, like a mass. Some people think that the Idea of smallness designates what is contracted, indivisible and unified in the universe, but this is their opinion.[36] 3

4 Nos argumentationem iam disponamus. Sit ergo, si licet fingere, ipsa parvitas idealis dividaturque in partes duas, duobus quibusdam distribuendas ut per eas duo haec parva reddantur, duo interim sequentur errata. Primum quidem, quod ipsa parvitas idealis evadet magna, dum ad partes proprias comparabitur ipsa tota minores. Nos vero nunc ipsam parvitatis rationem seorsum consideramus, cui nihil oppositae magnitudinis sit admixtum. Secundum, quod illa quibus post ipsius sectionem sectarum partium fit additio, aut maiora quam prius per additionem fient, aut forte minora. Si maiora, quemadmodum probabile quoque videtur, frustra fingebas haec per ipsam parvitatem parva futura. Sin minora, quod ipse quaerebas, stultum erit dictu, aliqua per additamentum fore minora. Socrates paulatim per haec instruitur, ut participationem idearum sublimiore quadam ratione quam corporea cogitet. Cui quidem eruditioni ipse facile assentitur, utpote ad hanc natura propensus.

: XX :

Ideas non convenire cum materialibus neque natura neque conditione.

1 Cum enim ideas tres modo dictas caeterasque consideramus quaslibet sui participantibus adesse eodem modo posse, sive maiora sint sive minora, seu in oriente seu in occidente, sive nunc sive alias, facile possumus coniectare eas neque dimensionibus neque

Let us lay out the argument as follows. Let us imagine, if we may, that there is an Idea of smallness, and that it is divided into two parts to be distributed in two different things, so that these two things become small through participating in these two parts. Two errors will follow. Firstly, the Idea of smallness will become great, as a whole, when compared to its parts, which are smaller. Yet we consider the rational principle of smallness in the abstract, to which no element of its opposite, greatness, may be added. Secondly, the two things to which two divided parts of smallness have been added following the division of smallness will become either greater than before by virtue of this addition, or they will perhaps become smaller. If they become greater, which seems probable, then it was vain to imagine that things become small by virtue of participating in smallness. If they become smaller, which is precisely what we were looking for, it means that things will become smaller by virtue of an addition, which is absurd. It is by virtue of these arguments that Socrates is progressively led to conceive participation in Ideas in a way that is superior to corporeal participation. He readily agrees to learn in this way, since he is naturally inclined to it [131C–E].[37] 4

: XX :

The Ideas are not aligned with material things either in nature or condition.

For when we consider that the three Ideas mentioned above, as well as any other given Idea, can be present in the same way in the things that participate in them, whether these things are greater or smaller, are positioned to the east or to the west, exist now or at another time, we can easily infer that these Ideas are not subject to 1

locis neque temporibus addictas esse, sed ab his omnibus absolutas, et quoniam post temporales alterationes ideae formas in generationibus speciales momento praeparatis iam subiectis exhibent, plane constat illas procul ab omni divisione, loco, motu, tempore esse impartibiles, immobiles, aeternas, ubique praesentes, ita praesentes, ut cuiuslibet ideae proprietas quaedam ad ultimas perveniat mundi formas.

2 Tales enim Platonici rerum series ab ideis hucusque deducunt, nempe sub idea[19] solis, lunae, leonis sunt eiusmodi stellae, daemones deinde tales, similes quoque animantes, eiusmodi metalla, lapilli. Iam vero cum in ultimis etiam idearum atque caelestium proprietates reperiantur, multo magis mediis inesse necessarium est, unde sane contingit ut per eiusmodi membrorum mundanorum contextum, summa infimis, infima summis compatiantur atque consentiant. Sed de his satis in libro *De Vita* tertio diximus.

3 Meminisse vero nunc oportet formas in materia non proxime ab ideis, sed per vires seminales naturae illinc infusas effici, formasque materiales cum eiusmodi seminibus non in natura quidem communicare (sunt enim incorporea semina), sed in conditione quadam particulari admodum atque mobili; cum ideis autem neque natura neque conditione communicare, sed relatione et dependentia quadam atque cognomento, quia videlicet certae rerum formae a certis proficiscuntur ideis quas et potissimum sequuntur et praecipue repraesentant. Neque tamen propterea tertia res quaedam exquirenda est, in qua res istae cum ideis convenire dicantur, sicut nec speculares imagines aut umbrae cum corporibus suis in re tertia congruunt.

dimensions, places or times, but are absolutely separate from all these. In addition, given that, posterior to temporal change, the Ideas appear instantaneously as the forms of species in the world of generation, once the substrate has been prepared,[38] it is clear that they are separate from any division, place, movement and time, and that they are indivisible, motionless, eternal, omnipresent — present in such a way that the property of each Idea extends down to the lowest forms of the world.

Such are indeed the series of things that the Platonists draw 2
from the Ideas down to this world: under the Ideas of Sun, Moon and Lion are the corresponding stars, then the demons, as well as other animate beings, and the corresponding metals and stones. In addition, since the properties of Ideas and celestial things are to be found at the lowest levels, then they are necessarily even more present at the intermediate levels. Consequently, by virtue of this tightly interwoven series of cosmic components, concordance and sympathy clearly exist between the highest and the lowest levels, and vice versa. But we have sufficiently spoken about this in Book III of the *De Vita*.[39]

At present we ought to bear in mind that forms-in-matter are 3
not directly created by the Ideas, but through the seminal powers that are infused into nature by the Ideas; material forms do not communicate naturally with seeds of this kind, since the latter are incorporeal, but through a highly particular and changeable condition. By contrast, material forms do not communicate with the Ideas naturally or by means of a condition, but through a kind of relation and dependence upon them and their name, because the forms of things proceed each from a particular Idea, which they follow more than any other Idea and represent above all.[40] It is not for this reason, however, that one should postulate the existence of a third unity, in which these things might be said to accord with the Ideas, just as reflections in a mirror or shadows do not accord with the bodies they represent via a third unity [131E–32B].[41]

: XXI :

Non debemus ex qualibet multorum communione, unam illorum ideam excogitare.

1 Quod Socrates per quasdam rerum multitudines in uno quodam certo convenientes, scilicet ratione formali, speciali, naturali, perfecta, una uniuscuiusque specialis multitudinis ideam excogitaret, Parmenides, tamquam Pythagoricus idearum cultor, non retractat, sed Socraticum impetum corrigit, ne forte confiteatur quamlibet praeterea rerum communionem ad ideam propriam referri debere, etiamsi in adventicia quadam vel relativa dumtaxat conditione vel defectu quovis vel figmento quodam vel cognomento convenire invicem videantur. Ita enim et multorum praeter naturalem rationem accidentium certae quaedam in natura rationes forent et ideae iam infinitae. Quod autem Parmenides argumentatur in multis, magnis atque ipsa magnitudine, idem intellege de multis hominibus et ipsa humanitatis idea. Haec enim singula cum idea in nomine quidem conveniunt, quoniam haec proprie sunt ex illa et ipsam praecipue referunt, in natura vero et conditione nequaquam. Non igitur haec cum illa invicem in tertia quadam specie congruunt, per quam ad superiorem ideam sit ulterius procedendum iterumque ab illa simul atque istis ad aliam et absque fine deinceps. Hactenus Socrates sit admonitus non ex qualibet apparente communione ideas novas effingere.

: XXI :

The mere fact that an association between many things exists should not make us assume the existence of a single Idea common to them.

Parmenides, who is a Pythagorean and cultivator of Ideas, does not reject Socrates' supposition that there exists an Idea for each specific multitude whenever pluralities of things have a particular unity in common (that is a formal, specific, natural, perfect, and unique rational principle). But he checks Socrates' impulsiveness, to prevent Socrates also admitting that any association whatsoever between things must be ascribed to the existence of a proper Idea [for these things], even in cases where these things appear to share in an association that is solely adventitious or relative, or in a defect of some kind or an image or a name. For if this were the case, there would be particular rational principles for the many accidents within nature, besides those pertaining to the natural order, and the number of Ideas would be infinite. One should understand that the argument presented by Parmenides about the many, the great and greatness itself also applies to the multitude of men and the Idea of humanity.[42] For these individual things severally accord with an Idea in name, since they receive their proper existence from that Idea and refer principally to it, yet do not accord with it in terms of their nature and condition. Thus there does not exist a third species through which things accord with the Ideas, thanks to which one must postulate a further Idea, then another Idea again from the association between that Idea and these things, and so forth *ad infinitum*. So far Socrates should be warned that one should not invent new Ideas from the fact that there is an apparent association between things [132A–B]. 1

: XXII :

Oportet a speciebus quae fiunt ab anima ad species ascendere, quae naturaliter insunt animae, ab his insuper ad divinas.

1 Socrates igitur, ne forte substantiales species infinitas in ipsa rerum natura ponere cogeretur, tamquam adolescens neque satis adhuc eruditus, ad communem quandam de singulis conceptionem confugit a nostra intellegentia factam, quam appellat 'noema,' nos commodiore vocabulo 'notionem.' Dicitur autem noema ab intellectu. Nec est intellegentia quaelibet proprie, quamvis more communi appellare etiam possimus intellegentiam, neque rursus intellegibile primum, sed quasi medium quoddam inter utrumque, conceptus quidam circa rem intellectam definitivus, in quem intus intellegentia definit,[20] sed super conceptus huiusmodi quotidie nobis excogitatos. Nostris mentibus insunt noemata naturaliter infusa divinitus, species videlicet quaedam mediae insuper inter intellegentiam atque intellegibile, quoniam intellegentia nostra per eiusmodi species quandoque ideas ipsas, quae praecipua intellegibilia sunt, agnoscit.

2 Species has nobis ingenitas esse multis in *Theologia* rationibus comprobamus, hic unica et hac quidem brevissima contenti erimus: quanto intellectus praestantior et verior est quam sensus, tanto intellegibilia sensibilibus perfectiora sunt atque veriora. Intellegibilia vero sunt ad quae naturaliter convertitur intellectus quotiens est[21] expeditus, hae vero sunt communes quaedam rerum absolutaeque rationes. Si igitur sensibilia substantiae quaedam sunt in ordine rerum, multo magis eiusmodi rationes. Sed

: XXII :

One should ascend from the species produced by the soul up to the species that are naturally in the soul, and from these up to the divine species.

Therefore, to avoid having to posit an infinite number of substantial species in nature, and because he is a young man who is not yet sufficiently schooled, Socrates takes refuge in [a definition of Idea as] a common conception produced by our intelligence about individual things, which he calls *noema,* and which we more conveniently call "notion" [132B–C]. The term *noema* derives from the term *nous,* intellect. It is not properly speaking an intelligence (although we could also call it "intelligence" in accordance with common usage), nor is it the first intelligible, but it is a sort of mean between the two, a concept that serves to define the intellected thing, in which the intelligence produces definitions from within,[43] but which is above our everyday concepts. The *noemata* are naturally infused into our minds by God, as the intermediary species between the intelligence and the intelligible object, because it is through species like this that our intelligence sometimes recognizes the Ideas, which are the first intelligible objects. 1

We establish by many arguments in the *Theology* that these species are naturally within us;[44] here we will limit ourselves to bringing in one argument, which will be extremely brief: inasmuch as intellection is superior to, and truer than sense perception, so the intelligible objects are more perfect and truer than sense objects. Yet the intelligible objects are those toward which the intellect naturally reverts, each time it liberates itself from the impediments of the body; they are rational principles that are both common to things and separate from them. Therefore, if sense objects are substances within the natural order, it will even more be the case 2

hae neque esse nisi penes intellectum quendam possunt neque primae omnium sunt, quae a nobis nuper concipiuntur. Mobiles enim sunt et intellegentia nostra posteriores. Vera autem intellegibilia et immutabilia sunt et intellegentiam antecedunt. Primae igitur eiusmodi rationes sunt in mente divina, sed in nobis quoque, ante adventicios quos dixi conceptus, rationes sunt naturaliter insitae, per quas et conceptiones eiusmodi parimus, et hinc ascendimus ad ideas.

3 Inesse vero animae penetralibus rationes eiusmodi ipsi tunc maxime declaramus, quando res quasdam absolute definituri a singulis externis confugimus, ad communia et intima mentis penetralia petimus, ubi nobis occurrunt intellegibilia proxima. Ideae vero intellegibilia sunt remota. Proxima quidem haec intellegibilia tamquam perfectiora a sensibilibus tamquam imperfectis collecta non sunt, sed a primis infusa, perque horum ipsorum virtutem, dum particulare aliquid circumspicimus, rationem specialem, quae in singulari non est universalis, universaliter cogitamus resque corporeas ad incorporeas causas recta ratione reducimus.

4 Denique quod Socrates ad notiones illius modi confugerit Parmenides revera non reprobat, sed quod in eis gradum sistere videatur. Studet igitur eum per hanc notionum novarum mentionem iam speciebus naturaliter insitis propinquantem, deinceps non solum ad has ipsas species revocare, sed etiam ad divinas.

for these intelligible rational principles. But the species that we just conceived can only exist within an intellect, and cannot be the first among all species, since they are in motion and subsequent to the activity of our intelligence, whereas true intelligible things are unchangeable and prior to the activity of the intelligence. Therefore, the first rational principles of this kind reside within the divine mind; however, prior to what I have called adventitious concepts, there are also rational principles that are naturally implanted within us, whereby we generate these conceptions, and ascend therefrom toward the Ideas.[45]

We ourselves are an especially clear example that rational principles like these reside in the innermost place of our soul, when, to define some things in an abstract way, we leave aside the individual external objects, have recourse to the elements these objects have in common, and reach the innermost and intimate part of the mind, where we encounter proximate intelligible objects. Yet the Ideas are remote intelligible objects. These proximate intelligible objects, which are perfect, are not collected from sense objects, which are imperfect, but are infused by the first principles. It is by virtue of their very power that, when we observe a particular thing, we conceive in a universal way the rational principle related of its species—which is not universal in the particular thing—and that we reduce corporeal things to their incorporeal causes by right reason. 3

Finally, Parmenides does not really condemn the fact that Socrates has recourse to these notions, but rather the fact that he seems to end his investigation at this point. His concern, therefore, is to guide Socrates further (who, by mentioning these new notions, already hastens himself toward the naturally implanted species) not only toward these species, but also the divine species. 4

: XXIII :

Primae rerum species, quae etiam sunt principalia intellectus obiecta, intellegentias antecedunt.

1 Sic ergo subintellege Parmenidem argumentari: quemadmodum verus sensus circa sensibile quiddam versatur, quod et revera existit et antecedit sensum ac denique cum sensu iam sentiente coniungitur, sic intellegentia vera, quam nunc nominat notionem, ad intellegibile suum dirigitur, revera existens atque praecedens et magis cum notione coniunctum quam cum sensu sensibile. Intellegibilia vero sunt speciales ipsae omnium rationes, communes, immutabiles, absolutae. Nostra igitur notio semper intellegit unum aliquid secundum speciem unam, ubique essentiam in se veram immutabilemque possidens, proprietatemque et appellationem suam singulis sub eadem specie comprehensis impartiens.

2 Id autem intellegibile neque est in singulis, alioquin iam divisum et mutabile foret, neque est ipsamet notio nostra nova, alioquin et mutabile foret atque figmentum neque iam esset intellegentia vera, neque rursus est praecipue notio illa superior menti nostrae naturaliter insita, haec enim rebus cognitis nihil tribuit neque communis est ullis. Est igitur id quod modo dicebam intellegibile, species quaedam in ipso intellectu rerum omnium conditore. Cuius speciei proles quaedam est et ratio seminalis circa quamlibet speciem universali[22] naturae illinc infusa et quaedam singulis sub eadem specie communiter tributa proprietas et notio nobis infusa divinitus.

: XXIII :

The first species of things, which are also the principal objects of the intellect, precede the intelligences.

This is the implication of Parmenides' argument: just as true sense perception is concerned with a sense object that truly exists, precedes sense perception and is ultimately joined to sense perception when sense perception is already perceiving, so true intelligence, which he now calls notion, is directed toward its intelligible object; this object really exists, precedes notion, and is more tightly joined with it than sense perception is with its sense object. Yet the intelligible objects are the rational principles themselves of all the species; they are common to them, unchangeable, and absolute. The notion within our soul, therefore, always knows one object by virtue of one species, always having within itself a true and unchangeable essence, while imparting its property and name to the particulars contained within the same species. 1

By contrast, the intelligible object is not within particulars, otherwise it would undergo division and change, nor is it that new notion of ours,[46] otherwise it would undergo change, be a figment of our imagination and cease to be a true intelligence; neither is it the notion that is superior to our mind and naturally implanted within us, for it does not impart anything to the objects of knowledge, and is common to none. It is that intelligible which I mentioned above, a kind of species within the intellect creator of all things. The offspring of this species are: a seminal reason related to any given species infused from heaven into universal nature, a kind of property imparted in common to particulars within the same species, and the notion infused into us from heaven. 2

3 Ubique vero intellegibilia intellegentias antecedunt, sicut sensibilia sensum, nisi enim praecederent, consequens profecto esset ut intellegentiae vicissim antecedentes intellegibilia, eo ipso priore momento, vacuae forent, in obiectum videlicet nullum directae, sed mox sibimet quod intellegerent conficturae. Quando igitur loquimur de ideis, non tamquam intellegentias, scilicet actiones quasdam, ideas excogitare debemus, sed tamquam obiecta et species viresque naturales intellectus primi essentiam comitantes, circa quas intellectus illius versetur intellegentia, sequens quidem illas quodammodo, sed mirabiliter ipsis unita. Haec clam significante Parmenide ipse nescit quomodo Socrates assentitur.

: XXIV :

Ideae non tam intellegentiae quam intellegibilia sunt atque haec intellegentias antecedunt.

1 Sed quoniam Socrates, antequam id manifeste consentiat, videtur quodammodo suspicari species ipsas rerum primas forsitan esse intellegentias quasdam, sive in nostro intellectu, sive superiore, Parmenides ita primum argumentatur: sicut quaecumque vitam vel sapientiam vera proprietate participant, vivunt aut sapiunt, ita quae intellegentiarum participia sunt, intellegunt. Omnia vero naturalia species participant primas, neque tamen omnia haec intelle-

Intelligible objects are always prior to intelligences, just as sense objects precede sense perceptions. For if the latter were prior to the former, assuredly it would follow that intelligences, being serially prior to intelligible objects, would be void during the moment that precedes the creation of their objects, i.e. directed to no object, and they would then have to invent an object of knowledge for themselves. Therefore, when we speak of Ideas, we should not conceive them as acts of intelligence, but as objects, species, and natural forces which accompany the essence of the first intellect, and toward which the intelligence of the first intellect turns itself, being in some sense posterior to them, while being joined to them in a miraculous way. This is what Parmenides secretly means, and—without really knowing how—Socrates assents to. 3

: XXIV :

The Ideas are not intelligences but intelligible objects, and they precede intelligences.

However, before openly agreeing with Parmenides' argument, Socrates appears to postulate that the first species of things might perhaps be themselves intelligences, and reside either in our intellect or in the superior intellect [132B]. For this reason, Parmenides first presents the following argument [132C]. Just as all the things that participate in life and wisdom through a real property live and are wise, so all the things that partake of intelligences are intelligent. Yet all natural things participate in the first species without, 1

gunt. Non igitur primae species formaliter intellegentiae sunt, sed intellegibilia quaedam, id est essentiales formalesque et verae rationes, omnium exemplares atque virtutes omnium effectrices, in uno videlicet omnium conditore, in quo praeter eiusmodi plenitudinem specierum et vita et intellectus existit et, quamvis omnes ibi species mox vivae et intellectuales existant, non omnia tamen ad species illas hic effecta, vivunt aut intellegunt, cum non idem omnino sit ibi species et intellectus et vita, sed quae praeter specialem formam illinc insuper vitali et intellectuali munere sunt donata. Sed haec alibi. Redeamus ad prima.

2 Intellegentia quidem formaliter actio quaedam est et quasi motus; species autem essentia est et virtus et terminus. Non igitur idem intellegentia speciesque prima per intellegentiam ubique percepta. Plerumque enim ad multa intellegenda unaquaedam communis intellegentia sufficit. Species autem intellegibiles quibus illa formaliter distinguuntur, ibi sunt multae, praesertim in superioribus intellectibus, quandoquidem et nos uno quodam intuitu formas saepe plurimas contuemur. Iam vero in intellectu primo intellegente seipsum, quod intellegibile est melius est quam intellegentia vel intellegens intellectus. Hic enim appetit, haec autem est appetitus, illud vero est appetibile. Illud igitur melius est tamquam summo bono cognatius. Quapropter universum hoc non tam ab intellectu vel intellegentia, quam ab intellegibilibus, id est ab essentia prima intellegibilium specierum virtutumque plena, sumpsit exordium. Ubique igitur essentiae speciesque sunt, non ubique intellegentia intellectusque omnibus distribuitur.

however, all being intelligent. The first species are not, therefore, formally intelligences, but they are intelligible objects, that is, essential, formal and true rational principles, which are the paradigms of all things and the efficient powers of all things; they reside in the unique creator of all things, where, besides this plenitude of species, there exist life and intellect, and although all the species yonder receive at once life and intellect, the things in our world that are produced in relation to these species do not all live and are not all intelligent (although species, intellect and life are not entirely the same thing yonder), but only the things that receive from the intellect life and intellect besides the form related to their species. But we treat of this elsewhere. Let us go back to what we were saying at the beginning.

Intelligence is formally a sort of action and motion, while spe- 2
cies is an essence, a power and a limit. Thus intelligence is different from the first species perceived by intelligence. For most of the time a unique common intelligence suffices to know a multitude of objects. But the intelligible species that formally distinguish these objects yonder are many, especially in the superior intellects, given that even we often contemplate a great many forms in one single gaze. In the first intellect, which knows itself, what is intelligible is superior to the intelligence or the knowing intellect. For the third desires, the second is desire and the first is object of desire. So the first is superior, because it is more cognate to the supreme Good. For this reason the universe does not so much originate with the intellect or the intelligence, as with the intelligible realities, that is the first essence, which is full of intelligible species and powers.[47] Thus there are essences and species everywhere, while intelligence and intellect are not distributed everywhere to all things.

: XXV :

Proprietas idealis una quodammodo est in tota serie, virtus autem varia.

1 Consideramus autem penes ideam quamlibet tum idealem ipsam proprietatem, tum etiam plenam architecti virtutem. Proprietas quidem illa per identitatem in totam seriem sibi succedentem similiter attribuitur, plenitudo vero virtutis per diversitatem sub diversis gradibus distribuitur. Nam quemadmodum diximus alibi, virtutes penes lunarem ideam ibi vigentes omnes quidem in lunam quodammodo descenderunt; in daemones vero lunares non similiter omnes; pauciores insuper, et hae quidem modo etiam remissiore, in homines in terra lunares; pauciores quinetiam debilioresque in bruta, plantas, metalla et caetera deinceps proprie subiecta lunae. Sic itaque virtus illa architecti, sapientia moderante, modis variis distribuitur; lunaris vero sub idea proprietas per quam et illa idea a caeteris differt ideis et naturae lunares dissentiunt a solaribus, vel una est in lunaribus deinceps gradibus omnibus, vel certe simillima. Per quam sane cognationem una quaedam series appellatur, in qua quidem serie graduum diversitas variam virtutum distributionem sequitur, illa interim unione servata. Hinc Aegyptii Apim cognovere lunarem piscemque Selinetem, lunam figura et motibus imitantes, lapillum quoque non solum virtute figuraque lunam, sed etiam augmento quodam et decremento sequentem. Denique si lunaris idealisque illa proprietas etiam apparet in ultimis, multo magis in superioribus eminet.

: XXV :

The property of the Idea in some way remains one in the whole chain, while its power varies.

Let us consider, within any Idea, the property itself of the Idea as well as the full power of the architect. By virtue of sameness the property [of the Idea] is evenly attributed to the whole series that is subsequent to the Idea, while by virtue of difference the fullness of [the Idea's] power is distributed differently according to the different grades [of being]. For, as we have said elsewhere,[48] the powers that thrive yonder within the Idea of Moon in some way descend in their totality into the Moon, yet not all of them descend in the same way into the lunar demons; into lunar men on earth a smaller number of powers descend, and these in a less intense way; and even fewer and weaker powers descend into beasts, plants, metals and then into all the others things that are subject to the Idea of Moon. So the power of the architect, with its guiding wisdom, is therefore distributed in different degrees, while the property of the Moon under the Idea of Moon, by virtue of which this very Idea differs from the other Ideas and moonlike natures differ from solar ones, remains one (or certainly most similar to one) at all the succeeding levels of the Moon chain. It is assuredly by virtue of such an affinity that a certain series is called one, in which [lunar] powers are distributed differently according to the different levels, while its unity remains unaltered. Hence the Egyptians knew the Moonlike Apis-bull and the Moonfish Selinete, which imitate the Moon's figure and movements, as well as a small stone which not only follows the power and shape of the Moon, but also its waning and waxing. Finally, if the property of the Idea of the Moon even appears at the lowest levels of the chain, it emerges to a much greater extent at the higher levels.[49] 1

: XXVI :

Ideae non sunt simplices notiones quaedam, sed species naturales, vim exemplarem efficientemque habentes.

1 Quod Parmenides Socratem non quasi certator insequatur passim atque refellat, sed obstetricis more provocet, adiuvet, foveat, dirigat et emendet, hinc plane perspicitur, quoniam hic adolescens non deficit paulatim, sed gradatim proficit deinceps ad meliora perductus. Iam igitur a Parmenide tamquam paedagogo ductus, veram certamque de ideis sententiam proferens ait eas 'tamquam exemplaria in natura consistere, caetera vero his similia fieri' nec esse aliud quam imagines idearum, 'nec aliter illas participare quam quod similia' fiant. Non species novas vel quomodolibet nostras hic ideas existimat nec extra nos per varios intellectus vel quomodolibet sparsas esse putat, ubi dicit ideas 'in natura consistere' — in natura, inquam, una, vitali simul atque intellectuali. Quam sane naturam Iovem nominat in *Philebo*, dicens in natura Iovis regiam intellegentiam animamque existere.

2 Praeterea dum hic 'naturam' nominat, admonet ne ideas existimemus notiones quasdam simpliciter esse, sed essentiales species viresque naturales. Nam si in naturis ultimis animarum naturales formae viresque membrorum sunt, et in ultima mundanae vitae natura sunt vires omnium seminales effectoriam vim habentes, multo magis in ipsa divinae mentis essentia sunt rerum species efficientes atque naturales. Quae quidem non solum tamquam

: XXVI :

The Ideas are not simple notions but natural species with a paradigmatic and efficient force.

Parmenides does not pursue and refute Socrates as if he were his adversary in a verbal contest, but he provokes, encourages, cherishes, guides and corrects him like a midwife. This is obvious from the fact that the young Socrates is not gradually losing ground, but is making progress step by step, and is led toward the apprehension of more correct concepts. So with Parmenides as his pedagogue, Socrates puts forward a true and firm opinion about the Ideas, and states that "they stand fixed as paradigms in nature," that "the other things come to be like them," and are nothing but the images of Ideas, and that "their participation in the Ideas is nothing but their being made like them" [132D]. Here, he does not consider that the Ideas are new species or species that in some way are produced by our soul in this world, nor does he think that they are scattered outside our souls by means of different intellects or in some random way, when he says that "the Ideas stand fixed in nature"—by nature, I mean the nature that is one, alive and intellectual, certainly the nature that he mentions when he talks of Jupiter in the *Philebus,* saying that a royal intelligence and a royal soul exist in the nature of Jupiter.[50] 1

In addition, by using the term "nature" in this passage, he invites us to think that the Ideas are not simply some notions, but rather essential species and natural forces. For if in the lowest natures of souls there exist natural forms and forces for the limbs, and if in the lowest nature of cosmic life there exist seminal forces for all things, which possess an efficient force, then it is even more the case that in the very essence of the divine mind there are efficient and natural species of things. These not only exist in [the 2

exempla quaedam ad haec effingenda extant architecto mundano, quod Socrates palam expressit, sed vim ad haec etiam efficientem habent conservantemque et unificam, quod minus expressisse videtur. Propterea Parmenides ad haec planius explicanda Socratem adducturus deinceps argumentis multis instabit. Socrates enim etsi virtutes huiusmodi clam significavisse videtur ubi ait ideas quidem in natura stare, scilicet tamquam aeterna rerum principia, haec autem fieri, scilicet ab ideis, et temporali conditione mutari, solam tamen virtutem, ut ita dixerim,[23] assimilantem manifeste protulit,[24] quae sola nunc expressa occasiones Parmenidi deinceps dabit argumentandi.

3 Tu vero interim, sicut alias te admonui, memento quae apud nos discreta sunt in anima, illic esse coniuncta ut intellectualis idea etiam efficacem virtutem habeat, quemadmodum seminariae vires in genitali natura non solum exemplarem, sicut artificiosae species in artifice vel quolibet intellectu, quamvis exemplare quidem munus[25] usque ad rerum species, effectoria vero vis usque ad singula protendatur.

4 Denique Socrates ubi ait inferiora haec ad ideas non aliam conditionem habere quam ut imagines, satis respondisse videtur interroganti quomodo participentur ideae, scilicet quod neque tota quaelibet idea neque pars eius corporea conditione suscipitur, neque ipsa ideae natura ad haec nostra transfertur, neque haec igitur in re ulla conveniunt cum ideis, sed solum illas referunt, quemadmodum specularis imago vultum.

mind of] the architect of the world as paradigms to shape these things, as openly put forward by Socrates, but also possess with respect to these things an efficient force of preservation and union; this is something that Socrates seems to have expressed less clearly. Therefore, in order to encourage Socrates to explain these matters more clearly, Parmenides proceeds in what follows to press him with a number of arguments. For even if Socrates appears to have secretly alluded to these powers when he said that the Ideas "stand fixed in nature," i.e. as the eternal principles of things, while things "come into being," i.e. are created by the Ideas and are submitted to temporal change, he openly brought forth only what I would call the Ideas' power of assimilation, which, by being the only power to be presently mentioned in the discussion, will provide Parmenides with an opportunity to progress with the argumentation.[51]

Meanwhile, you should remember, as I have pointed out to you 3
elsewhere, that the elements that are distinct in our soul are united in the intelligible realm. It follows that the Idea in the intellect also possesses an efficient power, like the seminal forces in the natural generation, and not only a paradigmatic power, like the artificially made species within the [intellect of] the artisan or within any intellect, although the paradigmatic gift is extended down to natural species, while the efficient force is extended all the way down to individual things.

Finally, when Socrates says that the inferior things are related 4
to the Ideas by no other condition than their being made in their image, he appears to have sufficiently answered the question "how do things participate in Ideas?": that Idea does not take on a corporeal condition either in whole or in part, nor is the nature itself of the Idea transferred to earthly objects. Thus earthly objects in no way merge with the Ideas, but are only related to them as a reflection on the mirror is related to the face it reflects.[52]

: XXVII :

Naturales formae dicuntur quidem ideis similes, ideae vero harum similes appellari non debent.

1 Parmenides extare quidem in natura primas rerum species non retractat, sed modum similitudinis horum ad illas diligenter inquirit. Tentatus itaque Socrates a Parmenide mutuam inter haec similitudinem temere nimium acceptavit. Hanc mutuam similitudinis sortem ille redarguit. Solet enim mutuum id consortium inter duo consimilia esse quae in eadem qualitate communicant, ab eodem videlicet auctore percepta. Inde fit inter illa conversio, sicut hoc illi, ita illud huic est simile. Si igitur inferiora haec eiusmodi coniugio et conversione reciproca idealibus speciebus similia forent atque his vicissim illae, proculdubio sequeretur haec una cum ideis tertia rursum specie quadam participare, atque in infinitum stulte procederetur.

2 Oportuit igitur Socratem respondere similitudinis modum esse duplicem. Nam hoc est illi simile aut quoniam ambo sunt ab eodem, aut quia hoc fit ab illo. Ibi quidem fit conversio, hic autem minime. Nam hic alterum quidem est exemplar, alterum vero similitudo. Sicut ergo quod est exemplari simile non habet exemplarem ad illud virtutem aut appellationem, ita quod est exemplar non habet ad similitudinem hanc suam similitudinis rursus conditionem. Hac itaque ratione inferiora haec ideis quidem similia sunt, quoniam inde dependent. Ideae vero ad haec quoniam in nulla qualitate conveniunt, non similia sunt, sed exemplaria tan-

: XXVII :

The natural forms are said to be "like" the Ideas, but their Ideas should not be called "like" them.

Parmenides does not reject the fact that the first species of things exist in nature, but he carefully inquires about how things are "like" the first species. This is why Socrates, as he was being put to the test by Parmenides, carelessly conceded that this relation of likeness was reciprocal. Parmenides rejects the existence of a mutual likeness between Ideas and natural forms [132C–33A]. For such a mutual association between two things that are alike usually occurs when things have some identical quality in common, that is, when they are produced by the same creator. Hence there comes to be a conversion between the two, so that the first is like the other and conversely. Thus if the inferior things were like their ideal species, and these species like the inferior things through a connection of that sort and a reciprocal conversion, it would undoubtedly result that the inferior things would in turn participate, along with the Ideas, in a third species, and this would absurdly go on *ad infinitum*. 1

Socrates should have answered, therefore, that the way things are "like" is twofold: one thing is like another either because both are created by the same principle or because one is created by the other. In the first case there is conversion, in the second there is not, because in the latter case the paradigm is one thing, the image another. Therefore, just as a thing that is like its paradigm does not have with respect to it a paradigmatic power or name,[53] so the paradigm does not in turn possess with respect to its image the image's condition. So in this way inferior things are "like" the Ideas because they depend on them, whereas the Ideas, because they are not convergent with inferior things by virtue of a quality, are not 2

tum atque principia. Modus ergo participationis idearum non fit per eam similitudinem, qua haec cum illis in communi quadam qualitate conveniant, sed quoniam haec formantur ab illis atque illas ideo repraesentant.

: XXVIII :

Contra Stoicos atque Peripateticos quod ideae divinaque omnia et natura segregata sunt et virtutem habent cunctis communicabilem.

1 Quoniam Socrates faciliorem idearum consecutionem existimabat atque ex sola rerum multarum communione definitioneque illas asseverabat, Parmenides admonet adolescentem ob hoc ipsum deinceps accuratius incessurum, ut cogitet in primis difficillime comprehendi posse quid sint ideae, ubi primo sint, quomodo et ad se et ad nostra se habeant, per quos gradus et quales earum vires ad nostra procedant, neque temere ex communione rerum qualibet affirmandas. Oportet sane revera duas ideam apud Platonem proprietates habere, primam quidem substantiam eminentem, videlicet neque commixtionem communionemve naturae neque inclinationem ullam ad naturales formas habentem, secundam vero virtutem actionemque per universum communicabilem suaque passim munera propria etiam praesentia diffundentem. Primam igitur appellamus eminentiam, secundam vero communicabilem providentiam.

like them, but are only their paradigms and their principles. Thus the mode of participation in the Ideas does not occur through a likeness whereby the inferior things merge with the Ideas by virtue of a common quality, but because they are formed by them and therefore represent them.[54]

: XXVIII :

Contrary to the doctrines of the Stoics and the Peripatetics, the Ideas and all divine beings are separated from nature and at the same time have a power communicable to all things.

Since Socrates was conceiving the sequencing of Ideas in too facile 1
a way, and proclaimed that the Ideas existed solely from the association and definition of many individuals, Parmenides on this account advises the young man to proceed more attentively thereafter and to consider first that it is "the most difficult thing" [133A–B] to be able to comprehend what the Ideas are, where they are in the first place, how they relate to one another and to earthly realities, through which levels and by virtue of which forces they proceed to earthly realities, and to realize that their existence should not be inferred rashly from mere association between things. Surely according to Plato the Idea must have two properties: firstly, a transcendent substance, that is, a substance that has no mingling or association with nature, nor any inclination toward the forms in nature, and secondly, a power and an action that can be communicated throughout the universe, and which diffuse everywhere the Ideas' gifts by virtue of their own presence. So we call the first property, transcendence, and the second, communicable providence.

2 Difficillimum autem nobis est in divinis utrumque servare. Nam Stoici quidem divinitatem eminentia sinceritateque privaverunt: providere enim illam et agere putaverunt per mundum usquequaque diffusam et instar spiritus ignei discurrentem. Quidam vero Peripatetici opinari videntur substantias divinas nec efficere sensibilia neque curare, sed omnino segregatas existere, caelestia vero per appetitum nescio quem ad illa movere, moveri, facere. Utrumque nos errorem in *Theologia* nostra refellimus. Contra Stoicos quidem multipliciter argumentamur quod tantum cum materia motuque commercium habet esse non posse primum; contra vero Peripateticos illos abunde probamus et substantias separatas, praecipue primam, agere, intellegere, curare sequentia et animas sphaerasque caelestes non alia ratione appetere, amare, imitari deum, nisi quoniam inde perficiantur, quoniam videlicet efficiuntur et inde. Praeterea nihil agere sterileque esse ad ultimum universi pertinet, non ad primum; media vero providenter agunt et quae superiora et[26] meliora, magis; prima igitur et optima, maxime; primum denique ipsumque bonum quam maxime facit et providet. Omnino vero dictu ridiculum est caelum tam operoso negotio imitari deum penitus otiosum. Iam vero si operari bonum est, quomodo deest operatio primo? Si non bonum, quonammodo sequentia operando optimum imitantur?

3 Parmenides igitur Socratem admonet ut circa divinas ideas observet utrumque et eminentiam naturae et virtutis communionem. Quod enim communicabilitas idearum sit eminens et absque habi-

For us, however, it is supremely difficult to preserve both these two aspects in considering divine things. For the Stoics, on the one hand, have deprived Divinity of its transcendence and purity: they thought that the Divinity exercises its providence and its efficient power by being diffused everywhere in the world, and spreads through all parts of the universe like a fiery spirit.[55] Some Peripatetics, on the other hand, seem to be of the opinion that divine substances neither act upon sensible things nor care for them, but are completely separate from this world, while celestial beings move, are moved, and act by virtue of some sort of desire for the divine.[56] We have refuted both errors in our *Theology*.[57] Against the Stoics we show by many arguments that what has so much commerce with matter and motion cannot be the first principle. Against the Peripatetics mentioned above we clearly prove that separate substances, especially the first one, create, know and care for the realities that follow, and that celestial souls and spheres desire, love and imitate God for no other reason than because they are perfected by Him, that is, because they are also created by Him. In addition, inactivity and sterility pertain to the last level of the universe, not to the first; realities located at the middle levels act with providence, those located at the superior and better levels act with more providence, and thus those at the first and best levels act with the greatest providence. Finally, at the first level, the Good itself acts with the maximum providence. It is utterly absurd to say that the heavens, which are so active, imitate a God that is completely at rest. In addition, if it is a good thing to be active, how can the first principle then lack activity? If it is not good, how could it be that the secondary things imitate what is best by being active?[58] 2

So Parmenides advises Socrates to note both of these two aspects pertaining to the Ideas: the transcendence of their nature and the immanence of their power. The fact that the communicable aspect of the Ideas is transcendent, without any proper dispo- 3

tudine propria et communione naturae in superioribus satis significavit, ubi alioquin quid absurdi sequeretur ostendit. Quod autem eminentia illa non debeat omni communicabilitate et qualibet habitudine vel proportione carere, ostendit deinceps per absurda quaedam ad quae hinc argumentando deducit. Primum quidem absurdum est quod ita nullo modo a nobis cognoscerentur, secundum quod nec ipsae nostra cognoscerent vel curarent. Utrobique cautum reddit adolescentem ut in ideis nec eminentiam sine ulla communione nec communionem seorsum ab eminentia cogitet.

: XXIX :

Quomodo ideae a nobis cognosci non possint, item quomodo possint.

1 Si quis tecum disputet de ideis et uterque vestrum solam idearum sinceram consideret excellentiam humana proportione superiorem, ex hac facile poterit qui tecum disputat demonstrare ideas a nobis cognosci non posse. Neque tu dubitans contra illum facile poteris redarguere vel emendare, nisi et natura aptus sis ad divina et in dialecticis naturalibusque et mathematicis eruditus et ad hoc ipsum certamen ardens atque perseverans. Nempe si ita ut fingo fueris institutus, denique respondebis ei vim hominis cognitivam actu quidem primo directoque ad humana et naturalia similiaque referri. Itaque haec a nobis per proprium scientiae modum cognosci posse, id est per conclusionem ex causis ad effectum rite

sition or association with nature, he has sufficiently indicated above, where he shows what absurd consequences would follow if this were not the case. The fact that this transcendence should not be completely deprived of all its communicable aspect and disposition or relation he then shows through the absurd consequences that he deduces by arguing as follows. Firstly, it is absurd to say that the Ideas would in no way be known to us, and secondly, to say that the Ideas would neither know nor care for our world. In both cases he makes the young Socrates consider carefully that in the Ideas there is no transcendence without association and no association without transcendence.

: XXIX :

How the Ideas cannot be known by us, and also how they can.

Let us imagine that you are having a discussion with someone 1
about the Ideas and that he considers solely the pure excellence of the Ideas, which transcends human proportion: in this case, he will be able to demonstrate easily on those very grounds that the Ideas cannot be known by us. And, if you wish to object, you will not be able easily to refute or correct his position, unless you have a natural ability for the consideration of divine matters, some experience in dialectical, natural and mathematical subjects, and an unwavering enthusiasm for the contest itself [133B].[59] Surely, if you were trained as I am imagining, you will eventually answer that human cognitive power relates to human, natural and suchlike matters through an act that is primary and direct. For this reason such matters can be known through the mode proper to scientific knowledge, that is, through a conclusion that is appropriately

collectam. Divina vero neque primo rectoque intuitu neque scientiae more comprehendi, sed vel actu quodam reflexo per haec velut imagines et effectus coniectari divina ideasque tamquam horum causas et exemplar, vel saltem ideas apprehendi posse, non per consuetam ratiocinationem scientiae causam, sed insolito more per simplicem quandam intellegentiam perfecte purgatam, rite exercitatam, divinitus illustratam.

2 Forte vero intellectuales quidem species intellectibus nostris superioribusque naturaliter insitae per industriam nostram certo sciri possunt, intellegibiles autem species et ideae primo intellectui naturales nostra quavis sagacitate certaque ratione apprehendi non possunt, neque rem hanc aliter se habere illi qui tecum disputet persuadere valebis. Numquam enim convinces ideas speciesve primas directa quadam a nobis vel propria virtute comprehendi, neque rursus poteris obtinere ipsam dei scientiam, qua deus intus contuetur ideas, sic ad nostra referri, ut intuitu quodam recto haec velut obiecta prima contueatur. Intellegit enim haec consequenter actu quodam revera reflexo per ideas ipsas quasi effectus et imagines idearum.

3 Proinde ubi Parmenides ait si sunt primae species in seipsis, sequi ut non sint in nobis, concedere debuit Socrates non ipsas quidem inesse nobis velut qualitates aliquas in subiectis, sed imagines illarum quasdam et perspicuas illinc mentibus nostris infundi et umbratiles in materiis resultare. Non enim steriles sunt, sed fecundae species illae primae, ac longe fecundiores quam naturales qualitates et formae caelestes. Si ita est, et nos certa possu-

drawn from causes to effect. By contrast, divine matters cannot be comprehended by a primary and direct gaze, nor in the manner of scientific knowledge; it is rather by a kind of reflexive act, through earthly things, which are the images and the effects [of the Ideas], that one can have an intuition of divine matters and of the Ideas, which are the causes and paradigms of these earthly things—or one can at least apprehend the Ideas, not through the usual ratiocination, which is the cause of scientific knowledge, but in an extraordinary way, through the simple intelligence that has been perfectly purified, appropriately exercised, and divinely illuminated.[60]

The intellectual species that are naturally implanted in our intellects and the superior intellects might be known with certainty through our own human efforts. But the intelligible species and the Ideas, which exist naturally in the first intellect, cannot be comprehended with certainty by human wisdom (whatever it may be), and you will not be able to convince your interlocutor that this is otherwise. For you will never convince anyone that the Ideas and the first species can be comprehended by us through a direct and proper power, and in turn you will not be able to sustain the view that God's knowledge itself, whereby God gazes inwardly at the Ideas, directly relates to human things, in such a way that He would gaze at them by a direct act, as if they were primary objects. Indeed, it is through the Ideas themselves, by a truly reflexive act, that He knows them inferentially,[61] as effects and images of the Ideas.[62] 2

As a result, when Parmenides said that if the first species are in themselves, they are consequently not in us [133C–D], Socrates had to concede that they are not within us in the way qualities are in subjects, but that certain clear images of them are infused into our minds from above and appear as shadows in material things. For these first species are not sterile but fecund, much more fecund than natural qualities and celestial forms. In this way, we 3

mus coniectare vestigia ad ideas investigandas et intellectus ille primus, idearum fecundissima plenitudo, per ipsas velut sequentium causas haec omnia cognoscit provideque dispensat. Tu vero inter haec, ubi primas species esse dicimus in seipsis, intellege non esse in primo intellectu velut partes in toto, vel qualitates aliquas in subiecto, sed quemadmodum in unitate numeri, in centro capita linearum, in solis luce radii vel colores, in geometria secundum actum perfecta necessariae propositiones eius, seminariae vires in genitali natura, si modo una cum efficacia genitali intellegentiam coniunxerint naturalem.

: XXX :

Quomodo ideae non referantur vel referantur ad nostra et haec ad illas ac de dominatione illic et servitute et relationibus idearum.

1 Si hinc quidem res nostras ut aliquid in se sunt, inde vero ideas ut prorsus in seipsis existunt consideremus, neque haec ad illa neque illa referuntur ad ista. Verum si rem hanc contemplemur ut factam et imaginem quandam, ideam vero ut efficientem atque exemplar, hac utique conditione mutuo referuntur. Item ubi idealem ipsam dominationem excogitamus, non debemus illam ad hanc servitutem nostram coniugata relatione referre, quemadmodum inter nos solemus dicere humanus dominus humani est servi dominus, sed

can conjecture the existence of certain traces that will help our investigation on the nature of the Ideas, while the first intellect, the supremely fecund plenitude of Ideas, knows and providently arranges all things through these Ideas, which are the causes of things posterior to them. But when we say that the first species are in themselves, you should understand that they are not in the first intellect in the way parts are in a whole or qualities are in a subject, but rather like numbers in unity, like the radii of a circle in its center, like the rays or colors in the sun's light, like the necessary theorems in perfectly actualized geometry, like the seminal forces in the generative nature, provided that they have joined natural intelligence to generative efficiency.[63]

: XXX :

How the Ideas relate, or not, to earthly realities, and how the latter relate to the Ideas. On mastership and slavery yonder, and on the relationships between the Ideas.

If we consider, on the one hand, the things in our world, inasmuch as they are to some extent in themselves, and, on the other, the Ideas, inasmuch as they exist entirely in themselves, we see that the former have no relationship with the latter, nor the latter with the former. But if we contemplate, on the one hand, a thing inasmuch as it is created and is an image, and, on the other, the Idea inasmuch as it is a creator and a paradigm, then surely we can see that under this condition they are related to one another. Similarly, when we conceive the Idea of lordship, we should not relate it to human servitude as if these were at the same level,[64] such as when we say with reference to our world that the human master is the master of the human slave, but we need to compare 1

idealem illam dominationem ad idealem servitutem quasi consortem conferre debemus, deinde ad dominationem nostram velut exemplar et causam ad imaginem vel effectum. Quod si nostrae dominationis consequenter et nostrae servitutis est auctor, tametsi servitutem nostram ad idealem servitutem proprie ut ad causam referimus et exemplar.

2 Proinde relationes in ipsis ideis non adventicias quidem collocare debemus (sic ut ego te circumeuntem mihi, modo dextrum dico, modo vero sinistrum), immo relationes aliquas naturales (sicut meam dextram ad sinistram meam comparo tamquam efficaciorem ad minus efficacem labore vel motu; item quemadmodum generantem ad genitum comparamus, naturali virtute facientem, naturali processu nascentem; praeterea sicut intellegentiam ad intellegibile et propriam quandam ad intellegibile proprium naturali quadam habitudine et proportione referimus). Similem quodammodo relationem ideae ad se invicem habere videntur, hoc tamen excepto quod non quemadmodum apud nos diversae eorum quae referuntur substantiae sunt, sed eadem. Una enim illic est genitoris idealis prolisque ipsius essentia, eadem intellegentis intellegibilisque substantia. Etsi omnes valde coniunctae sunt, maxime tamen quae sunt mutua relatione consortes. Idea quidem caloris necessario seorsum ab idea frigoris calores efficit, neque interim necessario generat eos cum humoris idea. Idea vero dextri quotiens facit dextra, agit haec simul cum idea sinistri interim faciente sinistra.

3 Est autem dominatio idealis ipsa vera dominandi ratio, per quam ubique naturaliter quod superius est et melius praeest inferioribus providetque minus bonis, horum opera utitur ad suum

the Idea of mastership with the Idea of slavery, which are at the same level, so to speak, and then compare the Idea of mastership with human mastership, as the paradigm and cause compared with its image and effect. Even if the Idea of mastership is the creator of human mastership and human slavery[65] in an inferential way,[66] nevertheless we properly relate the Idea of slavery to human slavery as its cause and paradigm [133D–34A].

As a result, we should not place within the Ideas adventitious 2
relationships (for instance, when I tell you to turn around me to the right, or to the left), but natural relationships (as when I compare my right hand with my left, the more efficient hand in labor and motion, with the less efficient hand; similarly, when we compare the creator with the creature, the former creating by virtue of a natural power, the latter being born by virtue of a natural process; as, moreover, when we compare intelligence to an intelligible object or an individual intelligence with its own intelligible object through disposition and proportion). The Ideas seem to relate to one another in quite a similar way, except, however, that in our world the substances of the sense objects that are compared are different, while the substance of the Ideas remains the same. For yonder the essence of the ideal creator and of his progeny is one, the substance of the knower and the knowable is the same. Even if all the Ideas are closely joined to one other, those that are joined in a reciprocal relationship are joined to one another to the highest degree. The Idea of heat necessarily produces warm objects separately from the Idea of coldness, yet it does not necessarily produce these objects together with the Idea of humidity; but every time the Idea of the right produces right things, it does so simultaneously with the Idea of the left, which meanwhile produces left things.

The Idea of mastership is the true rational principle of "being a 3
master," by virtue of which what is superior and better always rules naturally over inferior beings and exercises its providence

opus, haec conformat ad suum bonum. Idealis vero servitus vera subministrandi ratio, per quam quod minus bonum est naturaliter meliori ministrat. Similiter superiores ideae ideis quodammodo inferioribus praesunt. Dii daemonibus natura ultroque obtemperantibus imperant, daemones hominibus, sapientiores viri minus sapientibus naturaliter dominantur. Denique Socrates Parmenidi respondere debuit idealem dominationem atque servitutem non ad nos referri, sed invicem, prima dico coniugataque relatione, verumtamen consequenti quodam relationis modo ad nos quoque referri, quatenus omnis dominatio atque servitus tamquam effectus aliquis et imago dependet ex prima naturaliter dominandi serviendique ratione, per quam illa ad nostra consequenter et nostra referuntur ad illa.

: XXXI :

Quomodo ipsa simpliciter scientia ad ipsam simpliciter veritatem refertur, scientia humana ad humanam. Quomodo ideae ignotae vel notae.

1 In intellectu primo est idealis ipsa simpliciter scientia nihil aliud quam intellegentia certaque sui ipsius omniumque comprehensio. Est item idealis ipsa veritas, id est prima omnisque essentia naturaque, ipsius boni lumine fulgens. Quo quidem lumine et intellegentia spectat et cernit intellegibile suum, et universum hoc intellegibile, quod appellavimus veritatem, seipsum offert et infert

upon less good beings, makes use of their works to contribute to its own work and conforms them to its own good. The Idea of slavery is the true rational principle of "being a slave," by virtue of which what is less good naturally serves what is better. Similarly, the superior Ideas in some way rule over the inferior Ideas. The gods govern the demons, which are naturally disposed to obey them, the demons govern men, and the wise men naturally rule over the less wise. Finally, Socrates had to tell Parmenides that the Ideas of mastership and servitude do not relate to things in our world, but to one another [134A], that is by virtue of a primary and coordinate relationship; however, they also relate to us by virtue of an inferential mode of relationship, inasmuch as every mastership and slavery depend as effects and images on the primary and natural rational principle of mastership and slavery, whereby things in the intelligible realm relate inferentially to things in our world, and things in our world to the things in the intelligible realm.[67]

: XXXI :

How absolute knowledge is related to absolute truth and human knowledge is related to human truth. How the Ideas can or cannot be known.

The Idea of absolute knowledge in the first intellect is nothing else than the intelligence and the exact comprehension of the intellect itself and of all things. The same goes for the Idea of truth, that is, the first and whole essence and nature, which shines with the light of the Good Itself. It is through this light that the intelligence gazes at and sees its own intelligible object, and that this universal intelligible object, which we have called truth, offers and presents 1

ipsi intellegentiae penitus comprehendendum. Hinc multae quoque scientiae in sequentibus intellectibus similes sunt veritatesque consimiles et ad sua intellegibilia intellegentiae quaelibet referuntur, scilicet divinae ad divina et humanae ad humana similiaque, intuitu videlicet primo atque directo. Nam, ut in superioribus diximus, per consequentiam reflexionemque et dii nostra sciunt et nos divina percipimus, nos praesertim amatoria purgatione et illustratione quadam, quemadmodum Plato describit in *Phaedro*, animos scilicet purgatos et furore correptos ad sublimia deorum spectacula provehens. Quomodo autem per inferiorum rerum formas speciesve nobis innatas agnoscamus ideas quasi per imagines exemplaria est alibi dictum.

2 Nemo vero more quorundam dicat deum nostra per suam scientiam non attingere. Nam cum omnium causas in se perfectissime complectatur seipsum exactissime comprehendens, similiter complectitur omnia, praesertim quia si scientia prima scientiarum omnium scientia est, unde scientiae omnes, qua ratione scientiae sunt, dependent. Nimirum cognoscendo efficit omnes et faciendo cognoscit. Si scientiae omnes sibi notae sunt, consequenter et scibilia, ut ita dixerim, omnia sibi sunt cognita, coniuncta enim sunt scientiis suis scibilia quaeque. Deum vero non habere scientiam dictu nefas est, sicut quod dat vitam vita carere. Dico enim quicquid in ipsa scientia vitaque boni est non debere primo bono deesse.

3 Denique ipsae ideae primae quam plurimis ab anima nostra gradibus semotae sunt, neque nobis insunt per characterem aliquem expressissimum, neque circa nos sunt, id est nusquam nobis per absolutissimam imaginem offeruntur, neque igitur illas certissima ratione comprehendimus, immo neque intellectus angelici,

itself to the intelligence's total comprehension. Hence there are many similar bodies of knowledge and truths in the secondary intellects, and all intelligences are related to their intelligible objects (the divine to the divine ones, the human to the human ones, and so on [134A–B]) through a primary and direct gaze. Indeed, as we have said above, it is in an inferential and reflexive way that the gods know human things and that we perceive divine things, especially in our case, through some sort of erotic purification and illumination, as described by Plato in the *Phaedrus*, which lead purified and enraptured souls to the sublime spectacles of the gods.[68] We have explained elsewhere the way in which we know the Ideas through the forms and the species of inferior things that are implanted in us, as paradigms through their images.

One must not say, however, as some do, that God does not 2
reach human things through His own knowledge.[69] For as He comprehends the causes of all things within Himself with the utmost perfection, by knowing Himself with the utmost exactitude, even so He comprehends all things. This is especially so because the first knowledge is knowledge of all knowledges, and all knowledges, inasmuch as they are knowledges, depend on it. Surely God creates all things through knowing and knows all things through creating them.[70] If all knowledges are known to Him, then it follows that all knowledgeables, so to speak, are also known to Him, since the knowledgeables are each coordinated to their own knowledges. It is wicked to say that God has no knowledge, in the same way as one should not say that what gives life possesses no life. Indeed, what I mean is that everything sharing in good in terms of real knowledge and life must not be lacking in the first Good.

Finally, the first Ideas are distant from our soul by as many 3
levels as is possible, nor are they present within us through the clearest character,[71] nor are they around us (in the sense that they nowhere offer themselves to us through an utterly pure image), nor do we, therefore, comprehend their principle with the utmost

nedum nostri, illas ea perfectione definiunt qua deus ipse definit. Nam in intellectu divino, sicut et caeterarum rerum sunt ideae, sic est et ipsa scientiae ipsius idea, quae quidem vero coniugio ut obiecta propria tenet spectatque ideas. Ipsa vero scientia quam modo diximus idealis nedum in nobis nec proprie in ipsis est angelis, cumque in nobis multo minus, merito nec ideas quae eiusmodi sunt scientia comprehendendae comprehendimus. Cognoscimus autem per formas tum nobis obiectas tum innatas quandoque intellectuales ideas in mentibus post primam perspicue refulgentes, per quas denique praesertim a superioribus mentibus illustrati, post expiationem in *Phaedro* descriptam, ad ideas primas quae proprio nomine intellegibiles species nominantur, quoad fieri potest, ascendimus humana iam sorte superiores effecti.

: XXXII :

De modo divinae cogitationis atque providentiae.

1 Ubi Parmenides, per ea quae conceduntur ab adolescente, sequi probat ut neque nos cognoscamus ideas neque nos ideae cognoscant, subiungit interea graviter eos errare, qui quibuslibet argumentationibus confiteri coguntur nos penitus ignorare divina, quippe cum receptum sit ab antiquis animae rationalis substantiam esse divinam. Sed gravius erratum dicit superis negare providentiam humanorum ad quorum bonitatem necessario pertinet

certainty; indeed, not even angelic intellects (let alone human intellects) define them with the perfection whereby God defines them. For like the Ideas of all other things the Idea of knowledge itself resides in the divine intellect, and it holds and contemplates the Ideas truly bonded together, as objects belonging to itself. But the knowledge that we have just called ideal is not properly in the angels themselves, let alone us, and since it is within us to a far lesser degree, it is fair to say that we do not comprehend the Ideas that must be grasped by the ideal knowledge. But through the forms (both those that are objects of our thought and those that are innate in us), we sometimes know the intellectual Ideas, which shine brilliantly in the minds that come after the first mind, and by virtue of which, when we are finally illuminated, especially by the superior minds, after the expiation described in the *Phaedrus*, we ascend, as far as is humanly possible, toward the first Ideas, which are properly called intelligible species, when we are made to transcend the human condition.[72]

: XXXII :

On the mode of divine knowledge and providence.

In the passage where he demonstrates that, if the young Socrates admits these facts as true, it follows that we would not know the Ideas, and that the Ideas would not know us, Parmenides also adds that those who are forced to concede by any arguments that we are completely ignorant of divine matters commit a grave error [133B] — especially since it is an accepted belief of the ancients that the substance of the rational soul is divine.[73] But there is a graver error still, he says, that of denying that superior beings exercise their providence over human things [134C–E], since providence 1

providentia. Propterea Socrates hic diligenter exercitatur ut solvere discat dubitationes circa ideas, quae minus solutae providentiae divinae detraherent. Tu vero inter haec primo memento deum habere quoddam scientiae genus nullo modo cum nostra scientia in aliqua ratione conveniens, dominationem quoque nullo pacto cum dominatione nostra convenientem. Quatenus igitur rationem aliquam sciendi vel dominandi nostram aut nostrae quoquomodo similem cogitamus confiteri possumus deum nec ita neque similiter scire nostra vel dominari nobis, hactenus fuerit procul ab errore concessum. At vero si deum universae cognitionis dominationisque prorsus expertem dixeris, et a veritate et a Platonis sententia nimium aberrabis. Mitto nunc eos qui propter fortunam, cuius ordinem minime vident, providentiam negavere.

2 Sed agendum saltem breviter est contra nonnullos philosophos qui, cum deum ab omnibus materialium mobiliumque rerum conditionibus semotissimum esse sciant, inde statim argumentantur deum nullam harum rerum materialium cognitionem habere posse, si modo cognitio cum re cognita congruere debeat, ipsa vero divina cognitio nullam habeat cum rebus materialibus infra lunam mutabilibus congruentiam. Profecto si verum sit quod aiunt, vim cognoscendi oportere cum re cognoscenda congruere, in nostra forsan cognitione verum fuerit. Cum enim nos per cognitionem non simus auctores rerum, nulla forsan est ratio quare percipiamus eas, nisi proportio quaedam. Cum vero divina scientia sit causa prima rerum, non ideo res cogniturus est deus, quia congruat cum natura rerum, sed ideo cognoscit quoniam ipse est causa rerum. Qui cognoscendo seipsum principium omnium omnia statim et cognoscit et facit. Sed neque etiam in cognitione nostra verum est ipsum cognitionis modum pro ipso rerum modo esse debere,

necessarily pertains to the goodness of these superior beings. So here Socrates is carefully trained to solve the difficulties pertaining to the Ideas. If they were not solved, they would diminish belief in divine providence. Meanwhile you should above all remember that God possesses a genus of knowledge that is by no means and in no way in accordance with human knowledge, and a lordship that is by no means in accordance with human lordship. So, to the extent that we know a rational principle of knowledge or lordship that is human or in any way similar to the human one, we can concede that God does not know human matters, nor rule over us, in this or any similar way; to that extent, we should consider that the concession made by Socrates is correct. But if you say that God is totally deprived of cognition and lordship over all things, you will speak against the truth, and against Plato's opinion. I need hardly mention here those who have denied the existence of providence on account of fortune, whose order they little comprehend.[74]

But we must, at least briefly, refute certain philosophers[75] who, 2
knowing that God is absolutely separated from all conditions of things that are material and in motion, immediately reach the conclusion that God cannot have cognition of these material things, since cognition must be congruent with its object, and divine cognition has no congruence with things in the sublunar world which are material and in motion. Surely, if it were true what they say, that the knowing power must be congruent with the object of knowledge, this would perhaps be true in the case of human cognition: given that we do not create things by knowing them, we perceive them for no other reason than because there is a certain proportion between these objects and us.[76] However, since divine knowledge is the first cause of nature, it is not because God is congruent with nature that He will know it, but because He is its cause. By knowing Himself as principle of all things He at once knows and creates all things. But not even in the case of our cognition is it true that the mode of cognition itself must be

quandoquidem et efficientes causae pro modo suo, non pro conditione operis opus efficiunt. Homo enim nascens effectus quidem est unus: aliter vero ab homine fit, aliter et a sole; ab homine quidem particulariter atque etiam consultante atque sollicito, a sole vero universaliter neque ad hoc indigente consilio. Multo magis a prima causa absque negotio fiunt omnia. Sed de hoc alibi.

3 Nunc vero id quaerimus ut cum actio transiens in materiam non cogat causam pro modo effectus ipsius efficere, multo minus actio in agente manens, id est cognitio, adducit agentem, id est cognoscentem, pro ipso cognoscendorum modo cognoscere, quod omne cognoscens non simpliciter pro rei cognitae qualitate, sed pro ipsa cognitivae virtutis natura et forma et dignitate cognoscat et iudicet. Hinc apparet quia hominem nobis obiectum aliter quidem sensus exterior, aliter autem imaginatio iudicat, aliter item ratio, aliter intellectus. Sensus enim solam rem praesentem percipit et accidentia sola. Imaginatio et absentem repetit et quodammodo substantiam suspicatur, componit, dividit sola, summatim conficit quae singulatim quinque sensus. Ratio vero et haec efficit omnia et praeterea ad universalem speciem incorporeamque naturam argumentando se transfert. Intellectus denique simul quodam intuitu conspicit quae ratio multifariam argumentando circumspicit, quemadmodum visus obiectum globum semel percipit ut rotundum, tactus autem saepius attingendo.

4 Profecto natura visque superior percipit agitque quicquid inferior atque melius, et praeterea absque praesenti inferioris usu

in proportion to the mode [of being] of things, since even the efficient causes produce their work in proportion to their own mode of being, and not in proportion to the condition of their work. A man coming into being consists of one single effect, but the effect is caused in one way by the man [who generates him] and in another way by the sun.[77] He is generated by a man particularly, with deliberation and painstakingly, by the sun universally and without deliberation. It is with even less trouble that all things are created by the first cause. But we treat of these matters elsewhere.

Now this is what we are inquiring about: since an action that 3
passes through matter does not force its cause to effect something in proportion to the mode of its effect, it is even less the case that the action that remains within the agent (that is, cognition) leads the agent (that is, the knowing subject) to know in proportion to the mode [of being] of the objects of knowledge: any knowing agent does not simply know and judge in proportion to the quality of the thing known, but in proportion to the very nature, form and rank of its own cognitive power. Hence it is evident that the man who is the object of our thought is perceived differently by the exterior sense, the imagination, the reason and the intellect. For sense perception only perceives a thing when it is present, as well as accidents. Imagination also recaptures a thing that is not present, and in some way conjectures the nature of its substance; it assembles and divides the isolated sense perceptions, it gathers in a whole what was individually gathered by the five senses. Reason does all these things, and through reasoning it also turns itself toward the universal species and incorporeal nature. Finally, the intellect at once contemplates through a sort of gaze what reason viewed in multifarious ways through ratiocination, just as sight at once perceives a spherical object as round, while touch does so by touching the object more than once.

Surely a superior nature and force perceive and act upon in a 4
better way whatever is inferior to them; besides, without making

comprehendit et agit ea saepe ad quae inferior non ascendit. Quamobrem sicut circa idem percipiendum aliter vis inferior, aliter meliusque superior agit, et quod sigillatim quinque sensus attingunt, imaginatio quasi summatim, et quod hactenus individua corporeaque conditione perceptum est, ratio pro dignitate naturae suae iam speciali quadam et incorporea concipit ratione, intellectus autem iam quasi divinus unice immobiliterque saepe comprehendit quae ratio multifariam atque mobiliter (et multa praeterea quae ratio non attingit), sic intellectus primus longe aliter feliciusque quam ratio vel mens humana haec omnia et alia novit, neque rerum cognitarum conditiones, sed naturam ipse suam sequitur cognoscendo, naturam, inquam, uniformem, indivisibilem, immutabilem. Multa igitur forma unica contuetur, immaterialiter materialia, composita simpliciter, immutabiliter mutabilia, necessitate certa semel tenet quae nobis quotidie sorte contingunt.

5 Haec Boethius Proclusque confirmant ac, si liceat Procli exemplis uti, cogita, si placet, navem ventis circum et fluctibus agitatam, finge interim imaginationem tuam adeo potentem, ut, dum imaginaris mare, effluat inde mare, imaginaris navim, construatur eiusmodi navis, imaginaris multiplices ventos et fluctus et ictus, similiter ad imaginationem tuam statim singula consequantur. Si haec ita se habuerint, non cogeris circa haec perspicienda suspicari vel distrahi, sed unice, facile, semel confingendo facies pariter et cognosces. Similiter divinam intellegentiam ad inferiora conficienda

current use of this object, they comprehend and often act upon things to which the inferior object does not ascend. For this reason, just as in order to perceive one identical object an inferior force acts in one way, a superior force in another and better way; just as the objects that the five senses touch via an impression, imagination reaches as a whole; just as reason gathers in a specific and incorporeal way in proportion to the rank of its nature what has been hitherto perceived by virtue of an individual and corporeal condition; and just as the intellect, which is nearly divine, often comprehends in a unified and motionless way what reason does in a multiple and moving way (in addition to many other things that reason does not reach), so in the same way, the first intellect knows all these things, and the rest, in a way that is far different and more felicitous than that of human reason or mind. When it does so, it does not follow the conditions of the objects of knowledge, but its own nature, I mean its uniform, indivisible and unchanging nature. It contemplates, therefore, multiple things via a single form, material things immaterially, composite things simply, changing things unchangingly, and it holds at once and by virtue of sure necessity the everyday things that happen to us by chance.

5 This is confirmed by Boethius and Proclus.[78] If I may use Proclus' example,[79] please consider a ship that is tossed by the wind and the waves. Imagine meanwhile that your imagination is so powerful that at the very moment when you imagine the sea, the sea flows forth from your imagination; when imagining the ship, the ship is built by the very act of conceiving it; if you imagine the multiple winds, the waves, the jets of water, they instantly arise one by one from your imagination. In this way, you need not use conjecture or division to perceive them, but you simultaneously create and know them by the very act of conceiving them uniquely, readily and just once. So is divine intelligence disposed, accord-

simul et contuenda Proclus habere se putat. Qua vero ratione nostrum interim servetur arbitrium in *Theologia* diximus et Plotino.

6 Praeterea divinus intellectus cum sit universi conditor ideoque latissime vim suam per cuncta diffundat, merito formam habet amplissimam, quae videlicet virtutem habeat repraesentantem omnia simul et facientem et sicut perfecta ad illum effectio pertinet, ita pertinet et perfecta cognitio. Utraque vero perfecta est, non quae ad communia tantum et generalia confusaque venit, sed quae ad propria ubique distinctaque et ita demum iam exactissima pervenit, alioquin et operatio et cognitio fuerit imperfecta. Cognoscit igitur sicut efficit, non ulla quaedam solum, sed etiam singula suis invicem formis proprietatibusque distincta. Providet itaque singulis. Haec enim quattuor per cuncta aeque procedunt: virtus, actio, cognitio, providentia. Cognoscit proculdubio perfectissime ipsam bonitatis suae omniumque idearum suarum naturam atque virtutem. Scit ergo quot modis, quot gradibus, quousque procedere participarique possit. Res igitur infimas comprehendit certiore, inquam, cognitione quam sensus et opinio nostra. Quanto cognitio quae fit per omnes causas certior est quam cognitio quae non fit per causas, vel etiam non per omnes! Profecto si in illo est idealis essentia vitaque, sensus etiam est idealis, sed intellectualiter omnia. Per sensum igitur intellectualem sensibilia nostra perspicue sentit.

7 Hic illud Procli contra Peripateticos quosdam videtur opportune dicendum: si intellectus primus perfecte intellegit seipsum ut omnium effectorem et omnibus appetibilem, cum et effector ad

ing to Proclus, in order to create and contemplate at once inferior beings. The way in which our free will is meanwhile preserved we have described in our *Theology* and our commentary on Plotinus.[80]

In addition, since the divine intellect is the creator of the universe and thus diffuses most extensively its force into all things, it rightly possesses the form with the greatest extension, which has a power that at once represents and creates all things, and perfect cognition pertains to it as does perfect creation. The acts of creation and cognition are perfect when they not only reach the common, general, and mixed things, but also the particular and distinct things and finally the most fully realized things—otherwise its faculties of knowledge and operation would be imperfect. Thus the divine intellect knows in the same way that it creates: it knows not just certain [general] things, but also the particular things that are distinct from one another by their forms and properties. For this reason it providently cares for all things individually. For these four properties—power, action, knowledge and providence—proceed uniformly through all things. Doubtless it knows in the most perfect way the nature and power of its own goodness and of its own Ideas. Therefore it knows in how many modes, by how many degrees and how far it can proceed and be participated in. Therefore it comprehends the lowest things by virtue of a knowledge that is more certain, surely, than human sense and opinion. How much more certain is the knowledge that occurs through all causes, than that which does not occur through the causes, or not through all of them! Assuredly, if the Ideas of essence and life reside within it, so does ideal sense perception—but all of them in an intellectual way. It is by virtue of intellectual sense perception, therefore, that it perceives in a clear way the sense objects in our world. 6

Here it seems worth mentioning Proclus' opinion against some Peripatetics: if the first intellect perfectly knows itself to be the efficient cause of all things and the object of desire of all things, 7

effectus[27] et appetibile ad appetentia relative dicatur, necessario et eadem perfectione cognoscit et suos effectus omnes et quaecumque ipsum appetunt, non communiter tantum et confuse, sed ratione distincta. Sicut enim definita ratione seipsum tum effectorem omnium, tum omnibus appetibilem animadvertit, ita nimirum et ratione distincta quae inde fiunt et quae ipsum appetunt omnia prorsus agnoscit. Verumtamen scientia illa tamquam absolutissima intuitu recto, quemadmodum supra diximus, fertur in obiecta absolutissima, id est ideas speciesque primas. In quo quidem gradu fingi potest res nostras, non intueri. Contuetur enim eas subinde per consequentiam quandam conspectis ideis. Neque nos etiam intuitu scientiae recto alia praeter inferiora haec habemus obiecta; superiora enim consequenter quasi vaticinamur.

: XXXIII :

De dominatione et cogitatione divina atque de sex ordinibus idearum vel formarum.

1 Si quis negaverit deum nostra cognoscere, quoniam hic turpia multa sint et mala, intellectum vero forsan talium consideratione contaminetur, scire debet deum non ad haec aspicere, ut haec prospiciat, sed ad seipsum, ut intus inspiciat, penes quem omnia sunt pulcherrima. Quinetiam neque apud nos est quicquam simpliciter malum, sed huic vel illi malum aut turpe, aliis autem et

since it is said to be efficient relative to its effects, and to be an object of desire relative to the things that desire it, then it necessarily knows with the same perfection all its effects and all the things that desire it—not in a common and mixed way, but in a distinct manner. Indeed, just as it knows itself in a definite way as the creator of, and the object of desire for, all things, in the same way, surely, it knows in a distinct way all the things that are created by it and which desire it.[81] However, it is through a direct gaze, as we have said, that this knowledge, which is totally separate, moves itself toward the totally separate objects, that is, the Ideas and the first species. At that level [of being] it can represent but not gaze [directly] upon the things in our world. For it gazes at them in a secondary way, through a kind of inference, after having contemplated the Ideas. We too do not know other objects than those in our world through the direct gaze of knowledge: of the superior realities we have an intuition, so to speak, in an inferential way.

: XXXIII :

On divine mastership and cognition, and on the six orders of Ideas or forms.

If someone states that God does not know sense objects on the grounds that there are many ugly and evil things in our world, and that the intellect might be contaminated by considering them, one must know that God does not look upon these things to see them from the outside, but He looks upon Himself to see them from the inside—and within Him all things are most beautiful. Moreover, there is nothing simply evil in our world, but a thing is evil or ugly in relation to this or that thing, yet good and beautiful in I

universo bonum atque pulchrum. Rursus quae apud nos opposita sunt apud deum invicem sunt coniuncta et saepe ad formam et rationem unicam rediguntur, ut sub forma boni atque pulchri malum consequenter cognoscat et turpe. Nam et mens humana per boni formam auguratur saepe malum, et cognitio mali ita ferme est intellegentiae bona, quemadmodum et cognitio boni.

2 Parmenides autem non ex eiusmodi suspicione, quae nullius est apud ipsum, Socratem adducit in dubium, sed ex eo potius si quis solam ipsam divinorum consideret eminentiam, bonitatem vero communicabilem non advertat, alioquin dum omnem divinis communicabilitatem aufert, tollet et ipsis cognitionem et providentiam humanorum, quod quidem ita dictu absurdum est, perinde ac si negaveris deum inferioribus dominari.

3 Et recte quidem Parmenides dominationem divinam cum cognitione coniunxit admoniturus Socratem nullo modo negandum deum nostra cognoscere, sicut neque concedendum umquam nobis minime dominari, apud quem actio et intellegentia ita sunt idem ut quemadmodum actio praepotens supremae causae ad ultima quaeque procedit tamquam domina, ita et cognitio certa infimis quibusque provideat. Neque ab re inter disputandum Parmenides adiunxit 'cum dii sint,' quippe cum sciret intellectum merum si divinitatem praeterea nullam habeat, universalia quaedam naturaliter cogniturum ideasque similiter divinitatis expertes ad universalia tantum et species processuras. Quod autem et intellectus et ideae per cuncta vim suam et agendo et cognoscendo protendant, inde potissimum habent quoniam superioris illius principii, id est uni-

relation to other things, and from the point of view of the universe.[82] Once more, the things that are opposed in our world are joined to one another in God, and are often reduced to a single form and rational principle, so that He knows evil and ugly things inferentially, as contained under the form of the good and beautiful. For even the human mind often has conjectural knowledge of evil through the form of the good, and the cognition of evil, like the cognition of good, is virtually good from the point of view of intelligence.

But Parmenides does not lead Socrates to doubt by suggesting that God does not have knowledge of this sort, but rather by suggesting that one might solely consider the transcendence of divine beings, without taking into account the fact that they communicate goodness. In removing all communicability from divine beings, one will also remove their cognition of, and providential care for, human things, which is an absurd thing to say—as if one negated that God ruled over inferior realities [134D–E]. 2

And Parmenides rightly mentioned divine lordship together with knowledge, so that Socrates will realize that he should by no means deny that God knows human matters, nor ever admit that He does not rule over us, He within Whom action and intelligence are so identical that, just as the most powerful action of the supreme cause proceeds down to the lowest realities and dominates them all, so does exact cognition providentially care for them all.[83] It is not without reason that during the discussion Parmenides added "since they are gods" [134E5], knowing that if the pure intellect had no divinity besides being intellect, it would [only] know some universal things, according to its own nature, and similarly, if the Ideas were deprived of divinity, they would only proceed as far as universals and the species. In reality, the fact that both the intellect and the Ideas extend their power through all things by the act of creating and knowing stems precisely from the fact that they participate in this superior principle, unity and 3

tatis bonitatisque participes sunt per omnia longissime latissimeque procedentis. Tu vero inter haec, ubi Parmenides deo exactissimam supremamque scientiam tribuit, animadverte hanc propterea singula certissime cognituram. Et ubi audis nonnulla ad privationem negationemque pertinentia, negationem accipe non ut defectum aliquem, sed potius ut excessum. Ita enim saepe et Dionysius Areopagita nos admonet.

4 Forte vero Parmenides, ubi subiungit divina nobis prorsus incognita fore, ideas significat, si quae sunt in principio primo, non absolutis quidem, sed relativis tantum rationibus inter se distinctas, nullo modo vel nobis vel ullis intellegibiles, existentes videlicet super omnes ipsius intellegentiae terminos. Non enim intellegentia, sed occultiore quodam actu frui primo universi principio possumus. Sequuntur post eas ideae iam intellegibiles quidem simpliciter, nobis autem vix et tandem intellegendae, rationes scilicet rerum omnium in intellectu primo (ut nostri dicerent angelo primo) absolutis iam rationibus inter se discretae. Sunt tertio et intellectuales ideae in sequentibus intellectualibus a corporum commercio separatis. Quarto sunt animales in ipsis animarum vel divinarum vel etiam humanarum mentibus vel cogitationibus insitae. Quinto naturales ideae speciesque sunt in vegetali natura, seminales videlicet formarum corporalium rationes, in natura quidem et universalis animae et in naturis animarum superiorum atque nostrarum. Sexto formae sunt in materia, quae quidem, tamquam a superioribus omnibus dependentes, aliquid a singulis habent; a divinis occultum aliquid et divinum et unitatem atque bonitatem; ab intellegibilibus aeternitatem specialem distinctionemque necessariam; ab animalibus distinctiorem pulchritudinem et actionem atque motum; a naturalibus ortum et divisionem ulti-

goodness, which proceeds in the farthest and the widest way through all things.[84] Meanwhile, when Parmenides attributes the most exact and supreme knowledge to God, you should bear in mind that God's knowledge on this account will also know particular objects with utmost certainty. And when you hear some things related to privation and negation, you should not understand negation as a defect, but rather as an excess. For this is also what Dionysius the Areopagite often teaches us.[85]

When Parmenides adds that divine matters will be completely unknown to us [135A], he might perhaps mean that if some Ideas are within the first principle without being distinct from one another in an absolute, but rather in a relative way, then they are by no means knowable to us nor to anyone else, because they exist beyond all the limits of intelligence. For it is not by intelligence, but by a more secret act that we can enjoy the first principle of the universe.[86] Following these unknowable Ideas there are Ideas that are indeed simply knowable, yet are known to us with difficulty and at the very end [of the dialectical process]: these are the rational principles of all things within the first intellect (or the first angel, as our theologians would say),[87] which are absolutely separate from one another. Thirdly, there are intellectual Ideas in the subsequent intellects, which are separate from any relation with bodies; fourthly, psychic Ideas, which are implanted in the very minds and intellectual powers of divine souls, and even of human souls; fifthly, natural Ideas and species in vegetal nature, which are the seminal reasons of corporeal forms in the nature of the world soul and in the natures of superior and human souls. Sixthly, forms in matter, which depend on all superior beings and possess something of each of them: from the divine beings, they possess something that is secret and divine, unity, and goodness; from the intelligible beings, eternity for the species and necessary distinction; from psychic beings, a more distinctive beauty, action, and motion; from natural beings, birth, ultimate division, 4

mam atque processum. Ordines specierum quinque sub primo propter evidentem distinctionem mundi quilibet appellare potest. Quos forsitan quinque mundos apud Platonem Timaeus vaticinatur.

5 Denique in primo quidem sub unica forma sunt omnes ideae; in secundo ideae sunt multae formae, sed in paucissimo numero amplissima virtus ad faciendum atque cognoscendum; in ordine tertio specierum distinctio numerosior; in quarto insuper amplior in specialissimas species distributio; in quinto particularium iam et membrorum corporis seminariae vires; in sexto adventicia insuper sunt et praeter naturalem ordinem accidentia.

: XXXIV :

Nisi sint ideae penes deum et ideales in nobis formulae, peribit dialectica omnisque philosophia; non erit demonstratio vel definitio vel divisio vel resolutio.

1 Parmenides inceptum ab initio pium erga Socratem obstetricis officium ubique prosequitur, ingenium eius provocans ad exactissimam idearum contemplationem, dum ostendit passim ex opinionibus responsionibusque parum accuratis errata gravissima sequi. Item arduum opus et excellentis ingenii esse demonstrare ideas existere et quomodo se habeant et dubitationes incidentes recte dissolvere et auditorem perspicua ratione docere. Haec omnia

and procession. One could call them the five orders of species under the first principle, given the way in which the world is apparently divided—the five worlds, perhaps, celebrated by Timaeus in Plato.[88]

Finally, within the first principle all the Ideas are under one 5
single form; in the second principle, the Ideas are multiple forms, but the most pervasive power to create and know is distributed among a very small number of Ideas; in the third order, species are distinguished in greater number; in the fourth, there is a wider distinction into very specific species; in the fifth, there are the seminal forces of particular things and parts of the body; in the sixth, besides the natural order there are also adventitious states and accidents.[89]

: XXXIV :

If the Ideas are not within God and the ideal formulae are not within us, there will be no dialectic or philosophy; there will be no demonstration, no definition, no division, and no analysis.[90]

Parmenides continues the pious duty of midwife toward Socrates, 1
which he had undertaken at the beginning, and stimulates Socrates' mind to help him reach the most exact contemplation of the Ideas, while showing him that the most serious errors follow from inaccurate opinions and answers. Similarly, it is an arduous task which requires exceptional gifts, that of demonstrating that the Ideas exist and of explaining their status, of solving successfully the difficulties involved in the Ideas, and of instructing one's listener about them in a clear way [134E–35B]. All these observations

Socratem cautissimum accuratissimumque efficiunt. Ut autem inter haec admoneat adolescentem ne forte in hac investigatione ad negandas declinet ideas, sed conetur ad affirmandas, palam edicit nisi revera sint ideae tum in seipsis penes deum, tum etiam per earum veraces formulas mentibus etiam nostris naturaliter insitae, veram intellegentiam perituram, quandoquidem vera desint obiecta ad quae proprie dirigatur, scientiam quoque disserendi philosophiamque nullam fore.

2 Saepe iam diximus inter potentiam cognitivam et obiectum eius cognobile proportionem aliquam esse debere. Praeterea quanto verior praestantiorque intellectus est quam sensus, tanto intellectus ipsius obiectum praestantius et verius esse proprio sensus obiecto. Itaque formam rationemque universalem atque separatam veriorem perfectioremque particulari materialique forma necessario iudicandam. Proinde sicut sensus ad exteriora divertitur,[28] sic intellectus ad intima se convertit, si modo sit inventione iudicioque profecturus. Sicut igitur sensus obiectum est externum, ita proprium obiectum mentis est intimum. Hac utique aliisque permultis in *Theologia* rationibus formulas regulasque rerum esse menti etiam nostrae naturaliter insitas confirmavimus. Quae quidem cum ita mobiles sint ut ex habitu quodam otioso in actum cogitationis transeant[29] atque vicissim, probavimus eas tamquam nondum perfectissimas non posse ex seipsis existere, sed neque etiam a formis externis tamquam deterioribus procreari, ne forte infimum ipsius sensus obiectum sublime procreet mentis sensu superioris obiectum. Dependent igitur nostrae formulae, tamquam per se mobiles, non a sensibilibus formis quae semper aliunde moven-

make Socrates utterly careful and prepared. Meanwhile, in order to urge the young man not to be led astray and deny the existence of the Ideas, but to try to assert their existence, Parmenides openly declares that, if the Ideas are not truly within God and naturally implanted in our minds through true formulae, then true intelligence will perish in the absence of true objects on which to properly direct its attention [135B–C], and there will be neither dialectic nor philosophy.

As we have already said several times, there must be a certain proportion between the cognitive power and its object. In addition, the truer and nobler intellection is when compared to sense perception, the nobler and truer the object of intellection will be than the object of sense perception. So the form and the rational principle that are universal and separate should necessarily be considered truer and more perfect than the form that is particular and material. As a result, just as sense perception turns itself toward outward objects, so does the intellect (if it is to proceed with invention and judgment) convert itself toward the most inward objects. Thus just as the sense object lies outside sense perception, so the proper object of mind resides in the mind's inmost part. Surely we have demonstrated in our *Theology* with this and many other arguments that the formulae and patterns of things are naturally implanted in mind, even the human mind.[91] As we have shown, since these innate formulae are in motion in a way that allows them to change from a state of idleness to the act of cogitation and conversely, they cannot exist by themselves, since they are not yet in a state of highest perfection, nor are they created by external forms, since these are inferior, given that the lowest sense object cannot create the highest object of the mind, which is superior to sense perception. Inasmuch as they are in motion by themselves, therefore, our formulae do not depend on sensible forms, which are always moved by another, but they depend on the Ideas, which 2

tur, sed ab ideis quae nullo modo moventur, sed in eodem intellegentiae actu semper existunt.

3 Et quemadmodum sensibilium formarum numerus ad unam saepe redigitur seminariam rationem in natura vigentem, sic et intellectualium in nobis multitudo formarum ad unitatem stabilitatemque reducitur intellegibilium idearum. Quamobrem nisi sint ideae, nec in nobis erunt eiusmodi formulae quae quidem prima sunt et proxima et cognata nostrae mentis obiecta. Merito igitur, ut Parmenides inquit, nullam iam substantiam veram inveniemus ad quam mentis intuitum convertamus. Neque enim fas est ad superiora progredi nisi per intima, neque intima haec tamquam venerabilia ab externis profecto nimis abiectis accipere, neque fingendum est veridicum mentis intuitum ad novos quosdam conceptus a nobis pro arbitrio fabricatos se convertere, ubi de ipsa vera rerum natura atque etiam divinitate iudicaturi sumus. Conceptus enim eiusmodi figmenta sunt, deteriora quidem rebus externis et a speciebus divinis nimium dissidentia et a substantia naturaque rerum et ipsa veritate plurimum aliena, neque per haec tandem aliud quicquam praeter particularia et sensibilia quaedam perciperemus.

4 Liceat hic cum Proclo saepe nostro hunc in modum argumentari: demonstrationum fundamenta e medio iam tollentur, nisi in intellectu tam nostro quam divino species ideales exstiterint. Demonstrationes enim per illa procedunt quae sunt principia rerum demonstrabilium neque ad nos tantum, sed etiam secundum naturam priora simpliciter atque potiora. Sunt autem demonstrationum principia non particularia quaedam, sed universalia semper. Universalia igitur et antiquiora particularibus sunt et in principiorum ordine potiora. Definitio quinetiam quae demonstra-

are not in motion, but always remain in the same act of intelligence.

And just as a number of sensible forms is often brought back to a single seminal reason thriving in nature, so the multitude of intellectual forms within us is brought back to the unity and stability of intelligible Ideas. So if the Ideas do not exist, there will be no formulae within us, which are the first, closest and cognate objects of our mind. So it is right to say, like Parmenides, that we shall then find no true substance toward which to turn our mind's gaze [135B–C]. For it is wrong to proceed toward superior objects except by means of interior objects, nor can anyone apprehend these innermost objects, which are holy things, by means of external objects, which surely are too mean and sordid—nor should anyone imagine that the mind's true gaze turns itself toward some new concepts that have been arbitrarily fabricated by us, when we wish to consider the true nature of things and even their divinity.[92] For concepts like these are figments; they are even worse than outward objects, completely separate from divine species and totally alien to the nature and substance of things, as well as to truth itself. Through them we would in the end cognize nothing beyond a few particulars and sense objects. 3

Let us argue here along with our usual guide, Proclus, as follows:[93] the principles of demonstrations will be abolished, if the ideal species do not exist in both the human and the divine intellects. For demonstrations proceed through entities which are the principles of demonstrable things, and are simply prior and more powerful, not only for us, but also for nature. Yet the principles of demonstrations are not particulars, but always universals. Universals, then, are prior to particulars and more powerful in the order of principles. Moreover, if these species do not exist, then definition, which is the principle of demonstration, will be nonexistent, or certainly worthless. For definition does not pertain to some adventitious accident, nor to something particular, but to a natural 4

tionis est principium nulla erit aut certe vana nisi eiusmodi species extent. Definitio enim non ad accidens adventicium, non ad aliquid prorsus particulare, sed ad naturale quiddam pertinet et ad speciem multis aeque communem. Ubinam igitur hoc ipsum commune est a nobis sub ratione quadam immutabili definitum? Non quidem in rebus ad sensum pertinentibus particularibus prorsus atque mutabilibus, praesertim cum natura communis,[30] si qua consideratur in singulis, id est humanitas in hoc et in illo, neutrum comprehendat totum, sed utrobique partem.

5 Oportet autem hominem ipsum communiter definitum totum unumquodque comprehendere. Eiusmodi autem amplitudo non ad rerum materialium angustias, sed ad species pertinet absolutas, quae quidem et in intellectu divino sunt et in nostro divinitus. Profecto ipsa iusti ratio absoluta essentialisque et necessaria est in unoquoque nostrum, per quam et iudicare de iustis atque iniustis possumus et iustitiam definire. Verumtamen cum rationes eiusmodi in nostris mentibus multis sint et multae ad unumque commune conspirent, necesse est[31] eas ab una iustitiae ipsius idea superius dependere. Sub qua quidem per rationes eiusmodi nostra congruentes illi, similiter omnes species hominis definimus et leonis et equi, non speciem conceptu novo confictam, quae et mutabilis est et nihil pertinet ad essentiam atque naturam, sed idealem potius veritatem et in nobis expressam et extra nos effectu compertam.

6 Divisio quinetiam, quae definitionis principium est, idealibus speciebus sublatis similiter tolletur e medio. Quando enim generalem rationem per quasdam speciales distinguimus differentias, neque novos tunc conceptus nostros dividimus ad rationes rerum naturales minime pertinentes, neque sensibile aliquid distribuimus, quod particulare passim est atque mutabile, sed ad ideales species in nobis expressas intuitum dividendo dirigimus. Quamobrem si negatis omnibus semel idealibus speciebus consequens est

entity and some species that is common to many particulars. Where, then, does this common element defined by us under an immutable rational principle reside? Not in objects pertaining to sense perception, which are particular and changing, especially since a common nature, if any is considered as it exists in particulars (for instance, humanity in this or that individual), comprehends the whole of neither of these individuals, but a part of each of them.

5 Yet the common definition of man itself should comprehend each thing as a whole. An amplitude of this sort does not befit the confined spaces of material things, but the absolute species, which reside divinely in the divine intellect and in our intellect. Surely the absolute, essential and necessary rational principle of justice resides in each of us, and enables us to judge what is just and unjust, and define justice. However, since these rational principles reside in the multitude of our human minds and, being a multitude, have some unity in common, they necessarily depend on the Idea of justice above, which is one. Under this Idea, through rational principles like these, which align human things with this Idea, we define in the same way all the species (man, lion, horse) — not a species invented by means of a new concept, which is changing and does not pertain to essence and nature, but rather to the ideal truth, which is stamped in us and known outside us through its effects.

6 So if all ideal species are abolished, division, which is the principle of definition, will also disappear. For when we isolate the rational principle of a genus by looking at the specific differences, we do not isolate new concepts within us, which have nothing to do with the natural rational principles of things, nor do we isolate some sense object, which is always particular and changing, but through division we direct our gaze toward the ideal species that are imprinted in us.[94] So if, by denying at once the existence of all the ideal species, we consequently deny the existence of division,

divisionem quoque et definitionem demonstrationemque negare, immo et resolutionem veram a compositis ad simplicia procedentem. Quattuor vero haec totam continent dialecticam. Merito et dialectica simul tota cessabit, philosophia quoque peribit, usura videlicet necessario[32] dialecticis instrumentis, praesertim quoniam philosophia perfecta imperfectis causis non contenta ad perfectas ubique contendit, id est simplicissimas stabilissimasque ac penitus absolutas. Quae quidem nullae sunt nisi intellectualis, intellegibilis, idealis essentia fuerit. Maxime vero ad dialecticam quidem, ideales species insitae nobis attinent, ad philosophiam vero, divinae.

7 Denique si Platonicam disciplinam in *Epistola ad Syracusanos* traditam sequimur, concludemus per divisionem, definitionem, demonstrationem nos proprie ad cognoscendas ideales formulas pervenire in intellectibus post primum expressas, quae et intellectuales cognominantur, perque illas quoquomodo excogitatas etiam ad rerum materialium naturas rite descendere. Ideas autem intellegibiles, primas scilicet species in mente prima, quoniam a compositione motuque distantissimae sunt, non per illos dialecticos gradus qui in compositione motuque versantur statim posse cognosci, sed post eiusmodi discursiones, quae propinquius ad ideales formulas ducunt, purissimam in nobis mentem ideas iam primas per simplicem intellegentiam intueri, ad quam sane resolutoria facultas potius quam definitiva vel divisiva vel demonstratio confert.

definition and demonstration, we also deny the existence of true analysis,[95] which proceeds from composite to simple things. Yet these four stages constitute the totality of dialectic. We can rightly say that the whole of dialectic will also at once cease to exist, and philosophy too will perish, which necessarily needs to use dialectical instruments, especially since perfect philosophy does not content itself with imperfect causes, but always strives for perfect causes, that is, causes that are utterly simple, most stable, and completely separate. These causes do not exist if the intellectual, intelligible and ideal essence does not exist. However, the ideal species implanted within us are the primary concern of dialectic, while the divine species are the objects of philosophy.

Finally, following the Platonic doctrine transmitted in the *Letter* 7
to the Syracusans, we shall conclude that it is through division, definition and demonstration that we will properly reach knowledge of the ideal formulae, which are imprinted on the intellects that follow the first intellect, and are also called intellectual formulae.[96] It is through these (once they are in some way known) that we appropriately also descend into the natures of material things. As to the intelligible Ideas, that is, the first species within the first mind, since they are utterly remote from any composition and motion, they cannot be instantly known through these dialectical steps, which involve composition and motion. But, after these dialectical processes, which lead us closer to the ideal formulae, the purest mind within us (to which pertains the faculty of analysis, rather than that of definition, division, or demonstration) gazes at the first Ideas through simple understanding.

: XXXV :

De dialectica exercitatione per formas intellectuales ad species intellegibiles.

1 Cum Parmenides Socratem ad hoc ipsum dumtaxat in dialecticis exercitaturus sit, ne erret circa divina utque sciat dubitationes solvere in divinis, merito dialecticam formam tradet Socrati deinceps in eadem ipsa divina materia. Ita enim reddetur instructior. Exordietur autem ab uno tamquam causa idearum atque divinorum, significans in toto disputationis cursu ipsum unum producere entia omnia gradatim et entium unitates. Plato vero cum nec in *Philebo* nec in *Republica* turbam adolescentum ad dialectica libenter admittat, ne forsan insolentiores efficiantur, Socraticum tamen ingenium natura divinum etiam in adolescentia per Parmenidem ad disserendi artem plurimum exhortatur. Parmenides igitur in primis Socratem probat quod ad ideales species ultro se conferat, formas vero spernat materiales, quoniam, cum materiae ratio sit informitas ideoque sit opposita formae, nimirum forma materialis est imperfectissima forma, immo et nullae formae habentes mutabilitatem aliquam et mixturam materialibus quodammodo similem, sive in natura sive in anima sive[33] in aliquo intellectu sint, sunt formae perfectae.

2 Quoniam vero et generationis ordo gradatim nititur ad perfectum et ordo universi a principio perfectissimo ducit exordium, ad perfectissimas tandem formas pervenire debemus, id est ad ideales intellegibilesque species quae sint ab omnibus materia-

: XXXV :

On the dialectical exercise leading to the intelligible species through the intermediary of the intellectual forms.

Since Parmenides wishes to train Socrates in the art of dialectic for the sole purpose of helping him to avoid errors concerning divine matters and to learn how to solve difficulties related to divine matters, he is now rightly going to teach Socrates the form of dialectic which will be used from then on in that very same divine material. This is how Socrates will become wiser. Parmenides will start the inquiry with the One, *qua* cause of Ideas and divine matters, and in the whole course of the discussion he will show that the One creates progressively all beings and unities of beings. Although in the *Philebus* and in the *Republic* Plato does not readily admit the multitude of youth to the practice of dialectic, lest they become too arrogant,[97] he strongly exhorts Socrates, through Parmenides' intermediary, to take up the art of dialectic, and he does so despite Socrates' youth, because Socrates naturally possesses a divine gift.[98] So Parmenides first indicates to Socrates that he must apply himself of his own accord and turn to the study of ideal species, leaving aside material forms. Indeed, given that the rational principle of matter is formlessness, and is thus opposed to form, material form is assuredly the most imperfect form; moreover, the forms that are subject to change or result from composition in a way that is similar to material things (whether they exist in nature, the soul or any intellect) are by no means perfect forms. 1

However, since the order of generation tends toward perfection, and the order of the universe originates from the most perfect principle, we need to reach eventually the most perfect forms, that is, the ideal and intelligible species, which are totally separate from 2

lium formarum conditionibus penitus absolutae. In quibus ita sit pura formositas, sicut est et nuda prorsus informitas in materia, sed quemadmodum materia, sic et illa est difficillima cogitatu. Cogitur enim cogitaturus materiam omnem denique formam exuere, quod quidem est contra consuetum cognitionis effectum. Compellitur et ideas contemplaturus omnes materialium formarum nubes reliquiasque excutere, quod quidem a[34] communi cognitionis humanae more nimis est alienum. Illas igitur attingit tandem stabilis intellegentiae simplex intuitus ab omnibus materialium cogitationibus penitus segregatus. Sed ad ipsas interim dialectica facultas ingenium exercet et praeparat per animales intellectualesque conceptus et species artificioso quodam, ut ita dixerim, errore discurrens. Ideo facultatem hanc Plato appellat erraticam quasi vicissim longis ambagibus per opposita discurrentem. Eiusmodi Socrates pervagatione censet utendum circa intellectuales species potius quam sensibiles, quod et Parmenides proculdubio comprobat.

: XXXVI :

Regulae dialecticae supponentes esse vel non esse et quot modis dicitur non ens.

1 Potissimam argumentandi formam esse vult quae ex suppositione procedit, perpendens quid, affirmato quolibet vel negato, multis gradibus inde sequatur. Forma enim eiusmodi non machinis quibusdam confidit humanis, sed ipsa rerum naturalium divinarumque consequenti serie nititur praeceptoremque veritatis habet ip-

all the conditions pertaining to material forms. In them resides pure beauty, just as a naked, ugly formlessness resides in matter. Like matter, however, beauty is extremely difficult to know. For to know matter one has eventually to strip off all forms, a procedure in contrast to the usual workings of cognition; to contemplate the Ideas one is compelled to shake off all the clouds and remains of material forms, a procedure utterly alien to the usual mode of human cognition. The Ideas, therefore, are ultimately reached by the stable, simple gaze of intelligence, which is completely isolated from all cognitions of material objects. The dialectical method precisely exercises and prepares the mind for the consideration of the Ideas, through the intermediary of concepts and species formed in the soul and the intellect, by proceeding through an artificial "wandering," as it were. This is why Plato calls this faculty "wandering" [135E2], because it proceeds in long meanderings through contradictory propositions. Socrates thinks that one should use this "excursion" to apprehend the intellectual rather than the sensible species, which Parmenides approves without reservation.[99]

: XXXVI :

The dialectical rules of hypothesizing that a thing is or is not, and the different meanings of the term "not-being."

1 According to Parmenides, the most powerful form of argumentation is that which proceeds from a hypothesis and carefully considers, when one affirms or denies anything, what follows at the various levels of reality. For this form of argumentation does not trust in human devices, but relies on the successive grades of natural and divine things, and uses the order of the universe as the teacher of truth. According to Parmenides, however, one should

sum ordinem universi. Supponendum vero iubet non modo si est aliquid, verum etiam si non est, et animadvertendum quid utrimque sequatur. Nempe id observandum est ubi rerum accidentiumque cuique causas praecipuas et principia quaerimus. Ratio namque principii est ut hoc posito vel sublato ponatur vel auferatur effectus. Si enim posito tantum hoc, ponatur simul et illud, neque tamen auferatur ablato, ducit illam originem etiam aliunde. Praecipit inde inter consequentia utrimque quattuor considerare sive supponatur res quaedam (puta mens vel anima) esse sive non esse. Utrobique enim perpendi vult quid contingat hinc ipsi rei suppositae ad seipsam, quidve ad alia, rursus quid aliis accidat ad seipsa, quid ad illam. Sed ubi supponit mentem vel animam non esse, quonam pacto potest considerare deinde quid illi accidat non existenti? Respondendum non supponi in praesentia mentem vel animam omnino nihil esse, alioquin non quaereretur deinde quid sibi accidat, sed supponi potius rem hanc quae appellatur mens et anima non esse mentem proprie aut animam, sed quodvis aliud esse vel fingi. Platonici sane non ens dupliciter accipere solent aut simpliciter, id est prorsus nihilum aut secundum quid non ens. Id est autem quod vel non hoc quidem est, scilicet non homo, quamvis sit illud, scilicet equus, vel quod hac quidem ratione non est, licet sit alia, potentia videlicet quadam ens, non autem existens actu. Materiam non ens appellant, quia nihil sit actu formali; sensibile quodlibet etiam non ens, quia propter fluxum et divisibilitatem confusionemque non vere sit; mobilem quoque conceptionem animae non ens, quia non ens perfectum; alteritatem ipsam in intellectu vel primo quodammodo non ens, quoniam est origo ut

not only postulate that "something is," but also that "something is not," and examine what consequences follow in both cases [135E–36A]. This is indeed what one should consider when one is looking for the first causes and principles of each thing and each accident. For the rational structure inherent in a principle is such that, by postulating that it is or that it is not, one postulates that its effect is or is not: if by solely supposing that a thing A is, one simultaneously supposes that a thing B is too, but that B does not cease to be if A ceases to be, then A is not the principle of B. In this way, Parmenides teaches us to examine four consequences that follow when one supposes that something (for instance, the intellect or the soul) both is and is not. In both cases he wishes us to consider what consequences follow (1) for that thing in relation both to itself and (2) to others, and again what consequences follow (3) for others in relation to both themselves and (4) to the thing itself [136A–B]. But when one supposes that the intellect, or the soul, is not, how can one then consider what consequences follow for something that does not exist? The answer is that one does not actually suppose that the intellect or the soul are absolutely not, otherwise one could not then investigate what consequences follow for them, but one rather supposes that this thing called "intellect" or "soul" is not properly intellect or soul, but is, or is imagined to be, something else. Certainly the Platonists usually understand "not-being" in a double or in a simple way—absolute not-being, or not-being relative to something else: either something is not A, but B (for instance, what is not a man, but is a horse), or it is not in one way, but is in another (for instance, what is potentially, but not actually). The Platonists call matter not-being, because it is formally nothing;[100] any sensible object is also called not-being, because by virtue of the flux, the divisibility and the mixing it undergoes, it has no true being; the soul's moving act of comprehension is also called not-being, because it is not a perfect being; within the intellect (even the first intellect) otherness

hoc non sit istud et istud non sit illud; ipsum unum bonumque non ens quoniam ente superius. Multis ergo modis aliquid non esse supponere possunt,[35] dum tamen hoc ipsum de quo ens negant funditus non extirpant, ut cum fingunt si unum, si multitudo, si intellectus non sit, quaerentes quid ipsi sequatur aliisque, ex ipso non eradicant funditus quod supponunt sed, ut dixi, subintellegunt nonnihil interea a quo absit tamen ut sit unum vel multitudo vel intellectus.

2 Caeterum quidnam ad illud, ubi Parmenides supponit unum omnino non esse? Respondebimus, quantum in praesentia mihi succurrit, fingi posse quod unum dicitur omnino non esse unum, id est fingi turbam unitatis omnis prorsus expertem. De hoc quidem dubio in praesentia satis. Ad illud autem quod dicitur non ens, addendum est praeceptum Parmenidis in *Sophiste* narratum, ubi Melissus ait magnum Parmenidem praecepisse cavendum ne quando ipsi omnino non enti aliquid entis admoveremus, ne videlicet contradictionem maximam inter ens atque non ens temere concedamus. Ibi quidem non ens significare vult nec ipsum unum superius ente, nec materiam in ipsa entis integritate deficientem minimumque gradum entis habentem, sed omnimodam, ut ita dixerim, orbitatem. Quam qui fingit non debet deinceps ei quicquam quod ad ens pertineat adhibere. Cum vero numerus gradum non minimum in ente possideat, non licet, inquit, orbitati confictae vel multitudinem vel unitatem ad numerum pertinentem aliquam admovere, neque vel singulariter vel pluraliter eam pronuntiare vel cogitare aut dicere eam esse aliquid, siquidem aliquid dicitur ens aliquid, neque dicere eam unum aliquid, nam unum aliquid

itself is in some way called not-being, because it causes A not to be B and conversely; the One-and-Good is called not-being, because it is superior to being. There are many ways, therefore, in which one can postulate that something is not, as long, however, as one does not completely eliminate the existence of that which "is not." For instance, if one imagines that the One, the many, or the intellect are not, and investigates what consequences follow for themselves and for the others, one does not completely eliminate the existence of those things which "are not," but, as I said, one implies that there exists something else which those things lack in order to be one, many or intellect.[101]

To sum up, when Parmenides supposes that the One is absolutely not, we shall say, as far as this is helpful for the moment, that one can imagine that what is called "one" is not absolutely one, for instance, a multitude which is totally deprived of unity. On this delicate question this will suffice for the moment. Regarding what is called not-being, one must add Parmenides' precept mentioned in the *Sophist,* where Melissus says that the great Parmenides enjoined us never to attribute some being to absolute not-being, lest we admit without due consideration something that constitutes the greatest contradiction regarding being and not-being.[102] What Parmenides means here is that "not-being" does not designate the One, which is superior to being, nor matter, which lacks the very integrity of being and has the smallest degree of being, but any kind of what I would call privation of being. When one imagines the privation of being, one should not then apply to it anything that pertains to being. But since number does possess being in some degree,[103] one cannot, he says, apply the singular or plural of number to this imagined privation of being, nor utter in speech or mentally conceive this privation in a singular or plural way, or even say that it is something, given that something is "some thing that is," nor say that it is something that is one, since "something that is one" is either this "some thing that 2

est ens hoc unum aut ens illud unum. Ipsum vero primum unum, de quo nondum ibi fit mentio, non est ens unum, sed simpliciter unum. Alioquin si foret ens unum non esset unum simpliciter, sed iam aliquod unum quod cum ente convertitur. Sed de hoc diligentius in *Sophiste*.

: XXXVII :

Futura disputatio dicitur ardua, quia non solum logica est, sed etiam theologica.

1 Ex verbis Socratis et Parmenidis atque Zenonis sequentem disputationem colligimus fore 'opus grande et arduum pelagusque profundum' non tam propter ipsam dialecticam sive logicam dialogi formam quam propter subiectam huic materiam plurimum theologicam, alioquin minime decuisset tam magnificis verbis totiens hic praefari, neque rursus deceret Pythagoricum senem nudam logicam pertractare. Nonne Plato decorum profanum ubique servat et quae quisque tractaverat cuique tribuit, moralia, purgatoria, conversoria Socrati, amoris sacri mysteria sacerdoti, physica et mathematica Timaeo, de ente Melisso Parmenidis sectatori? Numquid ergo Parmenidi seniori magistro et entis intellegibilis idearumque prae caeteris assertori exercitationem tribuet puerilem?

is one" or that "some thing that is one."[104] The first One, however, which is not yet mentioned in the *Sophist,* is not the one being, but the absolute One; if it were the one being, it would not be the absolute One, but would already be some "one" that is convertible with being. But we treat of this in more detail in our commentary on the *Sophist.*[105]

: XXXVII :

Parmenides says that "the discussion will be arduous," because it is not only logical but also theological.[106]

From the words of Socrates, Parmenides and Zeno we conclude that the following discussion will be an "important and arduous task" [136D1] and a "deep ocean" [137A6],[107] not so much because of the dialectical or logical form of the dialogue, but because of the highly theological material that underlies it—otherwise it would by no means have been appropriate to announce this here so many times with such magnificent words; neither would it be appropriate for an elderly Pythagorean to treat entirely of basic logic. Is it not true that in all his dialogues Plato preserves common propriety [in the portrayal of his characters], and assigns to each philosopher the material that they have studied, to Socrates, matters relating to ethics, purification and conversion, to the priestess Diotima, erotic mysteries, to Timaeus, physics and mathematics, to Melissus, Parmenides' disciple, being? Would he really attribute, then, some puerile exercise to an elderly master, who has championed more than anyone else the existence of intelligible being and 1

Absit. Sed audiamus Platonem ipsum de excellentia Parmenidis librique huius divina testificantem. Socrates in *Sophiste* Melissum sic alloquitur: 'Utrum velis oratione perpetua nobiscum loqui, an potius interrogando, quemadmodum solebat Parmenides, quem ego adolescens audivi quondam ita disputantem admodum senem rationesque pulcherrimas afferentem?' Rursus in *Theaeteto* Socrates obsecratus ut eos refelleret, qui ens unum immobile posuerunt, non recipit se id facturum, ita respondens: 'Etsi Melissum atque alios, qui unum consistens universum dicunt, vereor ne forte immodesti videamur illos exagitantes, minus tamen quam unicum Parmenidem vereor. Parmenides enim, ut Homericis verbis utar, verendus mihi acerque videtur. Collocutus sum olim cum illo sene admodum adhuc adolescens mihique visus est profundam generosamque omnino sapientiam possidere. Formido itaque ne dicta eius vocesque nequaquam intellegamus et quod ipse verbis subintellegit multo magis nos lateat.' Denique quis non intellegat, dum promittit disputationem dialecticam, praestare interim theologicam, cum et apud Platonem idem sit utrumque et genera propriaque universi entis gradatim in medium afferantur? Quod autem dictum est disputationem eiusmodi turbae ridiculam fore, praesertim a sene tractatam, duplicem habet sensum: partim quidem propter praetextum logicum quem vulgus existimat verbis cavillationibusque nugari, ignorans videlicet artificium hoc esse veritatis et sapientiae clavem, partim quoque propter materiam qua de agitur theologicam paradoxis refertam. Quam videri turbae quidem

the Ideas?[108] Not at all! Let us listen to Plato himself attest the divine excellence of Parmenides and of his work. In the *Sophist,* Socrates addresses Melissus as follows: "Do you prefer to speak to us in an uninterrupted speech or to use the interrogative method in the manner of Parmenides? I once heard him debate in this way and develop splendid arguments. I was a young man then, and he was very old."[109] Similarly, in the *Theaetetus,* although enjoined to refute those who have postulated that the one being is motionless, Socrates refuses to do so for the following reason: "Although I have a fear of appearing immodest by criticizing Melissus and others, who state that the universe is one and motionless, I have greater fear still of criticizing one single man, Parmenides. For Parmenides seems to me, to use Homer's words, "venerable" and "severe." I once talked to him when I was still young and he was quite old, and he appeared to me to possess an absolutely profound and noble wisdom. So I am afraid we may not understand his words and may be still farther from understanding what he implied by them."[110] Finally, who would fail to realize that the dialectical discussion Plato promises us is actually a theological discussion, since Plato considers that dialectic and theology are identical, and the genera and properties of being are progressively adduced in this dialogue? In addition, the passage where it is said that "such a discourse will be ridiculous to the vulgar, particularly in a man of his age" [136D7–8] has a double meaning: on the one hand, it refers to the logical appearance of the dialogue, which the vulgar crowd considers to be a jest in words and quibbling, unaware that this logical artifice is the key to truth and wisdom; on the other, it refers to the theological and highly paradoxical material of the dialogue. That it seems ridiculous to the vulgar, but

ridiculam, sed sapientibus venerandam Plato in *Phaedro* et in *Epistolis* ad Dionysium Syracusanosque testatur. Neque fas est Pythagorico vel Platonico, praesertim qui in hac disciplina iam consenuerit, profanis divina mysteria divulgare.

2 Quid plura? Quicquid hactenus disputatum est longum est ad sequentia theologicumque prooemium, ut merito et quod sequitur futurum sit profecto divinum, non logica quaedam simplex absque ullo philosophico sensu, ut quidam dubitaverunt ante Proclum. Contra quos Proclus in *Theologia* inquit non ulterius pugnandum sibi fore, iamdiu enim a Platonica familia fuisse convictos. Ipse autem Syrianum secutus in singulis verbis singula putat latere mysteria, et quot sunt clausulae, ferme totidem esse numina. Ego vero mediam secutus viam arbitror tantum saltem theologiae subesse quantum admittit artificium, ut communiter dicitur, dialecticum, ideoque non ubique omnino continuatas, sed quandoque divulsas de divinis inesse sententias. Profecto si Platonis consilium fuisset solum in logicis argumentationibus erudire, non arduam hanc de uno et ente entisque generibus materiam accepisset discentibus impedimento futuram, sed facilem et in promptu cunctis expositam. Si contra decrevisset divina prorsus omnia hic ubique continuare mysteria neque logicam interim difficultatem introduxisset, per se haud modum venerandam dignamque numinibus, neque adolescentem hic elegisset erudiendum. Qui tamen tamquam natura divinus divina quaedam simul cum logicis postulabat, quae et

honorable to the wise is attested by Plato in the *Phaedrus* and the *Letters* to Dionysius and to the Syracusans;[111] it is not permitted, moreover, to a Pythagorean or a Platonist, especially if he is quite an elderly member of the school, to reveal the divine mysteries to the profane.

In short, what has been discussed thus far serves as a long theological introduction for what follows; so, appropriately, what follows will also undoubtedly be divine, rather than a simple logical exercise without any philosophical meaning, as some of Proclus' predecessors believed. Proclus says in his *Theology* that there was no longer any need for him to refute them, because they had long been defeated by the Platonic school.[112] Proclus himself, like his master Syrianus, thinks that mysteries are hidden in each word, and that the number of conclusions in the dialogue corresponds almost exactly to the number of divinities.[113] For my part I have followed a middle path, and I consider that there is at least as much theology in this dialogue as is permitted by the art that is commonly called dialectical. In my opinion, therefore, allusions to divine matters are not everywhere continuously present, but divulged on occasions. Surely if Plato had solely intended to teach us how to argue logically, he would not have chosen as his subject this difficult material on the One, being, and the genera of being, which would be difficult to grasp for the student, but a material that is easy and clearly accessible to all. Conversely, if Plato had wished to continuously expound throughout the whole dialogue all the divine mysteries without introducing logical problems from time to time (which in itself is neither honorable nor appropriate to divine beings), he would not have chosen as the dialogue's protagonist a young man who required instruction. Despite his youth, Socrates had a divine nature and kept asking to be instructed in 2

a Parmenide merito tradebantur futuram disputationem tamquam etiam divinam ex libris suis divina tractantibus opportune texente. Qui futuram disputationem ludum serium negotiosumque appellavit, quoniam sub dialectica vel logica specie divinam quandam materiam ex suis libris acceptam subesse volebat.

3 Denique librum hunc esse theologicum non solum caeteri Platonici praecipue probatissimi convenerunt, sed etiam Dionysius Areopagita confirmare videtur. Quotiens in ipsius unius incidit mentionem, totiens enim enti praeponit, distinguit unum ens ab ipso simpliciter uno ipsumque unum ait ipsius esse principium entisque unius procreatorem. Utitur quinetiam argumentationibus negationibus verbisque Parmenidis saepe quam plurimis in materia divinissima, testificans interea materiam Parmenidis esse divinam. Bonum quoque similiter ut unum ipsis Platonicorum rationibus semper anteponit essentiae. Sed de hoc alibi.

4 Confirmemus tandem alio quodam Platonis ipsius testimonio librum hunc non esse contentiosum, sed certe dogmaticum. Plato in *Theaeteto* Parmenidem Melisso Zenonique longe praeponit. In *Sophiste* Melissum Parmenidis sectatorem fuisse inquit a redargutionibus contentionibusque alienum, et ut deum veneratur[36] vel certe divinum. Nemo igitur suspicari debet Parmenidem ipsum seniorem ac longe diviniorem introductum a Platone fuisse quasi contentiosis redargutionibus incumbentem logicumve levem iuveniliterque ludentem.

divine as well as logical matters. These Parmenides was right to teach him, opportunely weaving together from his own work on divine matters the following discussion, which is also divine. And he called the following discussion "a serious and laborious game" [137B2],[114] because underlying the dialectical or logical appearance of the dialogue he wished to present some divine material drawn from his own work.

Finally, not only all the Platonists, especially the most honorable, agreed that this dialogue is theological, but Dionysius the Areopagite also appears to confirm it.[115] For every time he mentions the One he places it before being; he distinguishes the one being from the absolute One and says that the One is the principle of being and the creator of the one being. In addition, whenever he can he uses the arguments, the negations and the words of the *Parmenides*, and he does so when treating of the most divine matters, thereby testifying that the material of the *Parmenides* is also divine. Similarly, he always places both the Good and the One before essence, using the very arguments of the Platonists. But we treat of these matters elsewhere.[116] 3

One last testimony by Plato confirms that this dialogue is not eristic, but undoubtedly dogmatic. In the *Theaetetus* Plato grants a far greater preeminence to Parmenides than to Melissus and Zeno, and in the *Sophist* he says that Parmenides' disciple, Melissus, was alien to refutations and controversies, and honored like a god, or certainly like someone divine.[117] Nobody should imagine, therefore, that Parmenides himself, who is older than Melissus and far more divine, was presented by Plato as if he were involved in refutations for the sake of controversy or was playing a facile and juvenile game of logic for the sake of entertainment.[118] 4

: XXXVIII :

De suppositionibus Parmenidis et de uno bonoque quod ente et intellectu superius per verba Platonis.

1 Qua ratione Proclus aliique nonnulli novem suppositiones in hoc dialogo disposuerint narravimus in principio commentarii. Ubi etiam ex eorum sententia est addendum affirmationes negationesque a Parmenide circa unum factas ut utraeque verae sint. Oportere ipsum unum alia quidem significatione accipere, ubi negatur, alia vero, ubi affirmatur, puta si hunc in modum exponatur, ubi negatur unum, neque esse idem neque alterum, intellegatur de uno quod est ente superius, ubi autem affirmatur unum esse, et idem pariter atque alterum, intellegatur de uno quod habet cum ente coniugium. Alii vero nonnulli distinctionem eiusmodi non ubique probabant, ut quando consideratur si unum sit, quid hinc sequatur; item si non sit unum, quid et inde contingat. Oportere enim dicebant in hac ancipiti quaestione ipsum unum in eadem significatione utrobique sumere, alioquin auctoritatem unius ad consequentiam inde rerum intellegi numquam posse, nisi id certo sciamus ut uno quidem posito, consequenter talia quoque ponantur, eodem vero sublato, talia rursus auferantur. Sed ad hanc quaestionem alibi respondendum. Nunc vero quomodo ipsum unum sit ente superius et entis universi principium breviter perstringamus.

2 In *Philebo* probatur ab ipso uno rerum principio statim produci binarium, scilicet principia entium vel elementa duo, terminum

: XXXVIII :

On the hypotheses of the Parmenides and, following Plato's words, on the One-and-Good, which is superior to being and intellect.

The way in which Proclus and others have arranged the dialogue in nine hypotheses we have explained at the beginning of the commentary.[119] We should add that, following the doctrine of these same philosophers, the assertions and the negations formulated by Parmenides about the One are done in such a way that they are both true. We should understand the term "one" differently according to whether the hypothesis is "if the one is," or "if the one is not." For instance, in the proposition, "if the one is not, it is neither the same nor the other," we should understand "the One that is superior to being." But in the proposition "if the one is, it is both the same and the other," we should understand "the one that is united with being." Other philosophers, however, showed that a distinction like this between the various senses of "one" does not occur everywhere in the *Parmenides,* such as in the proposition "if the one is, what are the consequences?" and similarly in the proposition "if the one is not, what are the consequences?" For according to them, we should understand "one" in the same sense in both these questions, or else we might never comprehend the power of the One toward the succession of things that derive from it, unless we know as a fact that if the One exists, the other things consequently also exist, and if the One does not exist, these things do not exist. But we must answer this question elsewhere. For the moment let us briefly mention the way in which the One is superior to being and is the principle of universal being. 1

In the *Philebus* Plato shows that a dyad is immediately produced from the One, which is the principle of things. This dyad consists 2

scilicet infinitatemque, quod et Philolaus Pythagoricus introduxit. Ex quibus omnia prorsus entia componantur, sed ante aliorum entium compositionem primum ex his confici mixtum, scilicet ens primum in se continens ens universum, ut quemadmodum quodlibet ens ex suo quodam termino infinitoque conflatur, sic ens primum ex termino infinitoque primo sit praecipue mixtum. Ex his manifeste concluditur ipsum unum et ente et elementis principiisque entis esse superius. Aperte enim illic et infinitum appellat entium et terminum entium et ex his probat entia cuncta componi primumque ex his compositum vocat essentiam, auctorem vero unionis ipsorum inter se oppositorum[37] convenienter ipsum appellaturus est unum. Praeterea ibidem quaeritur summum animae nostrae bonum probaturque in primis tres summi boni proprietates existere, quibus videlicet sit omnino perfectum, sufficiens, expetendum. Per haec consequenter adducitur intellegentiam solam, quantumlibet in se perspicacem, non esse ipsum nobis bonum, quia suapte natura ipsas boni proprietates haud penitus complectatur. Non enim sufficit intellegentia nobis ad beate vivendum, nisi per ipsius boni praesentiam. Cum vero noster intellectus sit primi intellectus imago, sequi videtur ut quemadmodum intellectui nostro ipsa sua intellegentia non est ipsum sibi bonum, ita nec intellectui primo sola intellegentia simpliciter sit summum sibi bonum, alioquin si per solam intellegentiam primam bonum ibi definiretur, consequenter ubique intellegentibus omnibus sua simpliciter intellegentia sufficeret foretque summum unicuique bonum. Hac igitur ratione concluditur ipsum bonum primo intellectu superius esse, quandoquidem cuilibet intellegenti felicitas non per solam intellegentiam, sed per integram ipsius boni praesentiam definitur.

of two principles, or elements, of beings: limit and infinity, as the Pythagorean Philolaus also proposes.[120] Absolutely all beings are constituted from these two entities; however, preceding the composition of all these beings, there is the first mixture constituted from these two elements. This mixture is the first being, which contains within itself universal being. As a result, just as every being consists of a mixture of its own limit and the infinite, so the first being principally consists of a mixture of the first limit and the first infinite. Hence one clearly concludes that the One is superior to both being and the elements or principles of being. For Plato openly calls them "the infinite of beings" and "the limit of beings" in the *Philebus*, and shows that all beings are composed of them; and the first mixture he calls essence, while he will appropriately call that which is responsible for the union of these opposites, "the One."[121] In addition, when in the same dialogue Plato is looking for what constitutes the highest good for the human soul, he first shows that the highest good has three properties by virtue of which it is absolutely perfect, sufficient and desirable.[122] By these arguments it is concluded, therefore, that intelligence, however visionary it is in itself, cannot constitute the good for us, because it does not naturally contain the very properties of the good. In other words, intelligence is not sufficient to make us happy; the presence of the Good is necessary. But since our intellect is the image of the first intellect, it seems to follows that, just as our very intelligence is not the good for our intellect, so simple intelligence is not by itself the highest Good for the first intellect. Otherwise, if the Good was defined solely by virtue of the first intelligence, then each knowing being would be content with its own simple intelligence, which would be its own highest good. So the conclusion is that the Good is superior to the first intellect, since happiness for each knowing being is not defined by intelligence on its own, but by the pure presence of the Good.[123]

3 Audi praeterea comparationem Platonicam in sexto *De Republica* eadem manifestissime confirmantem. Quemadmodum sol in oculis et coloribus generationem virtutemque et actionem mutuam cum lumine praebet, ipse tamen sol nec oculus neque color neque generatio est, sed longe superior, sic ipsum bonum intellectibus intellegibilibusque essentiam et vim actumque mutuum cum ipso veritatis splendore largitur neque tamen est intellectus vel intellegibile vel veritas vel essentia, sed his omnibus dignitate et potestate superius. Rursus ibidem inquit ipsum ens in eodem gradu cum veritate pariter emicare. Cum igitur ipsum bonum veritati intellegentiaeque apertissime praeposuerit, pariter anteposuit enti.

4 In *Sophiste* rursus probatur in primo ente omnia esse quae ad perfectionem entis necessario requiruntur. Igitur habere vitam et intellectum formalesque entium omnium rationes, penes vitam quidem habere motum atque alterum, sed penes intellectum habere statum atque idem. Ibi haec quattuor essentiae addita inter se distingui formaliter, distingui quoque ab his essentiam interea cunctis admixtam. Igitur ipsum ens esse totum et multiplex atque unum ipsumque totum et ipsum ens idem penitus esse. Item ad rationem essentiae pertinere ut sit totum atque unum, et quae conveniunt toti convenire pariter enti, scilicet ut sit multiplex simul et unum. Hinc apparet ipsum ens ab ipso uno tamquam posterius discrepare, praesertim quia omne primumque ens, inquit, cum non ente permixtum. Nusquam vero ipsum unum miscuit cum non uno. Immo et in *Sophiste* significat et in *Parmenide* probat ipsum unum prorsus a non uno et ab omnibus entis generibus segregatum tamquam ente sublimius. Probatur denique in *Sophiste* ferme hunc in modum: ipsum primum et universum ens

Consider also the Platonic comparison in Book VI of the *Republic,* which confirms in the clearest terms what has been said above: just as the sun provides, through its light, the eyes and colors with their generation, strength and action (despite the fact that it is not itself eye, color, or generation, but is far superior to these), in like manner, the Good provides, through the very splendor of truth, the intellects and the intelligible objects with their essence, power, and acts (though it is not the intellect, the intelligible, truth or essence, but transcends all these in dignity and power). Again, in the same passage Plato says that being shines equally and in the same grade as truth. Therefore, since he has very clearly placed the Good before truth and intelligence, Plato has also placed it before being.[124] 3

In the *Sophist* too it is shown that all things are in the first being, since they are necessary for being to be perfect, and therefore possess life, intellect and the formal rational principles of all beings; within life, they have motion and otherness; within intellect, rest and sameness. Yonder, these four genera[125] added to essence are formally distinct from one other, and the essence that is mixed together with everything [in our world] is also distinct from them. Being itself, therefore, is whole, multiple and one, and the whole and being are totally the same thing. Similarly, it pertains to the rational principle of essence to be whole and one, and what is in accordance with the whole is equally in accordance with being, which is both multiple and one. It is clear, therefore, that being differs from the One and is secondary to it—especially given that all being and first being, Plato says, is mixed with not-being. But he never mixed the One with the not-one.[126] Even more so, as he hints at in the *Sophist* and demonstrates in the *Parmenides,* the One is totally separate from the not-one and from all the genera of being, because it transcends being. Finally, the superiority of the One over being is demonstrated in the *Sophist* more or less as follows: the first and universal being is subject to unity, both in its 4

patitur unum tum in partibus suis tum in toto. Non est igitur ipsum unum, quoniam ipsum unum neque patitur unum neque partes ullas habet nec est totum. Item entium multitudo sive contrariorum sive non contrariorum ab uno ente necessario proficiscitur, ipsum vero unum ens ab ipso simpliciter uno. Quando enim calidum aut frigidum, statum aut motum ens appellamus, non utique horum quodlibet tamquam sit ens ipsum asseveramus. Sive enim status sit ens ipsum, certe motus iam ens non erit, sive motus sit ipsum ens, profecto status appellationem entis amittet. Sed constat hoc esse et statui et motui et omni entium multitudini ab uno primo ente distribui. Ipsum igitur ens quod est omnibus essentiae causa ab omnibusque participatum particeps est unius. Propterea non sicut primo ens est sic est et unum primo, sed ipsum quidem ens existit neque secundum participationem est esse sortitum, participatione vero est unum. Propterea patitur quidem unum, est autem primo ens. Haec in *Sophiste*. Cum igitur per haec ostendatur ipsum unum universi principium ente superius esse necessario demonstratum est esse super vitam, intellectum, intellegibile, haec enim enti succedunt.

5 Denique in *Parmenide* quod et dicimus alibi, differentia inter unum et essentiam et esse verbis ponitur manifestis ibique ipsum unum ab omnibus generibus entis et ab ipsa tandem essentia tamquam sublimius segregatur, praesertim in primae suppositionis fine. Itaque multo magis, ut modo dicebam, ipsum unum primum superat intellectum. Iam vero in intellectu sunt entis illa genera propriaque a quibus absolvitur unum. Postremo neque posthabendum est eiusmodi corollarium, sicut Plato Parmenidem hic de uno disputantem anteponit ubique Melisso disputanti in *Sophiste* de ente, ita verisimiliter ipsum unum anteponit enti, si modo decorum sit ut utrobique in materiis personisque servaturus, quod ubique servare solet. Superioribus Platonis verbis persuasi familia-

parts and as a whole. Thus being is not the One, since the One is not subject to unity, has no parts and is not a whole. Similarly, the multitude of beings (whether these beings are opposed to one another or not) necessarily proceed from the one being, and the one being proceeds from the absolute One. For when we predicate hot or cold, rest or motion of being, we do not mean that any of these [predicates] is being itself: if rest is being itself, motion will certainly cease to be a being and, if motion is being itself, rest will assuredly cease to be called being. It is clear that the act of being is imparted to rest, motion, and to the whole multitude of beings by the first being, which is one.[127] Thus being itself, which is the cause of essence for all and is participated in by all, participates in the One. So being is not the first One in the same way as it is the first being, but on the one hand, it is being and receives the act of being without participation; on the other, it is one by participation. Thus it is subject to the One, but is the first being.[128] Thus in the *Sophist*. So, by showing through these texts that the One, which is the principle of the universe, is superior to being, it is also shown that the One necessarily transcends life, intellect and the intelligible, given that these come after being.

Finally, as we also say elsewhere, the *Parmenides* describes in an 5
explicit way the difference between the One, essence and being, and shows that the One transcends all the genera of being and, ultimately, essence itself, especially at the end of the first hypothesis [141E]. So, as I mentioned above, it is even more the case that the One transcends the first intellect, because the genera and properties of being from which the One is separate reside in the intellect.[129] Lastly, one should not neglect the following corollary: just as Plato always gives Parmenides, who discusses here the One, precedence over Melissus, who discusses being in the *Sophist*, in the same way he is very likely to give the One priority over being, since we would expect Plato to follow in the *Parmenides* the deco-

res eius unum bonumque essentiae intellegentiaeque praefecerunt et, ut narrat Proclus, probatissimi quique Platonici, Plutarchus, Ammonius, Plotinus, Amelius, Porphyrius, Iamblichus, Theodorus caeterique sectatores eorum. Ego vero id sensisse Platonem arbitror in quo schola illa vetus extra controversiam cum nova consentit, nova vero a Syriano et Proclo, magnis profecto viris, idem penitus sentientibus ducit originem, in qua post illos Hermias et Damascius Olympiodorusque praecipui numerantur.

: XXXIX :

Item quomodo Plato procedit ad primum. De nomine eius. De idea boni.

1 Proinde Plato in *Republica* et in *Philebo* et ubique sensibiles passim multitudines ad intellegibiles redigit unitates, id est ideas, scilicet unamquamque multitudinem rerum invicem cognatarum ad ideam unam, deinde unitates intellegibiles ad ipsum simpliciter unum, quod ita saltem intellegibilia superat quemadmodum ab his sensibilia superantur illudque vocat ipsum simpliciter bonum. Sed inter ideas collocat etiam ipsum non simpliciter, sed ideale bonum, a quo distinguit et ipsum ideale pulchrum, ut bonum ideale non pulchrorum sit causa, sed bonorum, nec essentiam primam rebus tribuat vel excellentissimam unitatem, sed perfectiones aliquas consequentes bonitatum nomine designatas. At ipsum super ideas bonum, ut in *Epistolis* inquit, est auctor omnium ut bonorum ita

rum he generally establishes in his dialogues between topics and interlocutors.[130] Persuaded by the words of Plato mentioned above, his disciples assigned the One-and-Good priority over essence and intelligence; according to Proclus, all of these are highly venerable Platonists: Plutarch, Ammonius, Plotinus, Amelius, Porphyry, Iamblichus, Theodorus,[131] and all their followers. I myself think that Plato did adopt this doctrine, since there is no controversy between the old and the new schools over the issue.[132] The new school originates with Syrianus and Proclus, eminent men indeed who were entirely in agreement; among their successors are the great philosophers Hermias, Damascius and Olympiodorus.

: XXXIX :

Likewise, how Plato proceeds toward the first principle. On the name of the first principle. On the Idea of good.

Thus in the *Republic,* the *Philebus,* and everywhere, Plato brings multitudes of sense objects back to intelligible unities, that is, to the Ideas (each multitude of related things back to a single Idea), then the intelligible unities to the absolute One, which transcends the intelligible unities at least as much as the sense objects are transcended by the intelligible realities, and this absolute One he calls the absolute Good. But among the Ideas he also places a good—not the absolute Good, but the Idea of good, which is also different from the Idea of beautiful, since the Idea of good is not the cause of beautiful things, but of good ones, and does not provide things with the first essence or the most excellent unity, but with some secondary perfections called "goodnesses." But, as Plato says in the *Letters,* the Good above the Ideas is the creator of all 1

pulchrorum atque sicut in *Republica* docet, sic essentias sicut virtutes atque perfectiones ubique distribuit nec in essentia est, aut essentia est vel intellegibile, sicut idea quaevis, sed essentiam et intellegibile antiquitate, dignitate, potentia superat, sicut sol generationem et oculos et colores. Cum vero sit prorsus incognitum intellectu atque ideo proprio nomine designari non possit, ex ideali bono utpote sibi simillimo appellatur idea boni. Simili ratione entis luminosissimum nuncupatur, cum tamen et super ens et super entis lumen, id est veritatem et intellectum, manifestissime sit assertum, in *Republica* videlicet, ubi dum probat ipsum bonum quod intellectus omnes cum intellegibilibus unit, non esse intellectum, non intellegibile, non veritatem, non scientiam vel cognitionem ullam, non essentiam, examussim imitari videtur negationes entium omnium circa unum in *Parmenide* declaratas. Lumen denique boni in omnibus tam intellegibilibus quam intellectibus et in universo ente vero nihil est aliud quam superessentialis unitas bonitasque divinis infusa divinitus.

: XL :

Rursus duae Platonis ad primum viae, duo nomina primi.

1 Plato per duas ad summum vias ascendit, per comparationes quidem in *Republica*, per negationes autem in *Parmenide*. Utraeque pariter tam comparationes quam negationes declarant deum esse tum ab omnibus entibus et intellegibilibus segregatum, tum etiam principium universi. Negationes autem aliae quidem sunt affirma-

things, both the good and the beautiful ones.[133] As he teaches in the *Republic,* it distributes to all beings essences, powers and perfections, although it does not reside in an essence, nor is it an essence or an intelligible, like any Idea, but it transcends essence and the intelligible world by its venerable precedence, rank, and power, just as the sun transcends generation, eyes and colors.[134] However, although it is completely unknown to the intellect and cannot, therefore, be designated by a proper name, it is called Idea of good by analogy with the ideal good, which is very similar to it. Likewise it is called the "most luminous part of being"[135] even though the *Republic* most clearly states that it transcends being and the light of being, that is, truth and intellect. When Plato demonstrates in that passage that the Good which unites all the intellects to their intelligible objects is not an intellect, nor an intelligible, nor truth, nor knowledge or cognition, nor essence,[136] he appears to imitate word by word the negations of all beings put forward in the *Parmenides* about the One. Finally, the light of the good within all the intelligible objects and intellects and in the universal being is the super-essential Unity and Goodness infused by God into the divine beings.[137]

: XL :

Once again, the two Platonic ways to ascend toward the first principle, and the two names of the first principle.

Plato ascends to the highest principle in two ways: by using com- 1
parisons in the *Republic,* and by using negations in the *Parmenides.* Both comparisons and negations equally indicate that God is both separate from all beings and intelligible objects, and the principle of the universe. Among the negations, some are superior to asser-

tionibus meliores, aliae vero consortes, deteriores aliae. Primae quidem fiunt quando probamus primum non esse ens, tamquam videlicet melius ente entisque principium. Secundae vero, quando non ens cum ente probamus admixtum, quemadmodum in *Sophiste* dicitur ipsum non entis enti saltem aequale videri, quo videlicet pacto quod est ipse status non est ipse motus, quod est identitas non est alteritas, quod calor non frigus, quod rationale non brutum, quod aurum non est ferrum. Tertiae negationes fiunt quando privationes et fluxus informemque materiam non ens appellamus, tamquam integro ente longe deteriora.

2 Comparationes autem vere significant similitudinem quandam et habitudinem non primi quidem ad sequentia, sed sequentium prorsus ad primum, quod sane cuncta multo eminentius superat quam caeterae causae, quantumlibet excelsae,[38] effectus quaeque suos. Neque magis hos ordines superat, minus illos, alioquin habitudinem ad hos quidem maiorem haberet, ad illos vero minorem. Habitudine vero si praeditum fuerit, non erit simpliciter unum nec penitus absolutum. Omnia igitur aeque superat, haec autem ad illud habitudine quadam affecta iam alia quidem propinquiora sunt illi, alia vero remotiora. Illud rursus per unicum individuumque quasi cardinem cuncta producit, haec autem ad ipsum, pro varietate naturae, aliter passim et aliter se ad illud habent atque convertuntur.

3 Proinde quemadmodum via duplici Plato noster ascendit ad primum, ita nominibus illud praecipue duobus appellat. In *Republica* quidem, ubi per comparationes scandit, appellat bonum. Comparationes enim ex similitudine rerum ad primum infusa bonitate ducuntur. In *Parmenide* vero, ubi per negationes incedit, no-

tions, some are on the same shared level, and some are inferior. We use the first type of negation when we demonstrate that the first principle is not being, meaning that it is superior to, and the principle of, being. We use the second type of negation when we demonstrate that not-being is mixed with being; for instance, in the passage in the *Sophist* where it is said that not-being seems at least equal to being,[138] Plato is explaining how what is rest is not motion, what is sameness is not otherness, what is heat is not coldness, what is rational is not brute, what is gold is not iron. We use the third type of negation when we call privations, flux and formless matter "not-being," because they are by far inferior to being pure and whole.[139]

As to comparisons, they truly indicate some similitude and relation, not of the first principle in relation to the beings that follow it, but of the subsequent beings in relation to the first principle, since the first principle transcends all beings more eminently than the other causes (however elevated these may be) transcend their own effects. The first principle does not transcend some orders of beings more than others, otherwise it would have a relation toward them that would vary in degree. Yet if it has a relation toward beings it will cease to be the simple and absolute One. Therefore, it equally transcends all beings, while all beings have a relation toward it, and this relation varies according to whether they are closer to or further from it. It produces all things through a unique and indivisible axis, as it were, while all things are disposed and turn toward it in different ways, according to the variety of their natures.[140] 2

In this way, just as our Plato ascends toward the first principle in a double way, he also principally calls it by two names. In the *Republic,* where he ascends toward the first principle through comparisons, he calls it Good, for comparisons are drawn from the similitude of things toward the first principle when goodness is infused into them. In the *Parmenides,* where he ascends toward it 3

minat unum. Negationibus enim deum principium omnium unicum, simplicissimum, eminentissimum esse designat. Iam vero negationes processum omnium inde significant, siquidem multitudo procedit ab uno tandem multitudinis omnis experte, comparationes autem conversionem omnium ad primum indicare videntur, quippe cum appetitu boni omnia convertantur ad primum. Caetera quidem ab aliis appetuntur, ab aliis negleguntur, bonum autem necessario exoptatur ab omnibus. Neque tamen duobus his nominibus vel nominamus ipsum vel geminamus, sed nos ad sequentia convertentes, dum multitudinis omnis inde processum consideramus, appellamus unum, dum vero conversionem, appellamus et bonum, sed etiam in processu bonum intellegimus propter fecunditatem et in conversione unum, quoniam ita reducuntur ad idem. Ideo Plato in *Republica,* ubi omnia convertit ad ipsum ut ad bonum, interea ipsum asserit intellegibilis et ipsius intellectus unificum.

: XLI :

Sequuntur discursus Platonici probantes unum esse principium omnium et esse ipsum unum bonumque superius ente. Primus discursus.

1 Ens universum vel unum est omnino vel omnino multa vel unum atque multa. Non quidem omnino unum, ne cogamur quae contraria sunt idem prorsus esse fateri negareque dimensiones esse, in quibus multae sunt partes ac principium et medium atque

through negations, he calls it the One, for he indicates by negations that God is the unique, simplest and most eminent principle of all things. Indeed, negations signify the procession of all things from the first principle, since multitude ultimately proceeds from the One, which is deprived of all multitude; comparisons seem to indicate the conversion of all things toward the first principle, since all things turn toward the first principle by virtue of their desire for the good. Most things are desired by some and disregarded by others, but the good is necessarily desired by all things. However, we do not talk about two principles when we use these two names, but when we turn toward the realities that follow it and we consider the procession of the whole multitude that derives from it, we call it One; when we consider the conversion of multitude toward it, we call it Good. Yet even in procession we understand that it is Good by virtue of its fecundity, and in conversion we know that it is One, since all things are brought back to the same principle. For this reason, when Plato brings all things back to it *qua* Good in the *Republic,* he also says that it unites the intelligible and the intellect.[141]

: XLI :

There follow the Platonic discourses demonstrating that the One is the principle of all things and that the One-and-Good[142] *is superior to being. First discourse.*[143]

Universal being is totally one, totally multiple, or one and multiple.[144] It is not totally one, otherwise we would be forced to say that opposites are alike, that dimensions do not exist (since dimensions contain multiple parts, the beginning, the middle and the end), and that there are no numbers for things, no various 1

finis, negare rerum numeros variasque formas atque figuras, repugnantes qualitates, motus, effectus, actiones et passiones, motuum differentias, mutationes temporum atque rerum, distinctiones inter causas et effectus agentes atque potentes. Neque rursus dicendum est universum esse omnino multa, unitatis omnis penitus expers, quia si nullum sit unum in quolibet vel in cunctis, certe neque multitudo erit ulla. Multitudo enim ex aliquibus necessario constat quorum quodlibet in se sit aliquid et aliquod unum. Nisi igitur sit unum, neque multitudo quidem erit. Item in multitudine cui nullum insit unum, quicquid excogitaveris aut nihil erit aut multitudo penitus infinita, similiterque de partium particulis infinite argumentari licet. Erit igitur multitudo illa in primis accepta infinita ex infinitis infinite undique turbis coacervata, erunt infinita plura atque vel tota multitudo prima maior erit caeteris turbis quasi partibus, itaque infinitum erit amplius infinitis, vel nihilo maior erit, ut absurde confiteamur totum partibus non esse maius. Immo neque totum aliquod erit neque partes, nisi sit unitas atque unio ad formam totius partiumque necessaria. Denique si multitudo sit innumerabiliter infinita, quod accidit uno sublato, certe innumerabiliter deinceps evadet multitudo maior atque ex opposito innumerabiliter multitudo minor. Infinite igitur hinc quidem infinita consurget turba, inde vero finita restabit, quod est absurdum, et omnis ordinis expers ubique futurum.

2 Item per ipsam unionis privationem similia erunt pariter atque dissimilia, ut alibi diximus. Similia quidem, quia privationem similem patientur, dissimilia quoque, quia per ipsam privationem, dum nihil habebunt unum, in nulla qualitate vel conditione convenient. Rursus per privationem unius simili ratione et eadem erunt

forms and figures, no opposite qualities, motions, effects, actions or passions, no differences between motions, no change of times and of things, no distinctions between causes and effects in actuality and in potentiality. Nor should we say, either, that the universe is totally multiple and completely deprived of any unity, because if there is no unity in each and in all things, surely there will be no multitude either. For multitude is necessarily composed of things, each of which is something in itself and a unity. Thus if there is no unity, there will be no multitude. Likewise, in a multitude deprived of unity, every conceivable thing will be either nothing or an infinite multitude, and so on *ad infinitum,* down to the smallest parts of parts. So the multitude that we considered infinite above, will be composed of infinite masses infinitely piled up on all sides; there will be an infinity of pluralities, and either the first multitude as a whole will be greater than the other masses that will constitute its parts (and for this reason one infinite will be greater than the other infinites), or it will not be greater than anything (and as a result, we will say that the whole is not greater than its parts, which is absurd). In addition, there will be no whole nor parts, if there is no unity or union, because these are necessary to the form of whole and parts. Finally, if multitude is innumerably infinite, which would be the case if there is no unity, it will then become infinitely greater and, conversely, infinitely smaller. So, on the one hand, it will infinitely rise as an infinite mass and, on the other, it will remain finite, which is absurd, and will be on all sides deprived of any order.

Similarly, by virtue of the very privation of union, things will be 2
both like and unlike, as we have said elsewhere.[145] They will be like, because they will undergo the same privation; they will also be unlike, because having no unity by virtue of this privation, they will not be in accordance with one another in any quality or condition. And again, by virtue of being similarly deprived of unity they will be both the same and different, since they will both undergo

et altera, dum et privationem patientur eandem et non habentia unum cogentur esse diversa. Ita multitudo per ipsam unius privationem neque stare potest neque moveri. Non stare quidem, si modo stare est in eodem unoque aliquo permanere, neque moveri rursus, quod enim fingitur omnino non unum, si mutetur unquam, certe ad oppositum permutabitur, id est ad unum, quod fingitur esse nusquam. Cum igitur res nulla per aliquid idem pati simul possit opposita, merito quae ex unius privatione contingentia modo narravimus impossibilia iudicantur. Quas ob res et universum et quodlibet ens est unum simul atque multa.

3 Quaeritur deinceps utrum in ente unum atque multa sint omnino seorsum, an invicem sint commixta. Si inter se fuerint segregata, eadem sequentur absurda, quae circa multitudinem orbatam uno paulo superius sunt adducta. Sunt igitur inter se perfecte conflata. Quapropter necesse est super haec extare causam principalem, auctore videlicet partim quidem huic uni ut sit unum et huic multitudini ut sit multitudo, partim etiam ut conciliata sint invicem. Neque enim multitudo haec uno quodam conglutinata, qua ratione multitudo est, uni huic opposita causa efficiens est unius neque rursus hoc unum, qua conditione unum a multitudine infectum est particepsque eius, primum multitudinis est principium neque unum hoc multitudoque inter se opposita ex seipsis conciliantur, sed aliunde, praesertim si neutrum sit a neutro. Sed neque putandum est fortuito haec invicem confluxisse, alioquin aliquando segregata forent.

4 Quaeritur iterum de auctore utrum sit unum prorsus vel multitudo quaedam. Multitudo quidem esse non potest, siquidem ex ipso varia ubique copulentur in unum, ac si multitudo sit, unionis

the same privation and be necessarily different, since they will have no unity. By virtue of being deprived of unity, multitude cannot be at rest or in motion. It cannot be at rest, since rest consists in remaining in the same and unique place; nor can it be in motion, for if that which we imagine to be not-one as a whole ever undergoes any change, it will surely be transformed into its opposite, the one, which we imagine to be nowhere. Since, therefore, nothing can simultaneously undergo opposite states by virtue of the same cause, it is fair to consider that the consequences resulting from the privation of unity, which we have just related, are impossible. For these reasons, any being, whether universal or individual, is both one and multiple.[146]

Another question is whether the one and the many within being are totally separate or are mixed with one another. If they are 3
separate from one another, the same absurd consequences will follow as those we just inferred above when we supposed that the multitude was deprived of unity. Thus they are perfectly combined. For this reason, there must be above them a principal cause, which creates, on the one hand, the one *qua* one and the multitude *qua* multitude and, on the other, causes them to be united with one another. For the multitude that is mixed with the one and is, *qua* multitude, the opposite of the one, is not the efficient cause of the one, just as the one, as a "one" that is corrupted by multitude and participates in it, is not the first principle of multitude. Since the one and the multitude are opposed to one another, they are not united by virtue of themselves, but by virtue of another source, especially if none of them derives its existence from the other. But one should not think that their union occurred by chance, otherwise they would occasionally be separate.[147]

Another question is whether the cause [of the union between 4
the one and the multitude] is indeed a one or a multitude. It cannot be a multitude, since it causes various things everywhere to be joined into one, and if it is a multitude it would be wrong to say it

expers dictu nefas. Si vel multitudo particeps unitatis vel unitas particeps multitudinis sit, non est unum simpliciter principiumque primum, sed definitum quiddam et desuper copulatum. Quod autem ipsum simpliciter unum sit cuiuslibet entis et universi causa patet inde, quia nihil rebus melius est quam et sua cuiusque unitas et unio rerum mutua. Per hanc enim fit, est, servatur unumquodque, hac amissa disperditur. Oportet autem in rebus optimum a primo principio proficisci. Unitas vero et unio diversorum non fit aliunde quam ab uno. Quod quidem hoc ipso quod unum est esse dat cunctis, siquidem per divisionem amittitur esse. Quod enim amittit unum perdit et esse, quod autem amittit vel non recipit multitudinem non statim necessario orbatur essentia. Ipsi enim uni oppositum est non unum, quod Graece dicitur *οὐδέν*. Ipsi vero multitudini aut multis opponitur non multitudo vel non multa. Si igitur non idem est unum atque multa neque rursus non multa idem erit atque non unum, id est *μηδέν*. Item non idem est essentia atque unum, siquidem per ipsam essentiae rationem res quomodolibet sunt, per rationem vero unius quaelibet res non solum est, sed est unum aliquid, partim in se ab aliis distinctum, partim subiens cum caeteris unionem.

5 Rursus dicere essentiam vel dicere unum nondum est sermo, sed dicere essentiam unum iam est sermo. Iam vero si idem est essentia atque unum, erit similiter multitudo atque non ens idem, quod quidem est impossibile. Nam et in essentia est multitudo et in non essentia unum. Sed numquid ens et unum, cum inter se differant in ordine universi velut aequalia tamquam duo principia disponuntur? Nequaquam. Binarius enim esse rerum origo non potest. Exigit enim superius unum. Si autem essentia sit superior uno, unum quidem tamquam particeps subibit essentiam neque

is devoid of union. If it is a multitude that participates in unity or a unity that participates in multitude, it is not the absolute One and first principle, but something particular, which is united by a superior principle. It is clear, however, that the absolute One is the cause of being, both indeterminate and universal, because nothing is better for things than their own unity and their mutual union. For it is through unity that each thing is created, exists, and is preserved; without union each thing perishes. Yet what is best within things must proceed from the first principle, and unity and union between different things do not occur through another source than the One. The One, by virtue of being "one," gives the act of being [i.e. their existence] to all things, since the act of being disappears through division. For what loses its unity also loses its being, whereas what loses or does not recover multitude is not automatically deprived of its essence. Indeed, the opposite of the One is not-one, which the Greeks call *ouden,* while the opposite of multitude or many is not-multitude and not-many. Since the One and the many are not the same, therefore, not-many will not be the same as not-one, that is, *mèden.* Similarly, essence and the One are not the same, since things *are* by virtue of the rational principle of essence, while by virtue of the rational principle of the One, each thing not only *is,* but is also a certain "one," which is partly distinct from the others, and partly undergoes union with the others.[148]

Now the purpose is not yet to designate essence and the One 5
[separately], but rather to designate the essence that is one. If essence and the One are the same, multitude and not-being will likewise be the same, which is impossible. For multitude is within essence and the One is within not-essence. But could it be that being and the One, which differ from one another, are disposed in the order of the universe as two principles, as if they were equal? Absolutely not! The origin of things cannot be twofold, for there must be a superior principle, which must be one. Yet if essence is superior to the One, the One will participate in essence, and will

vicissim, quia si ens sit ante unum, eo ipso momento primo quo iam est ens nondum existit unum, cum naturaliter dicatur esse posterius. Quod vero nondum existit participari non potest. Quicquid igitur unum erit, essentia pariter erit, nec e converso, quicquid erit essentia, statim erit et unum. Erit igitur aliquid ens nullo modo unum. Igitur aut nihil aut multitudo infinities infinita, quod est impossibile. Quapropter unum est superius ente.

6 Dicitur autem ipsum unum praeter essentiam non propter defectum quidem, sed excessum, quoniam est melius quam essentia. Sed numquid extat in essentia velut apex? Nequaquam. Foret enim participatum aliquid et alicuius et in aliquo neque foret primum omnium principium, quod esse oportet imparticipatum suique iuris et in seipso tantum, id est non in aliquo, ne cogatur aliunde pendere nec habere debet duplicem in se naturam, sed unum esse penitus absolutum.

: XLII :

Secundus ad idem discursus.

1 Item illud est omnium principium, cuius omnia participia quodammodo sunt ac propter participationem quandam appetitu quodam ad ipsum omnia convertuntur, habentia videlicet ad ipsum habitudinem quandam inde tributam, illuc sua omnia referentem, ut unde primo facta sunt, inde praecipue perficiantur atque serventur. Sed quidnam est munus hoc ipsius primi proprium et tamquam communis quidnam artificis omnium primi charac-

thus undergo essence rather than the contrary. Indeed, if being precedes the One, it means that at the moment when it is being, it is not yet one, since the One is said to come naturally after being. Yet what is not yet cannot be participated in. Thus everything that will be one, will likewise be essence; and on the contrary everything that will be essence will not automatically be one. Thus there will be some entity that in no way is one. Therefore that entity will either be nothing or an infinitely infinite multitude, which is impossible. Therefore the One is superior to being.[149]

The One is said to be without essence not by defect, but by 6
excess, because it is better than essence. But could it be that it exists in essence as a summit?[150] Absolutely not! Otherwise it would be something that is participated in, it would be *of* something and *in* something, and would not be the first principle of all things, which must be unparticipated, solely *of* itself and *in* itself, that is, not in something, lest it depend on something else or have within itself a double nature, rather than being the totally separate One.[151]

: XLII :

Second discourse on the same theme.[152]

Likewise, the principle of all things is that in which all things in 1
some way participate, and by virtue of participation and desire they turn themselves toward it, because they have a certain relation toward it, which they draw from it and which enables them to refer all their objects to it, so that the source that creates them is also and above all that which perfects and preserves them. But what is the function proper to the first principle, and what is the character of the first artisan of all things, which is common to all?

ter? Non quidem vita vel motus; non enim omnibus insunt. Neque etiam status, ipse namque motus, qua ratione motus, tamquam oppositus, statum in seipso non habet. Non igitur status omnibus est communis. Sed neque etiam intellectus qua ratione intellectus omnibus est communis, nec[39] enim intellegunt omnia vel cognoscunt, siquidem quibus adest proprietas intellectus inest et cognitio. Intellegentia enim est cognitio prima, cognitionis omnis principium, nec materia speciem habet ullam intellegentiae symbolum. Videntur sane essentiam omnia communiter in se habere, neque tamen omnino verum est. Quod enim fit, qua ratione fit, nondum est hoc ipsum quod fieri dicitur et cum primum iam est, hoc ipsum non fit amplius. Cum igitur adhuc fieri aliquid atque iam idem hoc ipsum esse invicem opponantur, merito quod fit, qua ratione fit, essentiam non habere putatur. Idcirco Plato in *Timaeo, Sophiste, Republica* et ubicumque de essentia disputat, eam tamquam longissime diversam a generatione distinguit et quae fluunt fieri quidem iudicat, sed non esse. Quo fit ut essentia non omnibus sit communis. Ipse tamen primi character communissimi omnium principii communissimus in omnibus qualibet ratione communiter inest.

2 Contemplare igitur omnia inter se quantumlibet opposita, idem, alterum, statum, motum, fiens, ut ita dixerim, factum atque similia: omnibus et singulatim et summatim inest unum et in ipsa multitudine, quae uni videtur opposita, unum ipsum conficit multitudinem. Quid enim aliud multitudo est nisi unum aliquod saepius repetitum et quonammodo ex multis conficitur aliquod sine unione totum, et quomodo est pars ulla totius aut numeri cuiuslibet nisi ipsa sit aliquid, id est nisi sit aliquid unum? Unum ergo communiter inest omnibus, quo sublato perditur unumquodque. Quapropter volentes antiqui omnifariam nihilum prorsus expri-

It is not life or motion, because these do not exist in all things. Neither is it rest, because motion, *qua* motion, is the opposite of rest and does not possess rest within itself. Thus rest is not common to all. But neither is intellect *qua* intellect common to all things, for not all things do think or know, since cognition is within the things in which the property of the intellect also exists. Indeed intelligence is the first cognition, the principle of all cognition, and matter possesses no species that is the mark of the intelligence. Now all things seem to share the fact that they possess essence within themselves—but this is not completely true. For what becomes, *qua* becoming, *is* not yet that which is said to become, and as soon as it *is,* it ceases to become. Therefore, since "yet becoming" something and "already being" that same thing are opposed to one another, that which becomes, *qua* becoming, is rightly considered as having no essence. For this reason in the *Timaeus,* the *Sophist* and the *Republic,* and in all the works where he talks about essence, Plato distinguishes essence from generation as two completely different things, and he considers that things in flux *become,* but *are* not.[153] Consequently essence is not common to all things. Yet the very character of the first principle, which is the commonest character of the commonest principle of all things, exists in all things in one way or another.

Let us contemplate, therefore, all things, however opposed they 2
are to one another: sameness, otherness, rest, motion, what is becoming, so to speak, what has become, and the others. The one exists in all of them, both individually and collectively—the one even creates multitude, which is considered as the opposite of one. For what is multitude, if not the repetition of a one, and how can a whole be composed of many without union? How can a part be of a whole or a number if it is not itself something, that is, something that is one? Thus the one is commonly within all things, and without it everything perishes. For this reason the ancients, wishing to express all the modalities of "nothing" have called it

mere dixere *οὐδέν*, id est ne unum quidem, quasi plus negetur dicendo non unum quam non ens—perinde ac si munus unius universa posterius quam essentia deserat idque sit in nihil penitus evanescere, videlicet unum prorsus amittere. Hoc igitur unum omnibus communissimum ab ipso tandem existit simpliciter uno omnium communissimo.

: XLIII :

Tertius ad idem discursus ac de simplicitate primi et ultimi.

1 In ordine universi ad primum pervenitur et ultimum. Utrumque necessario est unum atque simplex, multitudinis expers, alioquin neutrum erit primum simpliciter aut ultimum. In ipso enim simpliciter primo non debet esse posterius aliquid et in ipso simpliciter infimo non debet esse superius. Si primum aut ultimum in plura diviseris, utrobique reperies intus superius aliquid et inferius. Non enim dividuntur haec, si modo dividantur more continui, siquidem dimensio nec primum est nec ultimum universi. Sicut igitur in linea longa pervenitur utrimque ad punctum, nullo modo longum, sed prorsus indivisibile quantum ad dimensionem spectat, sic in universo ad primum ultimumque procedimus, unum prorsus et individuum etiam quantum ad existentiam pertinet et naturam. De primo quidem id nulli dubium esse debet. Infimum quoque, si dividatur in plura, non erit totum hoc infimum, sed il-

oudèn, that is, "not even one," on the grounds that we negate more by saying "not-one" than by saying "not-being." This implies that the power of the one ceases to pervade the things in the universe later [in the hierarchy of beings] than that of essence, and the very fact of losing unity means to completely disappear into nothingness. This one, which is the commonest *for* all things, ultimately derives, therefore, from the absolute One, which is the commonest *of* all things.

: XLIII :

Third discourse on the same theme. On the simplicity of what is first and last.

The order of the universe stretches from a first to a last level.[154] 1
Both are necessarily one and simple and deprived of multitude, otherwise neither of them will be simply the first and last levels. Indeed, there should not exist anything inferior in the simple first principle, and there should not be anything superior in the simple last level. If [*per impossibile*] you divide the first and last levels into several parts, you will find inside each of them something superior and inferior. [But this cannot be,] for these are not divisible (supposing they were divided in a continuous way), since dimension belongs neither to the first nor last level of the universe. Thus, just as on a line which has a certain length one gets at each extremity to a point which has no length, but is totally indivisible in dimension, in the same way we proceed to the first and the last degrees in the universe, which are totally one as well as undivided in their existence and nature. There should be no doubt concerning the first degree. Nor is there any doubt regarding the lowest degree: if it is divided into several parts, it will not be the lowest degree as a

lud potius in quod postremo resolutio fiet. Iam vero cum actio primi ulterius protendatur quam sequentium actiones, nimirum in infimo nullum inerit caeterorum munus, sed sola et simplicissima ipsius primi proprietas, ut praeter primi simplicatem unitatemque nihil possit infimo simplicius cogitari, praesertim cum nihil in seipso novum machinari queat. Quod autem est primo quam proximum, etsi simplex existit inde, sua tamen seipsum fecunditate multiplicat.

2 Praeterea omnis divisio, differentia, multiplicitas fit vel per formarum varietatem vel divisionem ad dimensiones numerosve spectantem. Haec omnia formalia sunt. In materia nihil est per se formale, nulla igitur multiplicitas inest. Est itaque maxime unum et, quoniam non habet ullum in se multorum, ideo potentia est ad multa suscipienda, sicut primum, quia multorum nullum est, ad multa sufficit facienda. Est certe materia maxime unum, scilicet formabile, sicut ens primum maxime unum est formale. Neutrum vero est ipsum simpliciter unum. Quis ergo dixerit unum atque ens idem prorsus existere, si modo consideret unum de maximo et de minimo ente pariter praedicari atque quatenus multitudo formalis negatur de materia, eatenus negari ens et affirmari unum?

3 Ac si ex eo quod infinitas subire formas potest et indefinita pariter est ad omnes, Plato in *Philebo* sub ordine infiniti materiam collocet, non tamen propterea eam existimabit esse minus unam, sed maxime unam, siquidem nullum infinitorum naturaliter habeat. Nam et ipsum infinitum ibi saepe nominat unum, quod quidem non ipsa ratione sui multitudinem habeat, immo sub se parti-

whole, but that in which analysis occurs last.[155] In addition, since the action of the first principle is extended farther than the action of subsequent beings, the power of the other beings will assuredly not reach the lowest degree—only the simplest property of the first principle will. As a result, after the simplicity and the unity of the first principle, nothing can be conceived that is simpler than the last degree, especially since it can create nothing new in itself. This lowest level, which is as close as possible [in simplicity] to the first principle, although it derives its simplicity from it, nevertheless multiplies itself by virtue of its own fecundity.[156]

In addition, any division, difference and multiplicity occurs either through the variety of forms or through division, which pertains to dimensions and numbers. All these are formal. Matter contains nothing formal per se, and therefore contains no multiplicity. For this reason, matter is one to the highest degree, and because it possesses in itself none of the many, it is the potentiality to receive the many, just as the first principle, because it is none of the many, is sufficient to create the many. Surely matter is one to the highest degree *qua* formable, just as the first being is one to the highest degree *qua* capable of giving form. But neither of them is the absolute One. Who would say, therefore, that the One and being are the same thing, if you take into consideration that "one" is equally predicated about "being" in the highest degree and "being" in the lowest degree, and, to the extent that formal multitude is negated of matter, "being" is thereby negated of matter and "one" asserted?[157] 2

It is true that in the *Philebus* Plato places matter under the order of the infinite, on the grounds that infinity can undergo forms and is equally indefinite toward all. This does not mean, however, that he will consider that matter is less "one," but rather that it is "one" to the highest degree, since it does not naturally possess anything infinite. In addition, he often calls the infinite "one" in this dialogue on the grounds that it does not contain any multitude by 3

cipantium gradatim contineat multitudinem. Ibi quinetiam sub infiniti nomine non materiam dumtaxat subiectam corporibus vult intellegi, praesertim quia dicit ex infinito entia cuncta constitui, neque tamen ex hac materia cuncta. Universa igitur formabilitas et ad quamlibet multiplicitatem subeundam indefinita potentia dicitur infinitum. Quamobrem materia ad ordinem infiniti redacta nec ibi nec alibi a Platone multitudo vocatur, sed unum in *Timaeo* ad suscipiendam multitudinem susceptaculum, probatque longius ab ente distare quam formam, quandoquidem forma, scilicet materialis, ens verum refert velut imago, materia vero non refert, nisi fortassis ut umbra vel potius ut oppositum, siquidem tam informis materia sit quam essentia vera formosa. Verumtamen, dum ita probat eam quam minimum entis habere, declarat unius habere non parum, dicens de hac vere pronuntiari posse 'hoc est istud' neque propter ingredientia varia umquam e sua identitate mutari.

4 Proinde Platonici, sicut per negationes ascendunt ad ipsum simpliciter unum, ita negando descendunt ad materiam simplicissimam, ut diximus, ens quidem minimum, si modo sit ens, sed maxime unum. Nempe, quemadmodum negando molem, figuram, superficiem, longitudinem pervenimus ad punctum, quod in dimensionis genere maxime unum est et dimensionis habet minimum, quia non est dimensio, sed dimensionis aliquid, id est terminus, sic et negando entia per formarum negationes descendimus in materiam prorsus unum, entis vero quam minimum, non quidem ens proprie, sed aliquid entis, scilicet possibilitatem, ut ita dixerim, ad ens ente formabilem. Ferme similiter a corpore procedimus ad eius imaginem specularem, quae quidem non est corpus,

virtue of its own rational principle, but rather progressively contains under itself the multitude of things that participate in it. Furthermore, by the term "infinite" Plato does not merely mean the matter that is subjected to bodies, since he says that all beings are composed of the infinite, but not all of them are composed of matter. Thus he also calls "infinite" the universal capacity to be formed and the indefinite potentiality to undergo any multitude.[158] For this reason, here and in all the other dialogues Plato does not call "multitude" the matter that is brought under the order of the infinite, but in the *Timaeus* he calls it the single receptacle capable of receiving multitude, and he shows that it is farther apart from being than form is, since form (I mean material form) relates to true being as its image, while matter does not relate to it, except perhaps as its shadow or rather as its opposite, since matter is as formless as being is full of forms and beauty.[159] However, while proving that matter has the minimal degree of being, Plato makes clear that matter has no small degree of unity, saying of it that we can truly assert about it that "this is that," and that its identity is never altered by the variety of things that enter into it.

Consequently, just as the Platonists ascend through negations 4
to the absolute One, in the same way they descend through negations to the simplest matter, which, as we said, is minimal being (if it is being at all), but maximally one. Certainly, just as by negating mass, figure, surface and length we reach the point, which within the genus of dimension is one to the highest degree and has the lowest degree of dimension (since it is not a dimension, but something, that is, the endmost point of a dimension), in the same way, by negating beings we descend through the negations of forms toward matter, which is totally one, but has the lowest possible degree of being—it is not properly a being, but something belonging to being, the potentiality, so to speak, to be formed and receive being. It is more or less in the same way that we proceed from a body to its mirror reflection, which is not a body, but

sed corporis aliquid, et hinc ad eius umbram, quae aliquid corporis est quam minimum. Simili ratione ab ideis, quae vera sunt entia, ad corporeas formas imagines entium, hinc ad materiam universi entis umbram, in qua informitas ipsa discretionem ullam admittens, dum prohibet essentiam esse formalem, cogit esse necessario unum. Iam vero materia, ut sit unum, aliquid definitum sortitur a forma, per quam subit unam hanc speciem aut illam, ut autem sit unum et id quidem indefinitum habet ab ipso simpliciter uno, quoniam ab hoc solo dependet ut penitus infinito. Sed de hoc et de his in *Philebo* diligentius disputamus.

5 Praeterea materialis forma auctore *Timaeo* non convenit cum essentia in ratione aliqua, sed in nomine, quia sit inde referatque illam velut imago. Longe igitur ab essentia cadit, scilicet ideali, velut specularis imago hominis ab humana natura, neque tamen similiter discedit ab uno. Nam etsi nihil de natura entis aut hominis sit in eius imagine, tamen non propterea imago haec minus unum quiddam est, videlicet unum hominem vel unam ideam singularem repraesentans ab aliis differentem. Servata quoque pulchritudine conservat et bonum neque pariter servat essentiam. Similiter oppositi inter se motus, etsi propter fluxum ab essentia decidunt, non tamen minus suum quisque unum habet per distinctionem propriam qua ab aliis distinguuntur, suum quoque bonum, quo diriguntur ad finem conferuntque ad bonum. Item neque materia neque forma ita distat a bono sicut ab ente. Forma enim et pulchritudine habet bonum et ad bonum provocat ut

something belonging to body, and from there to its shadow, which is something belonging to body in the lowest degree. Similarly, we proceed from the Ideas, which are true beings, to the corporeal forms, which are the images of beings, and from there to matter, which is the shadow of universal being, in which formlessness, which admits no division, by prohibiting the existence of any formal essence, makes the existence of unity necessary. Moreover, matter *qua* one is given some limit by the form, whereby it undergoes this one species or that one; but in such a way that it is one and has something unlimited from the absolute One, because it depends solely on the absolute One, which is totally infinite. This and other matters we discuss more in details in our commentary on the *Philebus*.

5 Moreover, according to the *Timaeus*, material form is not in accordance with essence in anything but name, because it derives its existence from it and relates to it as an image.[160] Thus it is far from ideal essence, just as the mirror reflection of a man is far from human nature, yet it is not far from the [absolute] One to a similar degree. For even if nothing of the nature of being or man is in its image, the image is not less something that is one as a result: it represents one particular man or one particular Idea, which are different from the others. In addition, when beauty is preserved, the Good is also preserved, but not [necessarily] essence. Similarly, even if opposite motions are far from essence on account of their flux, they do not each possess less unity, on account of their own distinctiveness, which differentiates them from the others, nor do they possess less of their own good, whereby they turn toward their end and converge upon the Good. Likewise, neither matter nor form are as distant from the Good as they are from being. For form possesses the Good by virtue of beauty, and as the

imago boni. Forte vero materia, totiens iudicanda bona, quot species appetit excipitque libenter quasi proportiones boni et quantum necessaria est huic universo boni ipsius operi, tantum forsitan est et bona. Per ipsam tamen formarum indigentiam per quam et appetit bonum et bono necessaria est, ut dixi, longissime distat ab ente ac per eandem incitatur et accedit ad bonum. Per ea quae diximus dogma Platonicum confirmatur, unum bonumque ente superius iudicandum.

6 Summatim vero unum quod est cum aliqua multitudine et participatum est et aliquod unum, id est multitudo una, et est cum apposita multitudine mixtum. Super hoc igitur extat unum imparticipabile, absolutum, purum, quod omnis multitudinis est principium perque unum multitudini infusum ordinat ipsam et conectit et revocat ad seipsum. Denique sicut supra formas passim mixtas oppositis vel alienis, sunt ideae in seipsis purae et super ens quodlibet quodammodo cum non ente permixtum, est ens ipsa sui prima ratione sincerum, ita super unum multitudini coniugatum, extat unum a multitudine penitus absolutum, in quo nihil est non unum, a quo dependet quicquid est unum simul atque non unum. Omne quidem eiusmodi, quoniam existit a primo, unum est; quoniam vero extra ipsum et inferius ipso, statim in se multitudinem explicat et distinctionis originem.

image of the Good it attracts beings toward the Good. But perhaps matter should be considered good every time it desires some species and readily accepts them as likenesses of the Good; perhaps, too, matter is good inasmuch as it is necessary to the universal work of the Good. However, it is through absence of forms (whereby matter desires the Good and is necessary to the Good, as I said) that it is the furthest apart from being, and it is through this same absence of forms that it is roused toward the Good and comes near it. Thus is confirmed the Platonic doctrine according to which the One and the Good must be considered superior to being.

In sum, the one that is joined to multitude is participated in 6
and is something one, I mean a multitude which is one and is mixed with the multitude that is added to it. Above it, therefore, there is the unparticipated, separate and pure One, which is the principle of all multitude and, through the intermediary of the one that is infused into multitude, orders multitude, holds it together and summons it back to itself. Finally, just as above the forms that are everywhere mixed with opposite or alien things there are the pure Ideas, and just as above any being that in some way is mixed with not-being there is the pure and separate being, so above the one that is joined to multitude there is the One that is totally separate from multitude, where there is nothing that is not-one and on which depends whatever is both one and not-one. Any such being, surely, is one, because it derives its existence from the first principle; but because it is outside the first principle and is inferior to it, it instantly unfolds within itself multitude and the original principle of difference.

: XLIV :

Quartus ad idem discursus et de contemplatione boni.

1 Unicum optimumque universi principium percepturi, cogimur in primis quaecumque maxime ab ipso diversa sunt, id est malum multitudinemque, deponere, atque in nostrum quendam unicum optimumque habitum pro viribus revocari, ad simplicem videlicet tranquillumque intellegentiae sublimis intuitum. Illic igitur, quantum divinae lucis in intellectu primo ideisque refulget, ita ferme suspicimus, quemadmodum in nocte serena stellas in firmamento, per intellegentiam videlicet nostram intellectum illum, per formulas item ideales ingenitas intellegentiae nostrae ideas pro viribus contemplantes. Quod si in eiusmodi contemplatione diu perseverantes proficiamus, ita demum ipsius boni nova lux et incredibiliter admiranda coruscat nobis ex alto, quemadmodum astronomis stellas usque ad diluculum observantibus solis iubar exoritur, ita mox stellas oculis mirabiliter auferens, sicut ipsius boni lux, si modo percipienda sit,[40] nos cogit intellegentiam formulasque eius et intellectum ipsum ideasque et intellegibilia[41] omnia posthabere. Proinde, sicut solem coniventibus oculis, sic ipsam boni lucem intellegentia conivente suscipimus vel potius veneramur. Neque enim licet neque fas est intellegentiae aciem in illud umquam quod intellegibili superius est dirigere.

2 Id igitur quasi sub coruscamine quodam augurati potius quam intuiti, mox ad intellectum intellegibiliaque, velut a sole ad firma-

: XLIV :

Fourth discourse on the same theme. On the contemplation of the Good.

To perceive the unique and most excellent principle of the universe, we must first get rid of all the things that are completely different from this principle, that is, evil and multitude, and be summoned back, as far as is humanly possible, inside the unique and most excellent disposition [of our soul], to the simple and tranquil gaze of the sublime intelligence. It is in this place,[161] therefore, that we receive almost as much divine light as shines in the first intellect and in the Ideas (just as during a fine night we see the stars that shine in the firmament), by contemplating, as far as is humanly possible, the intellect through our intelligence, and the Ideas through the ideal formulae that are within our intelligence. If we persevere long enough in this contemplation, a new light, the wonderfully admirable light of the Good, finally gleams out upon us from above. Just as the light of the sun appears to the astronomers who observe the stars until dawn, and the stars progressively and amazingly disappear from their sight, just so the light of the Good (if only we can perceive it) compels us to leave aside the intelligence and its formulae, the intellect, the Ideas and all the intelligible realities. Likewise, just as we contemplate the sun with closed eyes, we receive, or rather worship the light of the Good by closing the eyes of our intelligence, because it is forbidden and impious to ever direct our intelligence's gaze toward that which is superior to the intelligible. 1

Thus, having divined the Good beneath its gleaming, elusive light—rather than seeing it directly—we presently trace our steps back to the intellect and the intelligible objects (just as from the sun that we observed with closed eyes we go back to the firma- 2

mentum et stellas conivendo, regredimur, deinceps iterum ad rationales discursiones atque sermones. Huc autem postremo regressi quidnam de illo potissimum concipimus aut loquimur? Certe quod simillimum est statui mentis illuc usque progressae. Eiusmodi vero status maxime unus est et simplex atque optimus. Ideo deum ex hoc statu nominamus ut unum penitus atque bonum.

3 Dum vero unum bonumque dicimus, non duo quaedam, sed idem prorsus vaticinamur. Bonum namque, tamquam conservans omnia proptereaque appetibile, nimirum est essentiae omnis appetentis unificum, sicut malum dissipans vel dissipatio quaedam. Unde sua cuique bonitas unio quaedam est atque vicissim. Propterea ipsum unum bonumque idem prorsus esse conicimus, praesertim quia natura boni est quasi diffundere se per omnia per processum vicissimque per insitum singulis appetitum ad se unum omnia revocare ideoque universum summopere reddit unitum.

4 Sed ubi dicimus unum, non ens unum, immo unum simpliciter intellegimus. Cum enim non tam essentia unitatem quam unitas conservet essentiam, proptereaque aliud et inferius essentia sit quam unum, non debemus primum ipsum unum ens unum dicere, ne forte cum multitudine misceamus.

5 Rursus quando pronuntiamus bonum, non ens quidem bonum, sed ipsum simpliciter[42] bonum significare conamur. Cum enim non ens quidem perficiat bonum, sed contra, neque bonum appetat essentiam, sed vicissim, merito alia est superiorque natura boni quam essentiae entisque natura. Quapropter si quis ipsi bono coniugium entis addiderit, deterius applicans meliori, non solum red-

ment and the stars), and then again to discursive reasoning and discussion.[162] But when eventually we come back here, how can we possibly conceive and speak about the Good? Surely we must use a concept that is utterly similar to the tranquility of a mind that has been raised to that place. Yet that tranquility of mind is unified to the highest degree, and simple and most excellent. It is by analogy with this tranquility of mind, therefore, that we call God one and Good.

However, when we call Him One and Good, we do not divine two principles but one and the same principle. For the Good, inasmuch as it preserves all things and is therefore the object of desire, is surely the unifying principle of the whole essence which desires it, just as evil disperses, or is a dispersion of sort. Thus the goodness that is proper to every being is a union of sort, and conversely. For this reason we infer that the One and the Good are totally the same principle, especially since the nature of the Good consists in diffusing itself, as it were, into all things by procession, and conversely to convert all things to itself through the innate desire of each thing for it, thereby unifying the universe to the highest degree. 3

However, when we call God One, we do not mean that He is a being that is one, but the absolute One. For since it is not so much essence that preserves unity as unity that preserves essence, and since essence is therefore different from, and inferior to, unity, we should not say that the first One itself is one being, lest the One should be mixed with multitude. 4

Again, when we call God Good, we do not seek to designate a being that is good, but the absolute Good. For since it is not being that perfects the Good but the contrary, and it is not the Good that desires essence but the reverse, then surely the nature of the Good is different from, and superior to, that of essence and being. For this reason, if one adds being to the Good, thus applying that which is less good to that which is utterly Good, not only will the 5

det pro ipso bono quoddam bonum, sed etiam pro optimo iam non optimum.

6 Iam vero communis omnium consensus definiens bonum cuius gratia omnia et quod appetunt omnia vaticinari videtur illud nec ullius gratia esse nec aliud prorsus appetere, illud itaque nec ens aliquod esse nec aliquod bonum in ente. Omnis enim essentia bonum appetit, id est esse secundum naturam ac bene perfecteque sese habere. Bonum quoque in essentia forte videri potest illius ipsius substantiae gratia esse quaesitum, ut videlicet secundum naturam perfecte se habeat. Nec est bonum simpliciter omniumve bonum, sed alicuius dumtaxat et in aliquo bonum et propterea quiddam bonum. Ea profecto ratione quaesitum ut per hoc ad ipsum bonum propius[43] accedatur. Itaque praeter bonum, quod vel ens vel in ente vel entis est, extat bonum eminentius ente. Sicut enim quodlibet ens suum quodque bonum appetit, tamquam aliud, et suo quoque bono appetit ipsum bonum, sic ens universum consequenter ipsum bonum exoptat tamquam aliud atque superius.

7 Denique si quo pacto bonum ipsum describere licet, circumspice omnes in rebus perfectiones quarum gratia sunt appetendae. Harum itaque fons est ipsum bonum, quod intra omnia quae appetuntur latet tamquam centrum, partim quidem in rebus appetibilibus perfectiones proferens appetendas, partim vero per has velut escas appetentia omnia passim alliciens ad seipsum.

Good become a particular good rather than the absolute Good, but that which is utterly Good will also cease to be so.[163]

In addition, all philosophers agree in defining the Good as the end and the object of desire for all things. This agreement shows, it seems, that the Good does not tend toward anything, does not desire anything, and is not, therefore, a being or a good within being.[164] For all essence desires the Good, that is, to be in accordance with its own nature and to be disposed in a good and perfect way.[165] The good within essence might also appear to be desired for the sake of the substance of the good itself, inasmuch as it is perfectly disposed in accordance with its nature, but this good is not the absolute Good, or the good of all things, but only the good of a thing and within a thing, thus a certain good. It is desired precisely because through its intermediary we come nearer to the Good itself. Beyond the good which is being, in being, or of being, therefore, there is the Good that is superior to being. For just as every being desires its own individual good, as something which is different from itself, and through its own good also desires the Good, even so, and as a consequence, universal being desires the Good as something which is other than itself and superior to itself. 6

Finally, if one may in some way describe the Good, one should look around at all the perfections within things, on account of which these things are objects of desire. This is why their source is the Good, which lies hidden as a center inside all the things that are desired, partly carrying forth the desirable perfections within the things to be desired, and partly using them as baits to attract toward itself all the things that desire it.[166] 7

: XLV :

Quintus ad idem discursus et de appellatione primi.

1 Quando nominamus primum, solemus quibusdam perfectionibus communissimis appellare, scilicet essentia, vita,[44] mente, veritate, virtute. Haec autem accipi velut concreta possunt vel abstracta. Si ut concreta, scilicet ens, vivens et reliqua, non conveniunt simplicitati primi. Si ut abstracta, propter simplicitatem magis convenire videntur, ut essentia vel vita magis quam ens vel vivens. Sed haec rursus abstracta, si considerentur quasi formae quaedam rationesve formales in concretis, primo non competunt; sin considerentur extra, nec[45] essentia in se numero conducit vitam nec vita mentem, sed et illa ad istam et ista ad hanc appetitu contendunt. Ideo nec essentia nec vita primo competunt. Sed forte magis intellegentia? Nec ista quidem, quia non competit omnibus intellegere, et ipsa intellegentia contendit ad veritatem et per hanc ad bonum, bonum vero nusquam vertitur. Summatim vero inter illa superius numerata nec praecedentia primo congruunt, quia non includunt sequentia, sed ad illa nituntur, nec insuper sequentia sunt consentanea primo, quoniam et primorum participant neque sunt illa, et quoniam deinceps effectus producunt angustiores. Neque appellare decet primum hoc nomine, scilicet esse vel vivere, quoniam esse est actus quidam per essentiam suam in ente concreto, vivere

: XLV :

Fifth discourse on the same theme. On the naming of the first principle.

When we name the first principle, we generally use some of the commonest perfections, such as essence, life, mind, truth and power. These appellations can be understood as concrete or abstract terms.[167] If they are understood to be concrete appellations, such as "being," "living," and so on, they do not befit the simplicity of the first principle. If they are understood to be abstract appellations, they are, it seems, more appropriate to the first principle, because they are simple—for instance, "essence" or "life" is more appropriate than "being" and "living." But again, if these abstract terms are considered to be particular forms or formal rational principles lying within concrete things, they are not suitable to the first principle; if they are considered to lie outside concrete things, essence does not bring life within itself numerically, or life bring mind, but both essence and life strive toward life and mind, respectively, via appetite. For this reason neither "essence" nor "life" can suit the first principle. Might "intelligence" be more appropriate? Indeed not, because it does not befit all things to have knowledge, and intelligence itself strives toward truth and, through truth, toward the Good, while the Good does not turn itself toward anything. In sum, among the appellations mentioned above, the first ones do not befit the first principle, because they do not include the derivative ones, but tend toward them, nor are the derivative appellations suitable, because they participate in the first appellations and are not the first ones, and because the effects they in turn produce have less extension. Neither is it appropriate to call the first principle by the appellations "to be" or "to live," because "to be" is an act through its own essence within a concrete 1

actus in vivo per vitam. Si quis autem primum his nominibus appellare voluerit, causali quadam, ut ita dixerim, appellatione potius quam formali, id quidem libenter accipiemus tamquam a Platonicis non alienum et a Dionysio frequentius usurpatum. Quoniam vero primum haec habet munera, ut et unice perfectiones omnium complectatur et nihil ultra petat et omnibus suum impertiat proprium, solum vero id munus ipsum bonum unumque possidet, merito praecipua haec est appellatio primi.

2 Iam vero essentia non quidem suapte natura vitam includit, ut diximus, nec vita intellegentiam neque haec simpliciter veritatem. Tametsi essentia iam per bonum perfecta vitam habet, vita per bonum perfecta similiter habet mentem, mens perfecta per bonum veritatem, gaudium felicitatemque iam possidet. Nec rursus primum ipsum est ipsa veritas vel virtus haec aut illa, ne forte bonum quiddam definitum sit, nec bona omnia complectatur, nisi forte componatur ex cunctis, quod dictu nefas. Ipsum enim primum bonum simpliciter et singulariter est omne bonum.

: XLVI :

Sextus ad idem discursus et quod non eligitur simpliciter esse, sed bene esse atque bonum.

1 Essentia, vita, cognitio, appetitus, actio per quosdam oppositorum modos inter se distinguuntur: essentia quidem statui, vita vero motui similis, item vita quidem motui recto, cognitio vero reflexo.

being, while "to live" is an act within a [concrete] living thing through life.[168] But if one wishes to designate the first principle using these names via a causal, so to speak, rather than formal appellation, we would readily approve of it, as a practice that is not alien to the Platonists and has been very frequently taken over by Dionysius.[169] However, since the first principle possesses the gifts of containing in a single embrace the perfections of all things, seeking nothing beyond itself, and of imparting its own power to all, but is the sole principle to possess the gift of the Good and One, it is right to say that "Good" and "One" are the first names of the first principle.

Moreover, as we have said, by virtue of their own nature, essence does not contain life, life does not contain intelligence, and intelligence does not contain truth. However, essence possesses life once it is perfected by the Good, life possesses mind when it is perfected by the Good, and mind possesses truth, joy and felicity once it is perfected by the Good. Again, the first principle is not truth itself, nor any individual virtue (otherwise it would be defined as a certain good), nor would it embrace all good things [individually][170] unless it were composed of all things, which is a sacrilegious thing to say. For the first Good is the whole Good, in a simple and unique way. 2

: XLVI :

Sixth discourse on the same theme. That we do not choose simply to be, but to be well and good.

Essence, life, cognition, desire and action are distinguished from 1
one another through certain modes that are opposite. Essence is like rest, whereas life is like motion; similarly, life is like linear mo-

Praeterea essentia pariter atque vita solam suae formae tenent proprietatem, cognitio autem omnibus se conformat. Rursus cognitio res quemadmodum sunt in ipsa percipit, appetitus vero non ita petit, sed quemadmodum sunt in ipsis. Denique appetitus in appetente manet, actio transit extra. Quanto haec magis deinceps inter se differunt, tanto magis gradatim differunt ab essentia, ut non sint quidam quasi gradus essentiae, sed formalia quaedam addita, tamquam perfectiones eius et bona quaedam a bono superiore pendentia. Non enim vel haec per seipsa sunt, cum sint in alio, vel essentia naturaliter non perfecta perficit semetipsam,[46] sed a bono quod super essentiam est perficitur.

2 Praeterea sicut se habet sensus ad bonum sensibile, ita ferme se habet intellectus ad intellegibile bonum. Itaque sicut sensum boni sequitur appetitus boni, quod bonum et a sensu et ab appetitu differt, ita semper intellegentiam boni sequitur appetitus boni, qui sane appetitus inter cognitionem et bonum semper est medius. Certum vero est appetitum boni non esse ipsum bonum; certum igitur cognitionem, quamvis exactam, non esse ipsum bonum; certius quoque essentiam, quae cognitione inferior est, ipsum bonum esse non posse.

3 Iam vero cum nulla essentia, qua ratione simpliciter essentia est, in seipsa quiescat, sed actionem edat et per actionem pergat ad aliquid ratione boni, quaero quidnam appetat. Non quidem esse: iam enim est antequam appetat neque potest appetere nisi sit prius, neque rursus appetit magis esse vel aliud esse quam sit.

tion, whereas cognition is like reflective motion.[171] Moreover, both essence and life alike retain only the property of their own form, while cognition conforms itself to all. Similarly, cognition perceives things within itself as they are; by contrast, desire pursues them as they are in themselves. Finally, desire remains within the desiring subject, while action passes beyond the subject. The more they differ from essence (which they do, progressively), the more they subsequently differ from one another. As such, they are not degrees of essence, so to speak, but formal additions, inasmuch as they are perfections of essence, and good things depending on the superior Good.[172] For they do not exist by themselves, since they are in another, nor does essence, which is imperfect by nature, perfect itself, but is rather perfected by the Good which is above essence.

Moreover, just as sense perception is related to the sensible good, in the same way, so to speak, the intellect is related to the intelligible Good. So, just as the desire for the [sensible] good is dependent on the sensible perception of the good, and the sensible good differs from both sense perception and desire, so the desire for the Good is always dependent on the intelligible knowledge of the Good, and this desire is assuredly always in the middle between cognition and the Good. It is certain that the desire for the Good is not the good; it is certain, therefore, that cognition, however exact it may be, is not the Good; it is even more certain, then, that essence, which is inferior to cognition, cannot be the Good. 2

In addition, since essence, inasmuch as it is simply essence, does not rest within itself, but produces an action, and through this action proceeds to something following the rational principle of the Good, the question is: what does essence desire? It does not desire to be, for essence *is* before it desires; it cannot desire unless it is; and again, it does not desire to be more or to be something else than it is. For it would then seek to change species, which would 3

Quaereret enim contra naturam speciem permutare—mitto quod essentia vel esse non suscipit magis aut minus. Non igitur praeter id quod iam est affectat, nisi bene vel melius esse, id est melius se habere. Hoc vero nihil aliud est quam appetere bonum tamquam essentiae condimentum. Non est autem appetibile aliquid qua ratione ens vel esse, alioquin ens praesens appeteretur et quod quisque habet perpetuo quaereret et quod utcumque maius ens appareret amaretur et magis. Non ergo qua ens, sed qua bonum est appetibile. Bonum quidem et appetibile convertuntur, non ita profecto ens et appetibile convertuntur, et saepe absens aliquid et futurum, quod minus entis habet, magis quam praesens nobis est appetibile, tamquam melius. Non igitur est idem ens et bonum, sed bonum est eminentius, quia si bonum ad ens comparetur et esse, rationem finis semper habet atque motoris.

4 Habitus profecto rationem entis magis quam privationes habent, saepe vero ratione boni ita privationes eligimus, sicut habitus et quandoque magis. Non est igitur eadem natura entis atque boni. Nonne, sicut eligimus agere tamquam bonum, ita saepe non agere tamquam bonum, sicut sentire iocundum, ita etiam non sentire molestum, sicut scire gratum aliquid, ita etiamsi offenderit neque nosse, sicut vivere cum usu vel saltem cum spe bonorum, ita nec vivere quidam eligunt, omni spe bonorum penitus destituti, interim oppressi malis? Itaque et seipsos interimunt, respuentes videlicet et vitam et essentiam absque bono, quippe cum haec amaverint propter bonum.

be contrary to its nature, not to mention the fact that essence, or the act of being, does not undergo degrees of more or less.[173] Essence aspires to nothing else than that which it already is, unless it wishes to be good, or better, that is, to be better disposed. Yet this is nothing else than to desire the Good, which is what gives essence its spice, as it were. Yet a thing is not desirable because it is a being or an act of being, otherwise any present being would be desired and would perpetually seek what everyone has, and the greater a being would appear to be, the more it would be loved. It is not, therefore, *qua* being, but *qua* good, that it is desirable, for good and desirable are identical, while being and desirable are surely not identical in the same way, and it is often the case that a thing that is not yet or will be (and has less being) is more desirable than something that is present to us, inasmuch as it is better. Thus being and the Good are not the same, but the Good is superior, because if the Good is compared to being and the act of being, it always possesses the rational principle of an end and a mover.[174]

Certainly dispositions possess the rational principle of being more than privations do, and yet on numerous occasions we choose privations following the rational principle of the Good just as we do dispositions, and sometimes more so. So the nature of being and of the Good are not the same. Is it not true that, just as we choose action as a good, so we often choose inaction as a good: we choose to perceive what is pleasant and disregard what is painful, to know what is agreeable and to ignore what is offensive, and some people choose to live if they can use or at least hope for good things, but to die if they have absolutely no hope for good things, being crushed by evil fortune? For this reason they commit suicide, rejecting a life and an essence deprived of good—since they [only] liked them, assuredly, because of what was good in them.[175] 4

: XLVII :

Septimus ad idem discursus et quae differens ratio entis atque boni.

1 Essentia ipsa, qua ratione essentia est, magis minusve non suscipit. Bonum vero, tamquam aliud, magis suscipit atque minus. Saepe etiam quod magis essentiale est in rebus appetit ut finem aliquem quod in his est minus essentiale, id est actionem motumque aliquem, tamquam melius aliquid vel tamquam per quod melius quandoque se habeat, quasi essentia et bonum non sint idem. Praeterea rem externam et fruitionem eius res appetunt tamquam bonam, non quia sit vel maxime sit, sed quia maxime congruat prositque quod est esse bonam. Praeterea oppositum quidem entis est non ens, oppositum vero boni malum, sed malum non idem penitus atque non ens. Malum enim dicitur non solum omnimoda, ut ita dixerim, essendi privatio, sed etiam defectus quidam boni et habitus aliquis tibi contrarius et res in primis adversa tibi, quae quanto magis habere in se videtur entis, tanto tibi mala magis. Immo vero oppositum boni est non bonum, sicut non ens entis oppositum, sed non bonum non idem penitus atque non ens. Nam non bonum cuique non modo est ipsa essendi privatio, sed etiam defectus boni aliquis, atque id insuper quod est contrarium, quod quidem quanto magis videtur ens, ut diximus, tanto magis occurrit ut malum.

2 Proinde perfectio formalis ultima essentiae est intellectualis forma. Huius formae perfectio est actualis, ut ita loquar, intellegentia.[47] Haec vero plurimum sui entis habet quando certissima est. Certitudo vero, qua ratione certitudo est, non est intellegentiae

: XLVII :

Seventh discourse on the same theme. What the difference is between being and the Good.[176]

Essence *qua* essence is not susceptible of more or less.[177] By contrast, the Good, which is other than essence, is susceptible of more or less. It is also often the case that what is more essential in things desires, as an end, what is less essential in them (for instance, an action and a motion), on the grounds that it is a better thing, or something whereby their disposition might sometimes be bettered. This suggests that essence and the Good are not the same thing. Moreover, things desire to enjoy a good thing that is external to them, not because it exists, or exists to the highest degree, but because "well being" is harmonious and profitable. In addition, the opposite of being is not-being, whereas the opposite of good is evil. Yet evil and not-being are not at all the same thing. Indeed, not only the privation of being of any sort, so to speak, is said to be evil, but also any lack of good, any contrary disposition, and anything that is immediately adverse to someone—and the more this thing appears to have being within itself, the more evil it is. Besides the opposite of good is not-good, just as the opposite of being is not-being, but not-good and not-being are not at all the same thing. For not-good is not only the very privation of being, but also any lack of good, as well as the contrary of good which, as we have said, appears all the more evil the more it has being. 1

Likewise the ultimate formal perfection of essence is the intellectual form. The perfection of this form is what I would call the actualized intelligence. Yet the actualized intelligence possesses its being to the highest degree when it possesses certainty to the highest degree. Certainty *qua* certainty is not the end of intelligence, 2

finis, sed quando certe suum bonum percipit, non quiddam ut dicitur maxime ens, sed maxime consentaneum atque delectabile, tamquam ita bonum, quasi ratio entis et boni sit diversa. Nonne voluptas prae caeteris affectatur, quasi rationem boni plurimam habeat?[48] Non autem versatur in hoc ipso voluptas, ut certo sentias maximum ens et vehemens, sed ut congruum tamquam tibi bonum.

3 At si etiam suspiceris quod magis essentiae vel entis habet, id magis expeti, equidem non putabo te magis essentiam suspicari quasi mole maiorem vel numero plurem vel tempore diuturniorem vel gradibus quasi qualitatis intentiorem. Essentia enim suapte natura a magnitudine, numero, tempore, qualitate simpliciter est abstracta et haec quae modo narravi nonnumquam minus eliguntur quam opposita. Neque rursus substantialiorem, ut ita loquar, eam vocas. Magis enim atque minus non pertinent ad substantiam. Reliquum est ut illud magis ens et optabile magis iudicaturus sis quod ens est melius. Melius autem per ipsam bonitatem melius esse censetur. Sed quae bonitas est in essentia qualitas est essentiae entisque conditio. Super hanc igitur extat ipsum absolute bonum.

4 Accedit ad haec quod sicut materia ad formas contrarias est indifferens et genus ad oppositas invicem differentias, sic essentia ad vivum atque non vivum, ad sentiens atque non sentiens. Per aliud igitur ad ista producitur. Vita quidem est ad essentiam ut perfectio quaedam bonumque eius et sensus similiter ad vitam et intellectus ad sensum. Vita non magis est ens quam essentia per quam est

but the moment when intelligence perceives its own good with certainty—not something that is being to the highest degree, as they say, but something that is suitable and agreeable to the highest degree, and thus like a good. This implies that the rational principle of being and that of the Good are different. Is it not true that pleasure is desired more than anything else, as though it possessed the rational principle of the Good to the highest degree? Pleasure does not turn toward something because you clearly perceive it to be the highest and most intense being; it rather turns toward that which is in harmony with you, and so, apparently, good for you.[178]

Even if you were to suppose that what has more essence or more being is more desired, you will not, I should think, suppose that the expression "more essence" denotes anything that is larger in mass, greater in number, more lasting in time, or more intense in degrees of quality, as it were. For by its very nature essence is simply separate from greatness, number, time, quality, and the predicates mentioned above are sometimes desired less than their opposites. You do not say, either, that essence is "more substantial," so to speak, for the degrees of more and less do not pertain to substance. Consequently, you should consider as "greater being" and "more desirable" what is better being. Yet better being is considered better by virtue of goodness. But the goodness that is within essence is a quality of essence and a condition of being. Therefore, above it there is the absolute Good. 3

In addition, just as matter is indifferent to opposite forms, and genus is indifferent to opposite differentiae, in the same way essence is indifferent to living and nonliving, sentient and nonsentient.[179] So it is through the agency of another that essence is related to these things: life is related to essence as its perfection and its good; the same goes for sense perception in relation to life, and for intellect in relation to sense perception. Life is not "more being" than the essence whereby it exists; it is better. Sense does not "live 4

ipsa, sed est melius, sensus non magis vivit quam vita per quam vivit ipse, sed melius, similiterque deinceps. Gradatim vero melius se habere ubique fit per bonum. Non tamen fit per essentiam quae non per se ad melius umquam proficit. Proficit ergo per bonum ente superius.

5 Si vero dixeris bonum ipsum esse id omnino quod maxime ens est, respondeo primo quidem sicut in quolibet ente alia quidem est essendi ratio, alia vero bene essendi, sic aliam esse rationem ipsius maxime entis, aliam ipsius boni. Deinde quod maxime ens appellabas non fore simpliciter ens, sed cum additamento quodam per quod non simpliciter quidem sit, sed sit quam maxime, id est quam perfectissime, id est quam optime, scilicet per aliquam perfectionem bonitatemque ab ipso simpliciter bono prorsus infusam. Cum vero dicimus ipsum simpliciter bonum, dicimus omne sine limitatione vel compositione bonum.

6 Item perfectio bonitasve est gemina. Alia quidem formalis, alia vero finalis. Si quis ergo convicerit formalem bonitatem esse quasi quoddam augmentum essentiale, non tamen de finali quae est potissima et optima idem dicere poterit. Igitur bonum praeter essentiam censetur existere, idque saepe facit ut quod quasi accidentale est in re vel circa rem optabilius sit et melius eo quod essentiale magis, quod quidem fieri nequit absque condimento boni (sive id quidem formale sit, sive sit finale), praesertim quia quod quasi accidentale est ideo optabilius est quod circa bonum ipsum agit externum, alioquin optabilius numquam foret. Non enim potest accidens esse substantiae finis. Igitur finis eius est ipsum bonum penes quod substantia per illud accidens sese versat.

more" than the life whereby it lives, but lives better, and so on. Being progressively better disposed occurs always through the Good. By contrast, this does not occur through essence, which never makes progress toward the better on its own, and thus does so through the Good that is superior to being.

If you say that the Good is precisely what is "being to the highest degree," I respond that, firstly, just as in any being the rational principle of being differs from that of well-being, in the same way the rational principle of what is "being to the highest degree" differs from that of the Good. Secondly, what you called "being to the highest degree" will not be simple being, but a being that is provided with an additional element, through which it is not simple but "in the highest possible degree," that is, "the most perfect possible," in other words, "the best possible," by virtue of a perfection and a goodness that are infused by the absolute Good. By "the absolute Good" we mean the whole good without limitation or composition. 5

Similarly, perfection, or goodness, is double: in one sense it is formal, in the other final. Thus if one were to refute our argument on the grounds that formal goodness is some essential addition, one could not say the same about final Goodness, which is the most eminent and the best cause.[180] Thus the Good is thought to exist separately from essence, and, as a result, what is quasi-accidental in or about a thing is often more desirable and better than what is more essential, which cannot occur without the flavoring of the good (whether this good is formal or final), especially since what is quasi-accidental can only be more desirable because it acts toward the Good, which is extrinsic to it, otherwise it would by no means be desirable, since an accident cannot be the end of a substance. Thus the end of a substance is the Good, toward which the substance turns itself from within through the intermediary of an accident. 6

7 Praeterea essentia, vita, intellectus differunt inter se ratione formali: differentes enim definitiones habent. Nec idem haec inter se sunt, scilicet non ens, non vivens, non intellegens, et pluribus alia quam alia competunt. Neque per magis minusve differunt, quasi essentia primum gradum et secundum habeat atque tertium, sicut calor (est enim substantiale), sed forte differunt sicut siccitas et calor et lumen. Profecto nisi aliter ens distinguamus quam more qualitatis, per primum[49] eius gradum et secundum atque tertium latenter eo deveniemus, ut solam unam essentiam substantiamve fingamus ceu calorem unum modo remissiorem, modo vehementiorem, tollemusque substantialium formarum gradus distinctionesque rerum ad providentiam pertinentes.

8 Forte vero dicet aliquis essentiam quidem non magis minusve qualitatis modo suscipere, sed in quovis composito multos essendi modos esse posse, ut anima nostra primo quidem habet suum esse naturale, secundo suscipit esse tranquillitatis, tertio sapientiae, quarto felicitatis, totidemque procedere bonitatis gradus quot essendi modos. Nos id quidem libenter accipiemus, sed dicemus insuper unumquemque bonitatis gradum ab ipso essendi modo quem comitatur formali quadam ratione distingui. Nam ubique esse bonum appetit potius quam vicissim. Perficitur esse per bonum neque contra, et illud esse respueremus si omni prorsus bono destitueretur, bonum vero respuere numquam possumus. Summatim vero cum anima ultra naturale suum esse appetit sapientiam, non videtur eam appetere tamquam maiorem quendam entis vel essentiae gradum. Nam vel essentia non habet eiusmodi gradus, vel forte magis essentiale est esse primum, in quo tamquam substantia fundatur secundum atque tertium tamquam ali-

Moreover, essence, life and intellect differ formally from one another because their definitions are different. Their opposites, not-being, not-living, not-knowing, also differ from one another, and some agree with more things than others. They do not differ according to the more or the less—as if essence possessed a first, second and third degrees, like heat (i.e. the substance heat)—but they perhaps differ from one another in the same way as dryness, heat and light do. Surely if we do not distinguish being in any other way than by quality, we will inadvertently, through a first, a second and a third degree, get to the point of imagining one single essence or substance, like heat, to be at times moderate and at times intense, and eliminate the gradations between substantial forms and the distinctions between things, which are the concern of divine providence. 7

But one might argue that essence does not admit of more or less in the way that quality does, but that there can be multiple modalities of being in any composite. For instance, our soul first possesses its own natural being, then receives that of tranquility, then that of wisdom, then that of felicity, and it proceeds through the same number of degrees of being as there are degrees of good.[181] This is a view that we shall readily accept, but we shall add that every degree of goodness is formally distinguished from the mode itself of being that it accompanies. For everywhere being desires the Good, rather than the contrary; being is perfected by the Good, and not the contrary, and we would reject this being if it were totally deprived of the Good, while we can never reject the Good. In sum, when the soul desires wisdom beyond its natural being, it does not seem to desire it *qua* a greater degree of being or essence. For either essence does not have degrees of that sort, or perhaps the first being is more essential, and on it, as in the case of a substance, is based a second and third being, like something ad- 8

quid adventicium. Non expetit, inquam, sequentem gradum ut essentiae magis compotem, sed ut meliorem, ut magis boni participem, ut conferentem ad ipsum bonum. Propterea ubique primus gradus entis ad secundum dirigitur ut ad finem. Ens autem qua ens non est necessario finis, sed qua bonum. Ergo dirigitur ut ad bonum. Non enim primum appetit secundum idque tertium, nisi ut inde proficiat, ex quo ut ad bonum procedere confirmatur.

9 Denique si Platonicum dogma sectamur, conclusuri sumus unumquodque et ex primo principio dependere et ad illud se prorsus habere. Quantum igitur inde velut ab effectore pendet, ens existere atque dici; quantum rursus se habet ad illud ut ad finem, esse appellarique bonum, et hoc quidem duplici ratione: ut enim praecipuo quodam charactere refert[50] illud, naturale secum afferre bonum; ut autem ad idem quolibet appetitu convertitur, adventicium comparare bonum nonnumquam melius naturali. Sicut igitur aliud quidem est ex primo pendere, sive produci sive procedere,[51] aliud autem ad ipsum se habere vel referendo vel remeando, sic in quolibet aliud ens, aliud bonum, similiter extra quodlibet aliud ipsum ens, aliud ipsum bonum. Bonum vero ad ens ubique ac semper se habet ut finis. Bonum igitur ente superius, et ubique tanto superius quanto ratio finis rationem superat effectoris. Res vero, sicut diximus, ab ipso deo tamquam effectore sortiuntur essentiam et tamquam fine praecipue adipiscuntur bonum. Ipsum itaque bonum, ut dicebamus, ipso ente praestantius iudicandum.

10 Quod et Aristotelem non arbitror negaturum, si modo meminerit se descriptionem boni hanc a veteribus accepisse: bonum est

ventitious. The soul does not desire, as I say, a dependent degree of being on the grounds that it has a greater share in its essence, but because it is better, because it participates to a higher degree in the Good, because it contributes to the Good. For this reason the first degree of being everywhere tends toward the second degree as toward its end. But being is not necessarily an end *qua* being, but *qua* good. Thus it tends toward it as to the Good. For the first desires the second, and the second desires the third, only if they set out from the source whence they may be strengthened in their progress toward the Good.[182]

Finally, if we follow Plato's doctrine, we shall conclude that each thing both depends on the first principle and is disposed toward it. Therefore, inasmuch as each thing depends on the first principle as its originator, it is and is called "being"; inasmuch as it is disposed toward it as to an end, it is and is called "good," and this for two reasons: inasmuch as it relates to the Good through a principal character, it brings with itself its natural good, and inasmuch as it turns itself toward it through some desire, it relates its adventitious good, which is often better, to its natural good. Therefore, just as to depend on the first principle (whether by being created by it or by proceeding from it) and to be disposed toward it (whether by relating to it or returning to it) are two different things, so within any reality being and good are different, and likewise outside all these realities being and the Good are different. Yet the Good is everywhere and always disposed toward being as an end. Thus the Good is superior to being, and it is superior to being to the degree that the rational principle of its end exceeds that of the originator. Yet as we have said, things are allotted their essence from God as their originator, and obtain their good from Him especially as their end. For this reason, as we were saying, the Good must be considered superior to being.[183] 9

This is something that even Aristotle will not deny, I should think, if he remembers that he has adopted the ancients' definition 10

quod omnia entia appetunt. Cum enim alia quidem sint appetentia, aliud vero atque praestantius sit appetibile, certe bonum cunctis entibus expetendum ab Aristotele concedendum est esse tota entium universitate superius. Propterea deum inquit regere moveque omnia non aliter quam ut appetibile et amabile, id est ut bonum atque finem. Nec iniuria causam causarum una cum praeceptore suo nominabit bonum, finis videlicet cognomento, siquidem finalis causa caeteras antecellit. Sicubi vero ens uni bonoque facit aequale, illi forsan uni atque bono par iudicat, quod et ab intellectu percipi et ab ente capi potest. Quod autem Plato suus vaticinatur excelsius id, tamquam ineffabile penitus et incognitum, non verbis quidem prosequitur, sed potius silentio veneratur.

: XLVIII :

Principium universi est ipsum simpliciter unum, principium in quolibet ordine quod ibi est maxime unum. De sole, natura, intellectu.

1 Sicut pessimum omnibus est divisio ad exitium singula trahens, sic optimum est unio et partium invicem et ad totum et totius ad causam suam et originem atque naturam. Unio vero a summa tandem fit unitate. Quae quidem hinc esse principium universi cognoscitur, quod donum tribuit optimum et uniendo convertendoque singula perficit, utpote quae effecerit omnia producendo. Hinc efficitur ut in unoquoque rerum genere atque ordine id profecto sit principium, quod ibi est maxime omnium uniforme et ante omnia simplicissimum. Mitto nunc quomodo unitas quidem

of the Good: the Good is that which all beings desire.[184] For since the beings that desire differ from the thing that is desired (which is also more excellent), surely Aristotle must admit that the Good that all beings must desire transcends the whole universality of beings. So Aristotle says that God governs and moves all things precisely as an object of desire and love, that is, as their good and as their end. He will rightly call the Good "the cause of the causes," as does his master [Plato], and also give it the name of "end," since the final cause precedes all the others. So when he makes being equal to the one and the good, he might mean the one and the good that can be perceived by the intellect and comprehended by being. But the more eminent One, which his master Plato reveals as completely ineffable and unknowable, he does not approve of with words, but rather honors in silence.[185]

: XLVIII :

The principle of the universe is the absolute One, in any order the principle is that which is one to the highest degree. On the sun, nature and the intellect.

Just as division is the worst thing for all beings because it leads to the destruction of individuals, in the same way union—between individual parts, between parts and their whole, between the whole and its cause, its origin and its nature—is the best. Yet union ultimately is brought about by the highest Unity. Hence Unity is known as the principle of the universe, which provides the best gift and perfects individual things through unifying and converting them, just as it has produced all things by creation. As a result, in every genus and order of things the principle is surely that which is the most uniform and the simplest of all things. I 1

sit principium numerorum, signum vero dimensionum, momentum temporis, naturale minimum quodammodo sit principium corporis naturalis, uniformis ipsa seminaria virtus origo corporis omniformis.

2 Sed maiora sumamus: lumen videmus et a stellis quam plurimis et ab igne et ab oculis multis et a carbunculis similibusque profluere. Haec quidem et specie et genere inter se valde diversa sunt. Lumen autem ex his emanans est ubique simillimum et, ut ita dixerim, maxime unum. Unum ergo principium postulat, non diversa, siquidem diversa facerent et valde diversum. Quid ergo? Sol unicus est luminis omnis mundani principium. Sub hoc, etsi plura videntur quasi quaedam principia luminis, per unam tamen naturam et virtutem proprietatemque solarem tam uniforme lumen effundunt. Si praeterea quaeramus in sole principium lucis potissimum, dicemusne ipsam solis molem lucis esse principium? Non certe, si rectam sequimur rationem. Multae namque globi illius partes lumina multa diffundunt. Erunt ergo principia multa. Nos autem requirimus unum atque primum. Lux enim, quae mundanorum omnium maxime una est et simplex incorporeaque et eminens, principium exigit unum simplex et incorporeum et excellens. Numquid igitur ipsa solis anima lumen generat? Ipsa profecto, sed non animali multiplicate sua, alioquin lumina diversa profunderet. Procreat igitur intellectuali luce visibile lumen, non intellectuali quidem varietate, sed unitate potius intellectus. Quae quidem unitas intellectuali illi animae praeest, quasi character il-

leave aside for the moment the way in which unity is the principle of numbers, the sign that of dimensions, the moment that of time, the way in which what is natural to the smallest degree, so to speak, is the principle of natural body, and how the uniform seminal power is the origin of multiform body.

But let us resume our discussion of the superior realities:[186] we 2
see light flowing forth from an infinite number of stars, from fire, from several eyes, from glowing embers and so on. These sources of light widely differ from one another in both species and genus. Yet the light that emanates from them is always and absolutely identical, and I would say one to the highest degree. Thus light requires one unique principle rather than several different principles, since different principles would create a light that would also be different in each case. What is this principle then? The sun uniquely is the principle for all the light in the world. Beneath it, even if there seem to be several principles of light, it is nevertheless through one nature, one power and one property, those of the sun, that these so-called principles pour forth such a uniform light. If we were to inquire, then, after the most eminent principle of light within the sun, would we say that the mass of the sun is the principle of light? Certainly not, if we follow a correct line of thought, because different parts of the solar globe pour forth different lights. There will then be several principles. We, however, are seeking the single and first principle of light. For light, which of all the worldly things is one to the highest degree, simple, incorporeal and eminent, requires a principle that is unique, simple, incorporeal and excellent. Is it the soul of the sun, then, that generates light? It generates light, certainly, but not through its own animal multiplicity, otherwise it would pour forth a number of different lights. Thus it is through intellectual light that it creates visible light—not through its own multiplicity, but rather through the unity of its intellect. This unity lies at the summit of the intellectual part of its soul, as the character of that absolute Unity which

lius simpliciter unitatis quae est universi principium, cui et intellectus ille per unitatem suam maxime est unitus. Per eandem est diciturque deus. Haec igitur divina solis unitas est uniformis luminis mundani principium, quemadmodum et ipsa simpliciter unitas atque bonitas est luminis intellegibilis auctor.

3 Similiter si quaeramus generationis universae principium, unum tandem inventuri sumus, quando et generationes omnes uno quodam ordine ad unam contendunt universi formam. Hoc vero principium est genitalis ipsa mundi vita. Cum vero in hac rerum semina sint quam plurima, unum autem oporteat esse principium, merito per principalem unitatem suam, per quam et ipsa divina est summoque deo prorsus unita, est generationis omnis mundanae principium.

4 Investigantibus praeterea quid primum cognitionis omnis principium sit, perfectissima cognitio, id est intellectus primus, protinus occurret ut princeps. Verumtamen non per multas species conceptionesque suas primum erit cognoscendi principium, nam unum tandem hoc esse debet, sed per unitatem suam, qua deus existit, tam sibi quam caeteris virtutem cognoscendi largitur.

: XLIX :

Primum rerum principium est unitas bonitasque super intellectum, vitam, essentiam.

1 Existimabit forte aliquis primum intellectum esse simpliciter primum. Tametsi oporteret eum qui sic existimat animadvertere se, dum dicit primum intellectum, significare id ipsum quod dicit non

is the principle of the universe and to which the intellect is also supremely united through its own unity. It is through this same unity that it is and is called God. Thus the divine unity of the sun is the principle of the world's uniform light, just as absolute Unity and Goodness are responsible for intelligible light.[187]

Likewise, if we inquire after the principle of universal generation, we will ultimately find the One, when all the generations tend in each order toward the single form of the universe. Yet this principle is the very generative life of the world. But since this life contains an infinite number of natural seeds and requires a single principle, it is rightly by virtue of its own principal unity—through which it is itself divine and completely united to the highest God—that it is the principle of all the world's generations.[188] 3

In addition, if we are to inquire after the first principle of all knowledge, we will instantly find that it is the most perfect knowledge, that is, the first intellect. However, it is not so much by virtue of its many species and concepts, since this principle must ultimately be one, but by virtue of its unity, whereby it is God, that the intellect imparts both to itself and to others the power of knowing.[189] 4

: XLIX :

The first principle of nature is the Unity and Goodness above intellect, life and essence.

Some will perhaps suppose that it is the first intellect which is the absolute first principle. The person who supposes that should realize, however, that in the very act of saying "first intellect" he is already indicating that this principle is not the "absolute" first prin- 1

iam esse simpliciter, sed certa quaquam conditione et definito quodam ordine, scilicet intellectuali, primum. Similiter neque quod ipsum intellegibile nominatur poterit simpliciter esse primum, praesertim cum proportionem habeat quandam cum intellectu quolibet a primo principio alienam. Sed dic quaeso, qui intellectum vis esse primum summumque deum, quanam ratione id munus habebit? Non qua intellectus est, alioquin cum omnia primi potentissimi auctoris omnium debeant reportare characterem, intellegentiam vel cognitionem quandam omnia possidebunt. Intellegentia enim est prima cognitio, si per intellegentiam ipsam proprie atque praecipue sint expressa, praesertim si illic intellegentia sit ipsa natura. Sicut enim vita naturaliter viventia generat, sic naturalis intellegentia naturaliter intellectualia vel cognoscentia facit. Praeterea intellectus ille primus, qua ratione est intellegens, ad intellegibilia iam existentia et ad ipsa quae dicuntur entia sese confert, nec aliud habet proprium, nisi illa quae iam sunt perspicue contueri. Non igitur hac ratione rerum principium esse potest, cuius proprium est omnia facere, servare, perficere. Quantum vero interest inter facere atque contueri, tanto intellectus intervallo saltem a primo rerum principio distat. Denique intellectus etiam sunt particulariter intellegentes animae, sive daemones sive angeli, neque tamen dii sunt, nisi praeterea universalis providentiae munus habeant. Non igitur eadem intellectus atque principii ratio est habenda.

2 Sed numquid intellectus ille primus, qua ratione vita est, appellandus est princeps? Minime, nam omnia viverent. Forte vero qua est essentia, sunt enim omnia? Neque id quidem; perfectior enim est qua intellectus existit aut etiam vita quam qua essentia. Si igitur non illa, neque ista ratione deus. Item nulla essentia in seipsa

ciple, but is first by virtue of a certain condition and a particular order, namely that of the intellect. Likewise, what is named as "intelligible" cannot be the absolute first principle, because it stands in a kind of proportionate relation to all intellects, and such a relation is alien to the first principle.[190] But tell me, please, you who wish the intellect to be the first and most eminent God, by virtue of which rational principle will the intellect possess this function? Not *qua* intellect, otherwise, given that all things must bear the mark of the first and omnipotent author of all things, they will all possess some intelligence or cognition. Indeed, intelligence is the first cognition, since things are expressed through intelligence in a particular and individual way, especially since in the intelligible realm intelligence is nature itself. For just as life naturally generates living beings, so natural intelligence naturally produces the intellectual or cognizing realities. Moreover, the first intellect, *qua* intelligent, is related to the intelligible things that already exist, as well as to the things that are called beings, and does not have any other proper role than that of contemplating with clarity the things that already are. So the intellect *qua* intellect cannot be the principle of nature, whose proper role is to create, preserve and perfect all things.[191] There is at least as much distance between the intellect and the first principle of things as there is between creating and contemplating. Finally, we should add that intellects also include in particular intelligent souls (whether demons or angels), but they are not gods, unless they also possess the gift of universal providence. Therefore, the rational principle of the intellect and that of the first principle should not be considered the same.

Is it *qua* life, then, that the first intellect should be called the 2
first principle? Not in the least, for all things would then be alive. But perhaps it is *qua* essence, since all things exist? Not even that, for it is more perfect *qua* intellect or even *qua* life, than *qua* essence. So if it is not *qua* intellect or life that the intellect is God, it is not *qua* essence either. Likewise, essence does not remain at rest within

quiescit, sed per actiones contendit ad bonum, neque aliquid simpliciter esse expetit, sed bene esse atque cum bono. Ex quo patet et super ipsam simpliciter essentiam esse aliud, id est ipsum bonum, praesertim quia, cum ens et essentia multiplicitatem possit admittere, quam unitas ipsa non potest, merito unitas est simplicior atque prior. Sed de his alibi. Praeterea non omnia esse suum habent propriamque essentiam, sicut quae omnino extrinsecusque contingunt simpliciterque fluunt et privationes informisque materia. Omnia tamen manifestum principii donum praeferre debent, donum, inquam, optimum, si modo principium sua proprietate facit omnia exprimitque potenter.

3 Quanam igitur conditione primus intellectus habet, ut sit principium aliquid atque deus, qua videlicet ferme cuncta sibi quodammodo similia reddit? Per unitatem bonitatemque omnibus distributam. Quodlibet enim est quodammodo unum atque bonum. Igitur qua unus est et bonus, per unitatem atque bonitatem. Verum haec non sunt in intellectu vel primo prima. Est enim ibi unitas bonitasque non simpliciter illa quidem, sed quaedam potius, id est intellectualis, pro intellectuali natura, pro capacitate sua, si modo alia semper atque superior unitatis bonitatisque ratio est atque intellegentiae ratio, quandoquidem intellegentia neque percurrit per omnia, sicut illa, neque seipsa contenta est, sed ad ipsum bonum expetit unionem estque particeps multitudinis compositionisque cuiusdam, quam prima unitas necessario refugit.

4 Ubi vero super intellectum ipsam simpliciter unitatem bonitatemque cogitamus, non duo quaedam, sed unicum contemplamur, siquidem ubique unire et benefacere idem est et tam unitas quam bonitas superius aliquid non admittit. Nihil enim vel unitate simplicius vel bonitate melius cogitari potest. Simplicissimum vero atque optimum est proculdubio primum, primum vero penitus

itself, but strives toward the Good through its actions; nor does something desire simply to exist, but to be well and accompanied by the Good. As a result, above the simple essence there is obviously something else—that is, the Good—especially since, as being and essence can admit multiplicity and unity cannot, unity is rightly [considered] simpler and prior. But of these matters we treat elsewhere. In addition, not all things have their own being and their proper essence, such as the things that are completely and externally contingent and simply flow, and privations and formless matter. Yet all things must manifest the gift of their principle, I mean its best gift, whenever the principle creates and eminently expresses all things by virtue of its own property.

Under what condition, then, could the first intellect be a prin- 3
ciple and God—through what condition could it in some way make almost all things like itself? By the Unity and Goodness imparted to all things. For everything is, in one way or another, one and good. It is *qua* one and good, then, by virtue of unity and goodness. But the first Unity and Goodness do not reside in the intellect, not even in the first intellect. For therein unity and goodness are not simple, but particular, that is, intellectual, according to their intellectual nature and according to their own capacity, provided that the rational principle of Unity and Goodness is always different from, and superior to, the rational principle of intelligence: intelligence does not pervade all things like Unity and Goodness do, nor is it self-sufficient, but it strives to be united to the good and it participates in a sense in multitude and composition, which the first Unity must necessarily avoid.[192]

But when we consider the simple Unity and Goodness above 4
the intellect, we do not contemplate two, but one single principle, since unifying and doing the good are always the same thing, and both Unity and Goodness do not admit anything that is superior to them. For one cannot conceive anything simpler than Unity or better than Goodness. Surely the first principle is utterly simple

unicum. Ad primum proprie pertinet incomparabilis ipsa simplicitas, quam ipsam dicimus unitatem; pertinet communicabilitas per omnia se diffundens, quam bonitatem ipsam cognominamus. Per unitatem quidem est maxime simplex. Ergo primum per eandem est maxime potens, siquidem unita virtus est ubique potentior. Per eandem rursus potenter per omnia se diffundit, unde est maxime bonum. Immo vero ut est ipsa simpliciter unitas, ita simpliciter ipsa bonitas.

5 Denique quia omnes etiam privationes et fluxus informisque materia quodammodo unitatis bonitatisque participia sunt et singula unionem bonumque appetunt, coniectamus ipsum simpliciter unum bonumque primum omnium esse principium. Utinam mirandus ille iuvenis disputationes discursionesque superiores diligenter consideravisset, antequam tam confidenter tangeret praeceptorem, ac tam secure contra Platonicorum omnium sententiam divulgaret et divinum Parmenidem simpliciter esse logicum et Platonem una cum Aristotele ipsum cum ente unum et bonum adaequavisse!

and good; it is the utterly unique first principle. To the first principle properly belongs incomparable simplicity, which we call Unity, as well as an all-pervading capacity to communicate, which we call Goodness. By virtue of Unity it is simple to the highest degree, thus it is also by virtue of Unity that it is powerful to the highest degree, since the power of Unity is always more powerful. Again, it is by virtue of Unity that it powerfully pervades all things, whence it is good to the highest degree—I should rather say: it is absolute Goodness just as it is absolute Unity.

Finally, since even privations, flux, and formless matter all participate in some way in Unity and Goodness, and since they each strive toward union and the Good, we conclude that the absolute One and Good constitutes the first principle of all things. I wish that admirable young man had considered with attention the arguments and discussions above, before attacking his master with such audacity and claiming without fear, in opposition to the doctrine of all Platonists, that the divine *Parmenides* is simply logical and that Plato, like Aristotle, has identified the One and the Good with being![193]

Note on the Texts

TEXT OF THE COMMENTARY

The text of the commentary proper is based on the *editio princeps* printed in Florence in 1496. Ficino's corrigenda from the 1496 edition have also been incorporated. Typographical errors have been corrected without comment; the spelling has been modernized (with the *u/v* and *e/ae* distinctions), abbreviations and diacritics have been silently expanded, fusions such as *siquis* and *siquid* have been disaggregated, and the punctuation has been modernized. Spelling of names has been regularized according to modern use. The subdivision in chapters and paragraphs is based on that of the 1496 edition; however, the editor has adopted a continuous chapter numbering, and has supplied the division in paragraphs in instances where there is no paragraphing in the 1496 edition (chapters 1–36). The text in the three editions of Ficino's *Opera omnia* (1541, 1576, and 1641) has been dismissed as too corrupt to be of any value, although some of the emendations of the 1576 edition have been adopted.

TEXT OF THE ARGUMENT

Ficino's argument to the *Parmenides* exists in three different versions, which correspond to three chronological stages in Ficino's interpretation of the dialogue.[1] In 1463–64, Ficino completed a first draft of the arguments to the first ten Platonic dialogues he translated at the request of Cosimo de' Medici. This draft, which is autograph and heavily corrected, is preserved in two separate fragments, now in Paris and Parma;[2] the *Parmenides* argument is preserved in the Paris manuscript. In 1464 Ficino had several amanuenses copy his translation of the ten dialogues, incorporat-

ing (with some variants) the introductions that he had drafted in the Paris and Parma fragments. This version is now in MS Canon. class. lat. 163, in the Bodleian Library in Oxford.[3] Ficino then revised this version when he published the *editio princeps* of his translation of Plato's complete works, printed in Florence in 1484.[4] The *editio princeps* contained a large number of typographical errors, as indicated in the list of *emendationes* added at the end of the second volume; these *emendationes* were subsequently incorporated in the text of second edition, printed in Venice in 1491.[5] Ficino revised the *Parmenides* argument one last time for the publication of the *Commentaria in Platonem* in 1496, where the argument is followed by the full-scale commentary on the *Parmenides*.[6]

In the Canonicianus, as well as in the first two printed editions of Ficino's *Platonis opera omnia*, the argument serves as an introduction to the Latin version of the *Parmenides*. By contrast, in the *Commentaria in Platonem*, which does not contain Ficino's translation of Plato's dialogues, the argument precedes the commentary. Although the argument still contains the final sentence announcing the dialogue ("Let us proceed to the dialogue, bearing in mind these preliminary remarks"), the structure of the commentary suggests that by this time Ficino considered the argument as an epitome of the commentary; in Chapter 38.1, for example, when he states that "the way in which Proclus and others have arranged the dialogue in nine hypotheses we have explained at the beginning of the commentary," Ficino is referring to the argument rather than to the preface or the commentary proper.

The argument to the *Parmenides* shows that by 1463 Ficino was already familiar with Proclus' interpretation, according to which the *Parmenides* contained the supreme expression of Plato's theology and was divided into nine hypotheses. The argument draws upon both Proclus' *Platonic Theology* and his *Parmenides* commentary. This shows, moreover, that by 1463 Ficino had a profound and precise knowledge of Proclus' *Platonic Theology* and of his *Par-*

menides commentary. (The latter Ficino read either in the original version or in Moerbeke's translation, more probably in both). We know that Ficino read and annotated Proclus' *Platonic Theology* in Florence, Biblioteca Riccardiana, MS Ricc. 70,[7] but Ficino's Greek copy (or copies) of Proclus' *Parmenides* commentary has not come down to us.

The present text is based on the 1496 edition of the *Commentaria in Platonem*.[8] It has been collated with the two editions of Plato's complete works (Florence, 1484,[9] and Venice, 1491[10]), and the five extant manuscripts in Paris,[11] Oxford,[12] Florence, the Vatican City,[13] and London.[14] Since the present edition follows consistently the text of the *editio princeps*, however, it does not record the variants of the other editions and manuscripts. A detailed account of all variants can be found in Francesca Lazzarin's edition of the text.[15]

NOTES

1. On the textual history of Ficino's translation of Plato, see P. O. Kristeller, *Supplementum Ficinianum. Marsilii Ficini florentini philosophi platonici opuscula inedita et dispersa*, 2 vols. (Florence, 1937), 1: cxlvii–clvii.

2. Paris, Bibliothèque Nationale de France, MS Nouv. acq. lat. 1633, ff. 5–7, and Parma, Biblioteca Palatina, Carteggio di Lucca, Casseta 5. On the history of these two fragments, see Kristeller, "Marsilio Ficino as a Beginning Student of Plato," *Scriptorium* 20 (1966): 41–53, esp. 48–49.

3. On the history of this manuscript, see H. O. Coxe, *Catalogus codicum manuscriptorum Bibliothecae Bodleianae*, 3: *Canonicianos* (Oxford, 1864), col. 182; Kristeller, "Marsilio Ficino as a Beginning Student," 44–46; *Marsilio Ficino e il ritorno di Platone. Mostra di manoscritti stampe e documenti*, ed. S. Gentile, S. Niccoli, and P. Viti (Florence, 1984), 113–115, no. 89. For a comparison of the different versions of Ficino's translation of Plato, see G. Boter, The *Textual Tradition of Plato's* Republic (Leiden, 1989), 270–78; G. Jonckers, *The Manuscript Tradition of Plato's* Timaeus *and* Critias (Amsterdam, 1989), 305–9; C. Brockmann, *Die Handschriftliche Überlieferung*

von Platons Symposion (Wiesbaden, 1992), 220–29; B. Vancamp, "La tradition manuscrite de l'*Hippias Majeur* de Platon," *Revue d'histoire des textes* 25 (1995): 1–60; E. Berti, "Osservazioni filologiche alla versione del *Filebo* di Marsilio Ficino," in *Il "Filebo" di Platone e la sua fortuna. Atti de Convegno di Napoli, 4–6 novembre 1993*, ed. P. Cosenza (Naples, 1996), 93–171; S. M. Tempesta, *La tradizione testuale del* Liside *di Platone* (Florence, 1997), 155–77; P. Megna, *Lo* Ione *platonico nella Firenze medicea* (Messina, 1999), 58–142; M. Vanhaelen, "Marsilio Ficino's Version of Plato's *Euthyphro*," *Scriptorium* 56, no. 1 (2002): 20–47.

4. On the history of the 1484 edition, see Kristeller, "The First Printed Edition of Plato's Works and the Date of Its Publication," in *Studia Copernicana* XVI: *Science and History, Studies in Honor of Edward Rosen* (Wroclaw, 1978), 25–35; *Marsilio Ficino e il ritorno di Platone*, 117–19, no. 91; Hankins, *Plato in the Italian Renaissance*, 1: 300–18.

5. See Kristeller, "Marsilio Ficino as a Beginning Student," 43; *Marsilio Ficino e il ritorno di Platone*, 119–20, no. 93.

6. On the different stages in Ficino's interpretation of the Platonic corpus, see Hankins, *Plato in the Italian Renaissance*, 1: 318–21.

7. See Introduction, p. xiv.

8. *Commentaria in Platonem* (Florence: Laurentius de Alopa, 1496 = ISTC ip 00152000). I have used the exemplar of the Bodleian Library (Auct. Q 4. 27). The *argumentum* is at ff. 2r–v; the emendations added at the end of the volume do not include any that are relevant to the *Parmenidis argumentum*.

9. *Platonis Opera* (Florence: Laurentius de Alopa, [1484–85] = ISTC ip00771000). I have collated the text of the *editio princeps* from the exemplar of the Bodleian Library (Auct. K. 3. 22); the *Parmenides* is at ff. 34r–v. At the end of the volume, the list of *emendationes* mentions two errors in the *Parmenidis argumentum*.

10. *Platonis Opera* (Venice: Bernardinus de Choris, de Cremona, and Simon de Luere, for Andreas Torresanus, de Asula, 1496 = ISTC ip00772000). I have collated the text of this edition from the exemplar of the Bodleian Library (Auct. O 3. 28) at ff. 22r–v.

11. Paris, Bibliothèque Nationale de France, MS Nouv. acq. lat. 1633 [1463–64]. I have collated the text by autopsy. The *Parmenidis argumentum* is at ff. 6r–7r.

12. Oxford, Bodleian Library, MS Canon. class. lat. 163 [1464]; the MS contains the first version of the introduction. I have collated the text by autopsy in the Bodleian Library. The *Parmenidis argumentum* is at ff. 65r–66r.

13. Florence, Biblioteca Mediceo-Laurenziana, MS Plut. 82.6 [1482–1484], and Vatican City, Bibliotheca Apostolica Vaticana, MS Urb. lat. 185 [1482–1484]. The latter two MSS are the personal copies, respectively, of Lorenzo de' Medici and Federico da Montelfeltro; both contain the version that was used for the *editio princeps*. I have collated both manuscripts from microfilm copies supplied by the Laurentian and Vatican libraries. The *Parmenidis argumentum* is at ff. 45v–46r in the Laurentian MS, and at ff. 66v–67v in the Vatican MS.

14. London, British Library, MS Harl. 3481 [ca. 1491]; this was copied from the 1491 edition. I have collated this manuscript from a microfilm copy provided by the British Library. The *Parmenides* is to be found at ff. 45v–46r.

15. Lazzarin, "*L'argumentum in Parmenidem* di Marsilio Ficino," especially 23–31 (this article also contains the Italian translation of the *argumentum*, 32–33, and a close analysis of the text, 7–22). On the *argumentum*, see also Allen, "Ficino's Theory of the Five Substances," esp. 24–28; idem, "The Second Ficino-Pico Controversy," esp. 432–37; Etienne, "Marsile Ficin, lecteur et interprète du *Parménide* à la Renaissance," esp. 157–63, and Lazzarin, "Note sull'interpretazione ficiniana del *Parmenide* di Platone."

Notes to the Texts

SIGLA AND ABBREVIATIONS

E	*Commentaria in Platonem,* Florence, 1496
Ec	Ficino's corrigenda in E
corr.	The editor's emendations
add.	The editor's additions
e Bas.	The editor's emendations or additions based on Ficino's *Opera Omnia,* Basel, 1576
e Proclo	The editor's emendations or additions based on Proclus's *Parmenides Commentary*

1. hactenus *Ec*: hacteus E
2. particeps *corr.*: participes E
3. particeps *Ec*: participes E
4. dissimilia *corr. e Bas.*: dissimillima E
5. distinctio *corr.*: distincto E
6. distinctae *Ec*: disiunctae E
7. congrediantur *Ec*: congregantur E
8. possunt minus *Ec*: potius manus E
9. non *add.*: *om.* E
10. sunt *corr.*: iunt E
11. secundum *Ec*: sui E
12. quoddam *corr.*: quiddam E
13. unitam *corr.*: unita E
14. pedes *corr.*: pedis E
15. substantiarum *Ec*: sub earum E
16. cuicumque *Ec*: cuiuscumque E
17. speculare *corr*: speculabere E
18. signum impressum *corr. e Proclo,* In Parm. *IV,* 847. 5–6 (τυπώματα; typomata *Moerbeke*): picturam E
19. idea *corr. e Bas.*: ideae E
20. definit *corr.*: desinit E
21. est *add. e Bas.*: *om.* E
22. universali *Ec*: oculi E
23. dixerim *Ec*: diximus E
24. protulit *corr. e Bas.*: protuli E
25. munus *corr. e Bas.*: unus E
26. et *add.*: *om.* E
27. effectus *Ec*: effectum E
28. sc. devertitur
29. transeant *Ec*: transeat E
30. communis *corr*: communi E
31. est *Ec*: est igitur E
32. necessario *Ec*: numero E
33. sive *add. Ec*

34. a *add. e Bas*
35. possunt *Ec*: posterius *E*
36. veneratur *Ec*: veneraretur *E*
37. oppositorum *corr.*: oppositarum *E*
38. excelsae *Ec*: ex se *E*
39. nec *corr.*: neque *E*
40. sit *corr. e Bas.*: fit *E*
41. intellegibilia *corr.*: intellegentia *E*
42. simpliciter *Ec*: simplex *E*
43. propius *corr. e Bas.*: proprius *E*
44. vita *corr.*: ita *E*
45. nec *Ec*: haec *E*
46. semetipsam *Ec*: semetipsum *E*
47. intellegentia *Ec*: intellegentiae *E*
48. habeat *Ec*: habeant *E*
49. quam more qualitatis, per primum *Ec*: more qualitatis, primum *E*
50. refert *Ec*: referet *E*
51. procedere *Ec*: praecedere *E*

Notes to the Translation

ABBREVIATIONS

Allen (*In Philebum*)	Marsilio Ficino, *The Philebus Commentary*, ed. and tr. Michael J. B. Allen (Berkeley: University of California Press, 1975; repr. Tempe: Arizona Center of Medieval and Renaissance Studies, 2000).
Allen (*In Sophistam*)	Michael J. B. Allen, *Icastes: Marsilio Ficino's Interpretation of Plato's Sophist. Five Studies and a Critical Edition with Translation* (Berkeley: University of California Press, 1989).
Dillon	Proclus, *Commentary on Plato's Parmenides*, tr. Glenn R. Morrow and John M. Dillon (Princeton: Princeton University Press, 1987).
Dodds	Proclus, *The Elements of Theology*, ed. and tr. E. R. Dodds (Oxford: Clarendon, 1963; repr. 2000).
Hankins-Allen	Marsilio Ficino, *Platonic Theology*, ed. James Hankins and tr. Michael J. B. Allen, 6 vols. (Cambridge, MA: Harvard University Press, 2001–2006).
Henry-Hadot	Marius Victorinus, *Traités théologiques sur la Trinité*, ed. Paul Henry and tr. Pierre Hadot, 2 vols. (Paris: Editions du Cerf, 1960).
Kaske-Clark	Marsilio Ficino, *Three Books on Life*, ed. and tr. Carol V. Kaske and John R. Clark (Binghamton, NY: Renaissance Society of America, 1989).
Laurens	Marsilio Ficino, *Commentaire sur le Banquet de Platon, de l'Amour*, ed. and tr. Pierre Laurens (Paris: Belles Lettres, 2002).
Matton	Francesco Diaceto, *De Pulchro Libri III*, ed. Sylvain Matton (Pisa: Scuola Normale Superiore di Pisa, 1986).

Moerbeke	Proclus, *Commentaire sur le Parménide de Platon, traduction de Guillaume de Moerbeke*, ed. Carlos Steel, 2 vols. (Louvain: Presses Universitaires de Louvain-Brill, 1982–1985).
Op.	Marsilio Ficino, *Opera quae hactenus extitere et quae in lucem nunc primum prodiere omnia* (Basel: Heinrich Petri, 1576; repr. Turin: Bottega d'Erasmo, 1959 and 1962; Paris: Phénix Editions, 2000).
Saffrey-Westerink	Proclus, *Théologie Platonicienne*, ed. and tr. Henri D. Saffrey and Leendert G. Westerink, 6 vols. (Paris: Belles Lettres, 1968–1997).
Steel	*Procli in Platonis Parmenidem Commentaria*, ed. Carlos Steel, 3 vols. (Oxford: Clarendon, 2007–2009).
Westerink	Leendert G. Westerink, *The Greek Commentaries on Plato's Phaedo*, 2 vols. (Amsterdam: North-Holland, 1976–1977).

ARGUMENT

1. Following the downfall of the Medici in 1494, Ficino had to rely on other sponsors to finance his work. Niccolò Valori (1464–ca. 1530) was a pupil of Ficino and a close friend of Machiavelli. He was involved in an anti-Medici conspiracy in 1512 and later tried to win back the favor of the Medici by publishing a *Life of Lorenzo de' Medici*.

2. See Proclus, *Platonic Theology* 1.8 (ed. Saffrey-Westerink, p. 33.13–18).

3. See Proclus, *In Parmenidem* 1.617–18 and *Platonic Theology* 1.1 (ed. Saffrey-Westerink, pp. 6.7–9).

4. See Proclus, *Platonic Theology* 1.1 (p. 8.5–15) and *In Parmenidem* 4.926–28. There is a similar argument in Ficino, *In Parmenidem* 29.1, with reference to *Parmenides* 133b.

5. See Proclus, *Platonic Theology* 1.12 (ed. Saffrey-Westerink, p. 58.13–16). The conception that God is both immanent (i.e., within all things) and transcendent (i.e., outside all things) is central in patristic (e.g., Augustine, *De Civitate Dei* 8.30, where God is said to be both *nusquam* and

ubique) and medieval literature. It is often linked to the famous image of God as an infinite sphere, the center of which is everywhere, the circumference nowhere, attributed to Hermes Trismegistus in the twelfth-century *Book of XXXIV Philosophers*. Ficino, who was acquainted with this medieval tradition as early as 1458 (see his vernacular treatise *Di Dio et anima* [1458] in Kristeller, *Supplementum Ficinianum*, 2: 128–58) and had completed his translation of the *Corpus Hermeticum* by the time he undertook the *Parmenides argumentum* (1463), must have been struck by the similarities between these traditions and the Neoplatonic interpretation of the *Parmenides*.

6. According to Proclus, the succession Zeno-Socrates-Parmenides reflects the progression toward progressively more divine realities. See Proclus, *In Parmenidem* 1.672. The same argument is found in Ficino, *In Parmenidem* 3–4 and 16.

7. See Proclus, *In Parmenidem* 3.784.12–18 (ed. Steel, p. 194). This is treated in great detail in chaps. 4–35 of Ficino's *In Parmenidem*.

8. See Proclus, *Platonic Theology* 1.10 (ed. Saffrey-Westerink, pp. 41.7–42.2); *In Parmenidem* 6.1039.19–22 (ed. Steel, p. 2). See Ficino, *In Parmenidem* 38.

9. Proclus, *In Parmenidem* 5.1035.1–5 and 11–12 (ed. Steel, pp. 268–69) and 6.1039.22–25 (ed. Steel, p. 2). The same argument is found in Ficino, *In Parmenidem* 36.1 and 38.1.

10. As in Proclus (*In Parmenidem* 5.1035.7–9, ed. Steel, p. 268), the difference between these two hypotheses lies in the fact that the "others" are seen either as partaking of the One (hyp. IV) or as nonparticipant in it (hyp. V). As is convincingly shown by Lazzarin, "Note sull'interpretazione ficiniana del *Parmenide*," 28–34, Ficino implicitly follows Proclus, since he states below that hyp. V corresponds to the level of matter, which does not partake of the one being, but solely of the One.

11. Proclus, *In Parmenidem* 5.1035.5–15 (ed. Steel, p. 268) and 6.1040.1–14 (ed. Steel, p. 2).

12. Proclus, *Platonic Theology* 1.12 (ed. Saffrey-Westerink, pp. 59.8–22).

13. Proclus, *Platonic Theology* 1.12 (ed. Saffrey-Westerink, p. 58.8–22) and *In Parmenidem* 6.1040.25–1041.15 (ed. Steel, pp. 3–4).

14. I.e., the division established by Plutarch of Athens; see Proclus, *In Parmenidem* 6.1059.3–15 (ed. Steel, p. 27) and *Platonic Theology* 1.12 (ed. Saffrey-Westerink, pp. 56–58). See Ficino, *In Parmenidem* 51.

15. Proclus, *In Parmenidem* 6.1048.5–7 (ed. Steel, p. 13).

PREFACE

1. The combination of *natura*, i.e., natural, innate abilities, and *gratia*, i.e., divine illumination, is a leitmotif in Ficino's philosophy.

2. See Proclus, *In Parmenidem* 4.637. On the four dialectical methods (division, analysis, definition, demonstration), see Proclus, *In Parmenidem* 5.982. This statement signals Ficino's refutation of Pico's thesis according to which the *Parmenides* is solely a logical exercise.

3. Perhaps a hit at Pico's great friend Poliziano, who affected Greek accusatives; Ficino aligns himself with more old-fashioned users of Latin philosophical vocabulary.

4. Plato, *Republic* 7.533b, and Aristotle, *Topics* 1.1.101a–b and 7.14.136a–b. Here Ficino attempts to establish an agreement between Plato's and Aristotle's philosophical methods. His source is Proclus, who mentions that some ancient scholars used to compare Parmenidean dialectic with the method described in the *Topics;* see *In Parmenidem* 1.635.2–17 (ed. Steel, pp. 20–21); 1.648.13–649.2 (ed. Steel, p. 34); and *Platonic Theology* 1.9 (ed. Saffrey-Westerink, pp. 35.24–36.3). However, Proclus clearly differentiates the Parmenidean method from the Aristotelian; see *In Parmenidem* 1.653.1–3 (ed. Steel, p. 39). Ficino's insistence that Plato and Aristotle are in agreement regarding dialectic should be read in the context of the controversy with Pico discussed in the Introduction, pp. xx–xxi.

COMMENTARY

1. Regarding the allusion to the Peripatetics, see Proclus, *In Parmenidem* 1.716–17.

2. Plato, *Theaetetus* 183e–84a.

3. In Plato's text, Zeno's argument is simply that if things are many, they must be both like and unlike (*Parmenides* 127e). Ficino's development of Zeno's argument derives from Proclus, *In Parmenidem* 2.725 and *Platonic Theology* 2.1 (ed. Saffrey-Westerink, pp. 6–7). Similar arguments can be found in Ficino, *Platonic Theology* 2.2–3 (ed. Hankins-Allen, 2: 96–113).

4. See Proclus, *In Parmenidem* 2.726–27 and *Platonic Theology* 2.2 (ed. Saffrey-Westerink, pp. 15–16).

5. *Sophist* 248a. See Proclus, *In Parmenidem* 2.729.20–26 (ed. Steel, pp. 131–32).

6. Ficino, *Platonic Theology* 11.4–5 (ed. Hankins-Allen, 3: 242–97) and *In Plotinum, ad Enn.* 5.7 (*Op.*, p. 1767), *ad Enn.* 5.9 (*Op.*, pp. 1769–71), *ad Enn.* 6.7 (*Op.*, pp. 1787–94).

7. On the comparison of nature and art and the notion of tools that are both separate from and linked with the agent's mind, see Ficino, *Platonic Theology* 6.1.6 (ed. Hankins-Allen, 2: 254–57) and 10.4.2–3 (ed. Hankins-Allen, 3: 146–49).

8. Radial species refer to planets or stars that project "living and perceiving" rays onto animals, humans, and objects, whence they derive the power to harm or kill through their evil eye. This ultimately derives from Al-Kindi's doctrine. See Ficino, *De Vita* 3.16 (ed. Kaske-Clark, pp. 322–25).

9. See Proclus, *In Parmenidem* 2.755–57.

10. Ibid. 3.812–13.

11. Ibid. 3.817–20.

12. Ibid. 3.822–23.

13. Ibid. 3.824–25.

14. Ibid. 3.826.

15. Ibid. 3.826–27.

16. Plato, *Republic* 10.567b.

17. See Proclus, *In Parmenidem* 3.828–29.

18. Ibid. 4.888.

19. Ibid. 3.828–29.

20. Plato, *Timaeus* 29e–30a.

21. See Proclus, *In Parmenidem* 3.829–31.

22. Ibid. 3.831–33.

23. See Proclus, *In Parmenidem* 3.835–38. This represents a theoretical justification for the practice of magic and theurgy.

24. Plato, *Theaetetus* 148e–51d.

25. See Proclus *In Parmenidem* 4.838–39. Ficino reproduces here the Proclean argument according to which Parmenides' criticism of the theory of Ideas should not be taken literally, since it primarily serves to encourage Socrates to articulate his thoughts more clearly.

26. Plato, *Timaeus* 28a–c and 50b–52b; *Sophist* 239d–40b.

27. See Proclus, *In Parmenidem* 4.839–42 and 845–48, who analyses his predecessors' modes of describing participation in Ideas, including the comparisons of mirror reflections, seal impressions, and images made by painting and sculpture. While he accepts the preparatory benefit of such comparisons, Proclus underlines the necessity to transcend them to grasp the true nature of participation. Before him Plotinus, *Enneads* 3.6.6–13, had drawn upon the *Sophist, Timaeus,* and *Republic* to use the same comparisons, while recognizing that these were inferior comparisons that would not lead to God (*Enneads* 6.7.36.6). See Ficino, *In Plotinum, ad Enn.* 3.6 (*Op.*, pp. 1718–19); *In Philebum* 2.1 (ed. Allen, p. 389); *In Sophistam* 46 (ed. Allen, pp. 271–77); *In Timaeum* 9 (*Op.*, pp. 1441–42).

28. See Proclus, *In Parmenidem* 4.846–48. One must read *signum impressum* instead of *picturam*. See ibid. 4.847.5–6 (ed. Steel, p. 13), which reads in translation (tr. Dillon, p. 217): things "are likenesses (*eikones*) of intellectual forms, reflections (*enoptra*) of the soul-forms, and imprints (*typômata*) of the physical forms."

29. See Proclus, *In Parmenidem* 4.842–45. See also Ficino, *In Timaeum* 9 (*Op.*, p. 1441).

30. An allusion to the retrograde motion of the planets. This phenomenon had been described by Aristotle and Ptolemy of Alexandria. Following a geocentric vision of the universe, these philosophers believed that retrograde motion was caused by a combination of epicyclic motion (i.e., planets move at a constant motion in circles called epicycles) and orbital motion (i.e., the epicycles' orbit around Earth).

31. Ficino, *Platonic Theology* 8.12.1 (ed. Hankins-Allen, 2: 342–45).

32. Plato, *Timaeus* 28a–29d and 92c; *Republic* 7.514a–18b.

33. Ficino refers to this doctrine in his *Philebus Commentary* 11 (ed. Allen, p. 141), relying upon Proclus, *In Parmenidem* 4.851–53 and *Platonic Theology* 1.29 (ed. Saffrey-Westerink, pp. 123–24). This doctrine, which is founded upon an interpretation of *Parmenides* 130e in the light of *Cratylus* 421c (where Plato distinguishes the first, essential names from the second, derived names), considers that divine names are *sunthemata* of the gods and thereby justifies the practice of theurgy.

34. According to Proclus, corporeal participation occurs either when a body incorporates the whole of another body (when one eats food) or when it incorporates only a part of the other body (when one participates in one of the Elements). When you drink the sensible substance called water, only part of that consists of (pure) elemental water.

35. See Proclus, *In Parmenidem* 4.856–66; Plotinus, *Enneads* 6.4–5.

36. Allusion to Proclus, *In Parmenidem* 4.871.10–20 (ed. Steel, p. 45), who considers that smallness is a Idea rather than an absence of greatness, and is the cause of indivisibility, contraction, and self-concentration.

37. See Proclus, *In Parmenidem* 4.866–73.

38. The instantaneous quality of species formation in a prepared substrate existing in the sensible world shows the immutable and eternal character of the Ideas. In other words, specific forms do not gradually emerge in the process of generation but are immediately present *in semine*, as it were. See Ficino, *Platonic Theology* 5.13.6 (ed. Hankins-Allen, 2: 82–83) and 10.5.1 (ed. Hankins-Allen, 3: 150–53). The passage draws upon Proclus, *In Parmenidem* 4.873.16–26 (ed. Steel, pp. 47–48).

39. See Proclus, *In Parmenidem* 4.873–75. Ficino, *De Vita* 3.14.

40. See Proclus, *In Parmenidem* 4.878–79.

41. This is tantamount to a rejection of the famous Third Man argument (*Parmenides* 132A–33A).

42. That is, the example taken up by Aristotle to develop the Third Man argument (*Metaphysics* 1.9.990b17).

43. The *noemata* refer to the intelligence's thought process, whereby the intelligence gives birth from within to forms and conceptions.

44. Ficino, *Platonic Theology* 11.3 (ed. Hankins-Allen, 3: 211–41) and 11.4.17–22 (ed. Hankins-Allen, 3: 270–77). See Proclus, *In Parmenidem* 4.893–98.

45. To account for both the human soul's capacity to produce its own rational principles and its illumination by the intellect during procession, Ficino considers, like Proclus, that there are two types of *noemata* in individual souls. The first *noema*, the one mentioned by Socrates, is conceived by the soul and is posterior to our intelligence, while the second *noema* is innate in our soul and exists before our intelligence. See Proclus, *In Parmenidem* 4.895–96.

46. I.e., the first *noema* conceived by the soul (to be distinguished from the one that is innate to our soul), as argued in 22.2–3 above.

47. See Proclus, *In Parmenidem* 4.905.

48. Ficino, *De Vita* 3.1–2.

49. See Proclus, *In Parmenidem* 4.903–4. See also *Elements of Theology* props. 97–102 and 110–12.

50. Plato, *Philebus* 30d.

51. See Proclus, *In Parmenidem* 4.906, who identifies the attribute "like" (*homoios*) mentioned in *Parmenides* 132d with the metaphysical concept of assimilation (*homoiosis*).

52. Ibid. 4.906–11.

53. I.e., a thing that depends on an Idea does not have an independent source of naming or reference within itself, but can only be named because of its relation with the Idea.

54. Ibid. 4.912.

55. *Spiritus* refers to the Stoic doctrine of the *pneuma*, the active and generative principle constituted of air and fire that infuses life into matter.

56. See Proclus, *In Parmenidem* 4.921.11–19 (ed. Steel, pp. 111–12).

57. Ficino, *Platonic Theology* 2.13 (ed. Hankins-Allen, 1: 192–211), where Ficino refutes Lucretius' doctrine.

58. See Proclus, *In Parmenidem* 4.920–23.

59. Ibid. 4.926–28.

60. On the scholastic terminology *actus directus/actus reflexus* to express the notion that knowledge varies according to the nature of the object of knowledge, see nn. 62 and 66 below.

61. *Consequenter* is a scholastic term (see the opposition *agere primo/agere consequenter*), meaning "through inference," used by Ficino to express the Neoplatonic doctrine according to which God can only know human matters in relation to the Ideas, both on an inferential (logical) level and in a manner corresponding to God's worth. The assimilation of logical relations to metaphysical relations of cause (for example) is typical of Neoplatonism. The view that God knows lower things inferentially through his own Ideas as their causes is also the position of Aquinas, an important influence on Ficino's theology; see *Summa theologiae* 1.14.5 and 6.

62. See Proclus, *In Parmenidem* 4.923–25 and 929. Here Ficino is using the scholastic terminology *actus directus/actus reflexus* (to distinguish the act of knowing expressed in the sentence "A is B" and the act of knowing expressed in the sentence "I know that A is B") to express the notion (adopted by Neoplatonic and medieval philosophers alike) that knowledge varies according to the nature of the object of knowledge. On the contrast between linear and circular motions, characteristic of Aristotelian epistemology, see *Platonic Theology* 8.9.2 and n. 26 ad loc. (ed. Hankins-Allen 2: 334–37 and p. 390), where Ficino uses the same distinction to compare the circular motion of thought with the linear motion of life.

63. See Proclus, *In Parmenidem* 4.930, which ultimately derives from Plotinus, *Enneads* 6.5.5 (lines and the center of a circle); 3.9.2; 4.3.4 and 9.5 (theorems and geometry).

64. *Coniugata relatione* seems to refer to a type of coordinate relationship; see Proclus' *homotagès* in *In Parmenidem* 4.943.21 (ed. Steel, p. 142).

65. See Proclus, *In Parmenidem* 4.943, which states that mastership presides over the whole chain of slavery.

66. Ficino uses the expressions *consequenter, per consequentiam* or *per reflexionem* to denote a noncoordinate, indirect relationship between realities that are not at the same level. *Per reflexionem* is the scholastic expression used to denote the intellect's indirect knowledge of the singular, in opposition to its direct knowledge of the universal; see Thomas Aquinas, *Summa theologiae* 1.86.1 and 4.

67. See Proclus *In Parmenidem* 4.933–34.

68. *Phaedrus* 247d. The notion that all knowledge is relative to the knowing subject is Proclus' answer to the objection raised in *Parmenides* 134a–c (that if God, who has perfect knowledge, only knows the Ideas, then He cannot know our world). See *Elements of Theology* prop. 124 and *In Parmenidem* 4.957. Given the influence of this doctrine on Thomas Aquinas, it is not surprising that Ficino expresses the concepts in scholastic terms, by using the opposition between "direct" and "reflexive" acts (*actus rectus* and *actus reflexus/per consequentiam*).

69. See Proclus, *In Parmenidem* 4.945, who refers to "some friends of Plato." Compare Thomas Aquinas, *Summa theologiae* 1.14.6, where the advocate of this false idea appears to be Averroes.

70. See Proclus, *In Parmenidem* 4.957. The notion becomes a topos in Christian literature. See, e.g., Augustine, *De Trinitate* 15.13.

71. *Per expressissimum characterem* is a Thomist expression, referring to the sign or figure imprinted in our soul by God. See *Summa theologiae* 3.63.3.

72. See Proclus, *In Parmenidem* 4.944.

73. This is the opinion of the *prisci theologi*, referred to in Ficino, *Platonic Theology* 6.1.7 (ed. Hankins-Allen, 2: 124–27).

74. See Proclus, *In Parmenidem* 4.954–55, who seems to refute some Epicureans or Peripatetics. Ficino uses similar arguments against Lucretius in *Platonic Theology* 2.13 (ed. Hankins-Allen, 1: 192–211).

75. Refutation of certain Stoics and Peripatetics; see Proclus, *In Parmenidem* 4.956–57.

76. Ficino here is invoking the late medieval theological dictum that there is *nulla proportio inter deum et hominem*, trying to show that it does not mean that God cannot know man.

77. See Proclus, *In Parmenidem* 4.956, which refutes Aristotle, *Metaphysics* 12.5.1071a. For Aristotle, the sun is a proximate cause of all generation beneath the moon.

78. Boethius, *Consolatio philosophiae* 4.6.12; Proclus, *In Parmenidem* 4.957–59.

79. See Proclus, *In Parmenidem* 4.958–59.

80. Ficino, *Platonic Theology* 2.13.10–11 (ed. Hankins-Allen, 1: 208–11); *In Plotinum, ad Enn.* 3.1, especially the *Summa Marsiliana* in *Op.*, pp. 1679–84 (= *Disputatio contra iudicium astrologorum*, in P. O. Kristeller, *Supplementum Ficinianum. Marsilii Ficini Florentini philosophi platonici opuscula inedita et dispersa* [Florence, 1937], 2: 16–21 and 51–52).

81. See Proclus, *In Parmenidem* 4.964. Proclus' argument is directed against Aristotle, as is Ficino's throughout this chapter; note that Aristotle's god has knowledge only of its own being.

82. Ibid. 4.963.

83. Ibid. 4.966.

84. Ibid. 4.967–68.

85. An allusion to (pseudo) Dionysius the Areopagite's negative theology, which ultimately derives from Proclus, and which distinguishes between negation by excess, whereby a principle "is not" because it "is superior to" that which it is not, and negation by defect, whereby a thing "is not" because it lacks that which it is not.

86. Ficino alludes to the scholastic debate on the highest human act, whether it was the intellect's knowledge of God or the will's love and

enjoyment (*frui*) of Him. This was a debate on which Ficino himself took various positions in the course of his life, but in his mature period, he sided with theologians in the Augustinian tradition who considered the will higher than the intellect.

87. Ficino, *Platonic Theology* 1.5–6 (ed. Hankins-Allen, 1: 59–91).

88. Plato, *Timaeus* 55c–d. See Allen, "Ficino's Theory of the Five Substances," and Allen, *Icastes*, chap. 2.

89. Here Ficino modifies Proclus' hierarchy of Ideas and forms; see Proclus, *In Parmenidem* 4.969–70.

90. I.e., the four stages of dialectic.

91. Ficino, *Platonic Theology* 11.3 (ed. Hankins-Allen, 3: 211–41) and 4.17–22 (ed. Hankins-Allen, 1: 270–77).

92. See Proclus, *In Parmenidem* 5.980.

93. Ibid. 5.980–83.

94. *Expressa* is a scholastic expression used to describe the process of sense perception whereby perceptions are both imprinted from outside (*impressa*) and exhibited from inside (*expressa*).

95. In medieval philosophy the term *resolutio* was used to render both the Greek *analusis* and *sunthesis; resolutio* here renders *analusis* (see Proclus, *In Parmenidem* 5.982.19, ed. Steel, p. 193), which is not understood in the Aristotelian sense (as an intrument for analyzing particulars into their basic elements), but in the Neoplatonic one, as a method to separate off the universal.

96. Plato, *Letter* 7.342a–44b.

97. Plato, *Philebus* 15c and *Republic* 537e.

98. See Proclus, *In Parmenidem* 5.992.

99. Ibid. 5.995–96.

100. I.e., in itself, it lacks actualized form.

101. See Proclus, *In Parmenidem* 5.999–1000.

102. Plato, *Sophist* 237a–b.

103. I.e., number is among the things that are.

104. Plato, *Sophist* 237b–38d.

105. Ficino, *In Sophistam* 17–18 (ed. Allen, pp. 228–31). Like Proclus, Ficino considers that the *Sophist* treats of the second principle, being, while the *Parmenides* treats of the first principle, the One.

106. Here there begins a section comprising thirteen chapters where Ficino interrupts his paraphrase of Proclus' *Parmenides* commentary and primarily draws upon Proclus' *Platonic Theology*. This section, which is clearly distinguished by a separate heading from the rest of the commentary, offers a point-by-point refutation of the position adopted by Pico in his *De ente et uno*, according to which the appellations "one" and "being" constitute two equally valid appellations for God. This section is very different in tone from that of the rest of the commentary; it contains rhetorical questions and adopts a question-refutation structure. Chap. 37 counters Pico's attempt to dissociate the Neoplatonists' interpretation from that of both Plato and (pseudo) Dionysius the Areopagite, and his claim that, contrary to the Neoplatonists' interpretation, Plato never defended the superiority of the One over being in the *Parmenides* and the *Sophist* (see Giovanni Pico della Mirandola, *De ente et uno* 2, and the Introduction).

107. *Tam profundum disserendi pelagus*: as in his translation Ficino follows Proclus' reading of the text (*pelagos logôn*; see *In Parmenidem* 1.633.24; 5.1018.11 and 1020.14) rather than the manuscripts (*plèthos logôn*).

108. See Proclus, *Platonic Theology* 1.9 (ed. Saffrey-Westerink, pp. 36.13–37.14).

109. Plato, *Sophist* 217b. See Proclus, *Platonic Theology* 1.9 (ed. Saffrey-Westerink, pp. 38.13–39.6). Ficino identifies the *Sophist*'s anonymous protagonist (the stranger from Elea, who is presented as a disciple of Parmenides and Zeno) with Melissus, a philosopher whom Plato refers to in the *Theaetetus* 183e–84a as a follower of Parmenides.

110. Plato, *Theaetetus* 183e–84a, with reference to *Iliad* 3.172. See Proclus, *Platonic Theology* 1.9 (ed. Saffrey-Westerink, pp. 37.20–38.13).

111. Plato, *Phaedrus* 275e; *Letters* 2.314a and 7.344c–d.

112. Proclus, *Platonic Theology* 1.8 (ed. Saffrey-Westerink, p. 33.15–18).

113. Proclus, *Platonic Theology* 1.10 (ed. Saffrey-Westerink, p. 42.9–20).

114. *Ludus*, "game," can also be translated "school."

115. On (pseudo) Dionysius the Areopagite and the reception of the works attributed to him, see the Introduction, p. xii.

116. I.e., in his commentary on the Areopagite's *Divine Names* (1490/92).

117. Plato, *Sophist* 216b. Ficino's use of the scholastic terms *redargutio* (which, in a disputation, refers to the denial of something previously granted or the granting of something previously denied) and *contentio* is directed against Pico, *De ente et uno* 2.

118. Platonic topos deriving from *Laws* 3.685a, alluded to by Proclus, *In Parmenidem* 6.1041.

119. Or rather in Ficino's *argumentum* to the *Parmenides*. See Note on the Texts, p. 238.

120. Plato, *Philebus* 23c. See Proclus, *Platonic Theology* 2.4. On the attribution of this doctrine to Philolaus, which ultimately derives from Proclus, *Platonic Theology* 3.8 (ed. Saffrey-Westerink, p. 30.15–18), see Ficino, *In Philebum* 2.1 (ed. Allen, p. 403), and *Platonic Theology* 17.2.11 (ed. Hankins-Allen, 6: 20–21).

121. Plato, *Philebus* 26d–e.

122. Ibid. 20d.

123. See Proclus, *Platonic Theology* 2.4 (ed. Saffrey-Westerink, pp. 35.10–36.11).

124. Plato, *Republic* 6.508c–9c. See Proclus, *Platonic Theology* 2.4 (ed. Saffrey-Westerink, pp. 32.1–34.8).

125. That is, the genera or kinds which, together with being, are the five Great Kinds of the *Sophist*.

126. Plato, *Sophist* 243c–45b. See also Ficino, *In Sophistam* 21, 26, 30–32, and 37–38 (ed. Allen, pp. 232–33, 238–41, 246–51, and 260–65).

127. Plato, *Sophist* 243d–e and 249e–50d. See Proclus, *Platonic Theology* 2.4 (ed. Saffrey-Westerink, p. 34.9–24).

128. Plato, *Sophist* 244b–45b. See Proclus, *Platonic Theology* 2.4 (ed. Saffrey-Westerink pp. 34.24–35.4).

129. See Proclus, *Platonic Theology* 2.4 (ed. Saffrey-Westerink pp. 36.12–37.3).

130. Ficino identifies the Stranger of the *Sophist* with Parmenides' disciple Melissus. The notion that the *Sophist* constitutes a preparation for the *Parmenides* derives from Proclus, *Platonic Theology* 3.21 (ed. Saffrey-Westerink, p. 73.10–12). On the conception that the topic of a dialogue should correspond to the personality of the protagonists, see Proclus, *In Parmenidem* 1.672. This allows Ficino to refute Pico's contention that neither the *Sophist* nor the *Parmenides* defended the superiority of the One over being.

131. The last five philosophers are mentioned in Proclus, *Platonic Theology* 1.1 (ed. Saffrey-Westerink, p. 6.16–24). Ficino adds the first two. As shown by Allen, for chronological reasons, we must assume that Plutarch is the Middle Platonist Plutarch of Cheronea (first–second centuries CE), rather than Proclus' teacher Plutarch of Athens (fourth–fifth centuries CE) mentioned in chap. 51 (Part II). Although the Neoplatonists were not in agreement with Plutarch's dualistic worldview, Ficino often associates Plutarch with the Neoplatonists. Ammonius Saccas was the master of Plotinus and is mentioned in Porphyry's *Life of Plotinus* (translated by Ficino in *Op.*, p. 1539).

132. *Pace* Pico, who distinguished between Plato's doctrine, which he showed to be in agreement with Aristotle's, and the Neoplatonists' doctrine, which he considered to be a distortion of Plato's words. On Ficino's interpretation of the history of ancient Platonism, see Allen, *Synoptic Art*, passim.

133. Plato, *Letters* 2.312e.

134. Plato, *Republic* 6.508e–9b.

135. Ibid. 7.518c.

136. Ibid. 6.508e–9b.

137. See Proclus, *Platonic Theology* 2.7 (ed. Saffrey-Westerink, pp. 45–48), who uses *Republic* and *Parmenides* in the same context. For the *Philebus* passage, see Plotinus, *Enneads* 6.7.25, who demonstrates the superiority

of the Good over the intellect by drawing upon the *Parmenides, Philebus,* and *Republic.*

138. Plato, *Sophist* 258b.

139. Ibid. 2.5 (ed. Saffrey-Westerink, pp. 38.18–39.5).

140. Ibid. 2.5 (ed. Saffrey-Westerink, p. 39.6–26).

141. Plato, *Republic* 507e–8c. See Proclus, *Platonic Theology* 2.6.

142. Since One and Good are appellations of one principle, God, as underlined at the end of chap. 40, the singular should be maintained in English.

143. Drawing upon Proclus' *Platonic Theology,* 2.1–2, Ficino's first two discourses answer the criticisms formulated in Pico, *De ente et uno* 7, where Pico draws upon Aristotle's *Metaphysics* (10.3.1054a20ff. and 6.1056b33ff.) and shows that the Neoplatonists' equivalence between the couples one/many and not-being/being (which leads them to equate one and not-being, many and being) is not valid.

144. See Proclus, *Platonic Theology* 2.1.

145. See chap. 3 regarding Zeno's thesis.

146. See Proclus, *Platonic Theology* 2.1 (ed. Saffrey-Westerink, pp. 4–9 and 11).

147. Ibid. 2.1 (ed. Saffrey-Westerink, pp. 12–13).

148. Ibid. 2.1 (ed. Saffrey-Westerink, pp. 13–14).

149. Ibid. 2.2 (ed. Saffrey-Westerink, pp. 21–22).

150. *Apex* renders the Greek *akrotès,* a term used by Proclus to characterize the henads, intermediate and participated unities between the absolutely transcendent One and the Ideas. See ibid. 1.3 (ed. Saffrey-Westerink, p. 15.3).

151. Ibid. 2.2 (ed. Saffrey-Westerink, pp. 22–23).

152. Ibid. 2.3. Refutes chap. 7 of Pico's *De ente et uno.*

153. Plato, *Timaeus* 27d, *Sophist* 245d, and *Republic* 6.509b.

154. See Proclus, *Platonic Theology* 2.3. Ficino demonstrates that the first and last levels of realities, i.e., God and matter, are one and not being. This refutes chap. 6 of Pico's *De ente et uno*.

155. *Resolutio* is one of the four stages in dialectic. In other words, the last level would be the last logical or dialectical stage rather than the last ontological level.

156. I.e., matter contains within itself "latent" seeds of forms (inchoation of forms). See, e.g., *Platonic Theology* 1.6.7 (ed. Hankins-Allen, 1: 86–87).

157. Application of the Neoplatonic principle that the higher the principle is, the further its action extends down through the hierarchy of being toward matter. See Proclus, *Elements of Theology* props. 57 and 72. So the absolute One is the only principle to reach the lowest level of the universe, matter. Unlike Plotinus, who considered matter as sterile and a principle of division (*Enneads* 3.6.6 and 19), Proclus considers matter as inherently one, although formless, and good (see Proclus, *In Alcibiadem* 326.13–15).

158. Here Ficino follows the Neoplatonic interpretation of *Philebus* 24b. See Ficino, *In Philebum* 2.1 (ed. Allen, p. 389). According to Proclus there are two infinites: the One, which is infinite by excess, as it transcends limit and limits all beings; matter, which is infinite by defect, *qua* limitless, is the limit of none, and is limited by all. See Proclus, *Platonic Theology* 3.8–10 and *In Parmenidem* 6.1118.

159. Plato, *Timaeus* 48e–51b. *Formosa*, beautiful, here alludes to both beauty and the plenum of forms, in opposition to matter's absence of form and beauty.

160. Plato, *Timaeus* 51a–b.

161. I.e., when we reach the one within us, whereby we can relate to God's Unity.

162. See Proclus, *Platonic Theology* 2.11 (ed. Saffrey-Westerink, pp. 64.10–65.26). Here Ficino provides against Pico a description of the soul's ascent toward God as the supreme One: it is only through the psychic one, the one within the soul, that we can have an intuition of God. The expressions *acies intelligentiae* and *acies mentis*, which correspond to Proclus'

akrotès tou nou, are used by Christian theologians to describe the process of the soul's mystic union with God. It refers to the highest part of the human intellect, which contemplates the divine intellect directly but can only have an indirect, nonintellectual intuition of the One.

163. The notion that the addition of being to the first principle would in fact diminish its simplicity and unity derives from Proclus; see *Platonic Theology* 2.2 (ed. Saffrey-Westerink, p. 23. 9–12) and 2.7 (ed. Saffrey-Westerink, p. 51.6–7).

164. *Vaticinari videtur* should be understood in the context of Ficino's principle that when all members of a species agree in some act, that is an indication from nature that something is the case. See Ficino, *Platonic Theology* 14.9.2 (ed. Hankins-Allen, 4: 294–97).

165. By referring to the "consensus of all philosophers," Ficino alludes to the Neoplatonic distortion of Aristotle's definition of the good, which Ficino analyzes in more detail in Discourse 7. This Neoplatonic definition is founded upon a reinterpretation of Aristotle's definition of the individual good, which will be later adopted by Thomas Aquinas (e.g., in *Summa theologiae* 1.6.2). Denying the existence of an absolute good, Aristotle defines the good as what each being *individually* desires. By contrast, Plotinus combines two passages of Aristotle to define the Good as the *universal* desire of all beings, in accordance with Plato's definition (*Enneads* 1.8.2.2–3): the divine intellect, as the prime mover of the universe, as an "object of desire" (*to orekton*), and as "final cause" (*to hou heneka*) in *Metaphysics* 12.7.1072b13–14; the individual good as "what each being desires" (*hou panata ta onta ephieta*) in *Nicomachean Ethics* 1.1.1094a3. This is closely related to Ficino's doctrine of natural desire (*appetitus naturalis*) as described in chap. 78 (Part II), and which derives from Proclus, *In Parmenidem* 7.509.10–26 (pp. 315–16 Steel). On *appetitus naturalis*, see Kristeller, *The Philosophy of Marsilio Ficino*, chap. X (VIII in the Italian edition).

166. See Proclus, *Platonic Theology* 2.7 (ed. Saffrey-Westerink, p. 51.16–19).

167. At this point, Ficino interrupts his paraphrasing of Proclus and refutes specific points of Pico's *De ente et uno*. In the following chapter, the arguments of which are further developed in chap. 58 (Part II), Ficino refutes *De ente et uno* 4–5. In chap. 4 Pico had established a distinction between concrete and abstract being (*ens concretum* and *ens abstractum*), in order to show that God can be called both pure (abstract) being and superior to (concrete) being, and can therefore be called both "being" (Aristotle, the scholastics) and "One above being" (the Neoplatonists). In chap. 5 Pico had claimed that God can be equally designated by the assertions used by the Peripatetics and by the negations used by the Platonists. See Introduction, pp. xxii–xxiii.

168. On Ficino's distinction between *ens, essentia,* and *entitas,* see *In Plotinum, ad Enn.* 5.5 (*Op.*, p. 1764); *In Sophistam* 34 (ed. Allen, pp. 255–57); *In Philebum* 2.2 (ed. Allen, p. 405).

169. This implies that although God is nameless, inasmuch as He is absolutely transcendent, He can nevertheless receive some appellations inasmuch as He is the cause of all things. See (pseudo) Dionysius the Areopagite, *On Divine Names* 1.5–6.

170. God contains all things in a single embrace, but cannot contain them individually.

171. The same image (linear/circular motion) is found in Ficino, *Platonic Theology* 8.9.2 (ed. Hankins-Allen, 2: 336–37).

172. Here Ficino uses scholastic terminology to defend the fact that the Good and being are different. See Thomas Aquinas, *Summa theologiae* 1.5–6, who uses the same reasoning to defend the opposite thesis, i.e., that the Good and being are the same in reality but differ only conceptually.

173. The expression "more or less" refers to Thomas Aquinas' distinction between substance, such as being, which does not admit a variation in degree, and accident, such as "white," which does admit degrees of more or less. See *Summa theologiae* 1.5.1.3. Incidentally, Thomas uses the distinction to defend the exact contrary of what Ficino is trying to show: the identity between good and being.

174. See Plato's definition of god as the final cause and Aristotle's definition of god as both final cause and prime mover.

175. Ficino's Neoplatonic distinction between being and well-being and his justification of suicide, which derives from Olympiodorus, *In Phaedonem* 1.9 (ed. Westerink, pp. 50–53), refutes the first part of chap. 5 and chap. 8 of *De ente et uno,* where Pico rejects Olympiodorus' distinction between being and well-being and establishes an equivalence between being and the Good. On the distinction between being and well-being, see also Ficino, *Platonic Theology* 12.3.7 (ed. Hankins-Allen, 4: 38–39).

176. This chapter is meant to refute chap. 8 of Pico's *De ente et uno.*

177. Unlike accidents, substance does not admit a variation in degree. See Thomas Aquinas, *Summa theologiae* 1.5.1.3.

178. *Voluptas,* pleasure, is here understood as *gaudium,* the supra-intellectual ecstasy that allows mystical union. On the identity of these two terms, see Ficino, *De voluptate* (*Op.*, p. 997). The argument developed by Ficino against Pico is that divine ecstasy derives from the Good rather than from the intellect. It draws upon a Neoplatonic interpretation of Plato's *Philebus,* which can be found in Proclus, *Platonic Theology* 2.4 (ed. Saffrey-Westerink, p. 36.7–11).

179. A scholastic expression; see, e.g., Thomas Aquinas, *De veritate* 8.12.

180. See Thomas Aquinas, *Summa Theologica* 1.6.1.

181. Here Ficino alludes to Pico's distinction between accidental and natural being and his contention that natural being and good are equivalent, since everything that is good is good inasmuch as it is (*De ente et uno* 8). Drawing upon Thomas' doctrine of variation of degrees, Ficino argues that an accidental thing (which has less being), if it is good, can be more desirable than a thing that has more being. It is the Good, therefore, not being, that makes a thing desirable.

182. Here Ficino rejects Pico's doctrine of multitude of beings as contrary to divine providence: being, life, and intellect differ formally, since their respective opposites are different; however, there are no degrees of being as there are degrees of heat.

183. Here Ficino refutes Pico's contention that being precedes Unity and Good within the creation, just as the efficient cause precedes the paradigmatic and the final causes (*De ente et uno* 8–9). According to Ficino, things created by the first principle are "being" inasmuch as they are created by God (efficient cause), and "good" inasmuch as they are naturally inclined toward Him (final cause). Thus, the final cause provides things with their individual good, while the efficient cause provides them with their essence. Such a distinction, Ficino concludes, demonstrates that the Good is superior to being.

184. This is based upon Plotinus' reinterpretation of Aristotle's definition of the individual good, harmonized with Plato's definition of the Good (see n. 165). Ficino shows against Pico that Aristotle's final cause, far from being an innovation, derives from a doctrine established by the ancient theologians. With the two introductory chapters (39 and 40) as a background, this passage counters Pico's contention that God's appellation of the One-and-Good above being does not constitute a mystery uniquely reserved for the Platonists but has also been adopted by Aristotle (*De ente et uno* 4).

185. In other words, *pace* Pico, the equivalence Aristotle explicitly draws between one and being concerns the second level rather than the first level of reality.

186. Here Ficino resumes his paraphrase of Proclus' *Parmenides* commentary, which he deliberately interrupted at chap. 38 to refute the arguments of Pico's *De ente et uno*. Here he uses Proclus' doctrine of henads (*In Parmenidem* 6.1044–51) to demonstrate that the principle of the genera and orders of all things is Unity rather than being.

187. See Proclus, *In Parmenidem* 6.1043.24–1045.19 (ed. Steel, pp. 7–9). Note, however, that Proclus appears to establish a strict separation between the sun's soul and the sun's intellect, while Ficino considers that the one is the highest part of the soul's intellect; Ficino actually combines Proclus' doctrine of henads with the doctrine of the *unum in nobis* to stress the soul's ability to reach the One though its unity. See Introduction, pp. xvii–xx.

188. Ibid. 6.1045.20–1046.10 (ed. Steel, pp. 9–10).

189. Ibid. 6.1046.11–1047.19 (ed. Steel, pp. 10–19).

190. In this chapter Ficino draws upon both Plotinus and Proclus to demonstrate against Pico that the intellect is not God *qua* intellect, life, or essence, but *qua* One.

191. Ibid. 6.1047.

192. See Plotinus, *Enneads* 6.7. Note that here Ficino establishes a strict separation between the One and the intellect.

193. This is the only explicit allusion to Pico della Mirandola, which ends the section devoted to the point-by-point rebuttal of the *De ente et uno*. *Mirandus ille* is a pun on Pico's surname, Mirandola.

Bibliography

Allen, Michael J. B. "Ficino's Theory of the Five Substances and the Neoplatonists' *Parmenides*." *Journal of Medieval and Renaissance Studies* 12 (1982): 19–44. Reprinted in Allen's *Plato's Third Eye: Studies in Marsilio Ficino's Metaphysics and Its Sources*, no. VIII. Aldershot: Variorum, 1995.

——. *Icastes: Marsilio Ficino's Interpretation of Plato's* Sophist. *Five Studies and a Critical Edition with Translation*. Berkeley: University of California Press, 1989.

——. "Marsilio Ficino on Plato, the Neoplatonists and the Christian Doctrine of the Trinity." *Renaissance Quarterly* 37 (1984): 555–84.

——. *The Platonism of Marsilio Ficino: A Study of his Phaedrus Commentary, Its Sources and Genesis*. Berkeley: University of California Press, 1984.

——. "The Second Ficino-Pico Controversy." In *Marsilio Ficino e il ritorno di Platone, Studi e Documenti* 2: 418–55. Edited by Gian Carlo Garfagnini. Florence: Olschki, 1986. Reprinted in *Plato's Third Eye*, no. X.

—— and Valerie Rees, eds. *Marsilio Ficino: His Theology, His Philosophy, His Legacy*. London: E. J. Brill, 2002.

Beierwaltes, Werner. *Denken des Einen. Studien zur neuplatonischen Philosophie und ihrer Wirkungsgeschichte*. Frankfurt: Klostermann, 1985. Italian translation: *Pensare l'Uno. Studi sulla filosofia neoplatonica e sulla storia dei suoi influssi*. Translated by Maria Luisa Gatti. Milan: Vita e Pensiero, 1992.

——. "L'interpretazione ficiniana del *Parmenide* platonico." In *Il Parmenide di Platone e la sua tradizione. Atti del III Colloquio internazionale del Centro di Ricerca sul Neoplatonismo, Università degli studi di Catania, 31 maggio–2 giugno 2001*, 389–410. Edited by Maria Barbanti and Francesco Romano. Catania: CUECM, 2002.

Dodds, E. R. "The *Parmenides* of Plato and the Origin of the Neoplatonic 'One.'" *Classical Quarterly* 22 (1928): 129–42.

Étienne, A. "Marsile Ficin, lecteur et interprète du *Parménide* à la Renaissance." In *Images de Platon et lectures de ses oeuvres: les interprétations de*

Platon à travers les siècles, 153–85. Edited by Ada Neschke-Hentschke. Louvain: Peeters, 1997.

Gersh, Stephen, and M. J. F. M. Hoenen, eds. *The Platonic Tradition in the Middle Ages: A Doxographic Approach*. Berlin: Walter de Gruyter, 2002.

Hankins, James. *Humanism and Platonism in the Italian Renaissance*. 2 vols. Rome: Edizioni di Storia e Letteratura, 2004–2008.

———. *Plato in the Italian Renaissance*. 2 vols. Leiden: E. J. Brill, 1990.

Klibansky, Raymond. "Plato's *Parmenides* in the Middle Ages and the Renaissance." *Medieval and Renaissance Studies* 1 (1943): 281–330. Reprinted in *The Continuity of the Platonic Tradition during the Middle Ages*. Millwood, NY: Kraus, 1982.

Kristeller, Paul Oskar. *Marsilio Ficino and His Works after Five Hundred Years*. Florence: Olschki, 1987.

———. *The Philosophy of Marsilio Ficino*. Translated by Virginia Conant. New York: Columbia University Press, 1943. Original Italian version: *Il pensiero filosofico di Marsilio Ficino*. Florence: Sansoni, 1953; revised edition Florence: Le Lettere, 1988.

Lazzarin, Francesca. "L'*Argumentum in Parmenidem* di Marsilio Ficino." *Accademia* 6 (2004): 7–34.

———. "Note sull'interpretazione ficiniana del *Parmenide* di Platone." *Accademia* 5 (2003): 17–37.

Malmsheimer, Arne. *Platons* Parmenides *und Marsilio Ficinos* Parmenides-*Kommentar. Ein kritischer Vergleich*. Amsterdam: B. R. Gruner, 2001.

Saffrey, Henri Dominique. "La philosophie néoplatonicienne, fruit de l'exégèse du *Parménide*." *Revue de Théologie et de Philosophie* 116 (1984): 1–12.

Vanhaelen, Maude. "The Pico-Ficino Controversy: New Evidence in Ficino's Commentary on Plato's *Parmenides*." *Rinascimento* n.s. 49 (2009): 301–39.

Vasoli, Cesare. *Quasi sit Deus. Studi su Marsilio Ficino*. Lecce: Conte, 1999.

Index

Note: Works are listed by author and title, so that the entries for works follow the main entry for the author; e.g., the entry for Plotinus is followed by the entry for Plotinus, *Enneads*.

Publication of this volume has been made possible by

The Myron and Sheila Gilmore Publication Fund at I Tatti
The Robert Lehman Endowment Fund
The Jean-François Malle Scholarly Programs and Publications Fund
The Andrew W. Mellon Scholarly Publications Fund
The Craig and Barbara Smyth Fund
for Scholarly Programs and Publications
The Lila Wallace–Reader's Digest Endowment Fund
The Malcolm Wiener Fund for Scholarly Programs and Publications